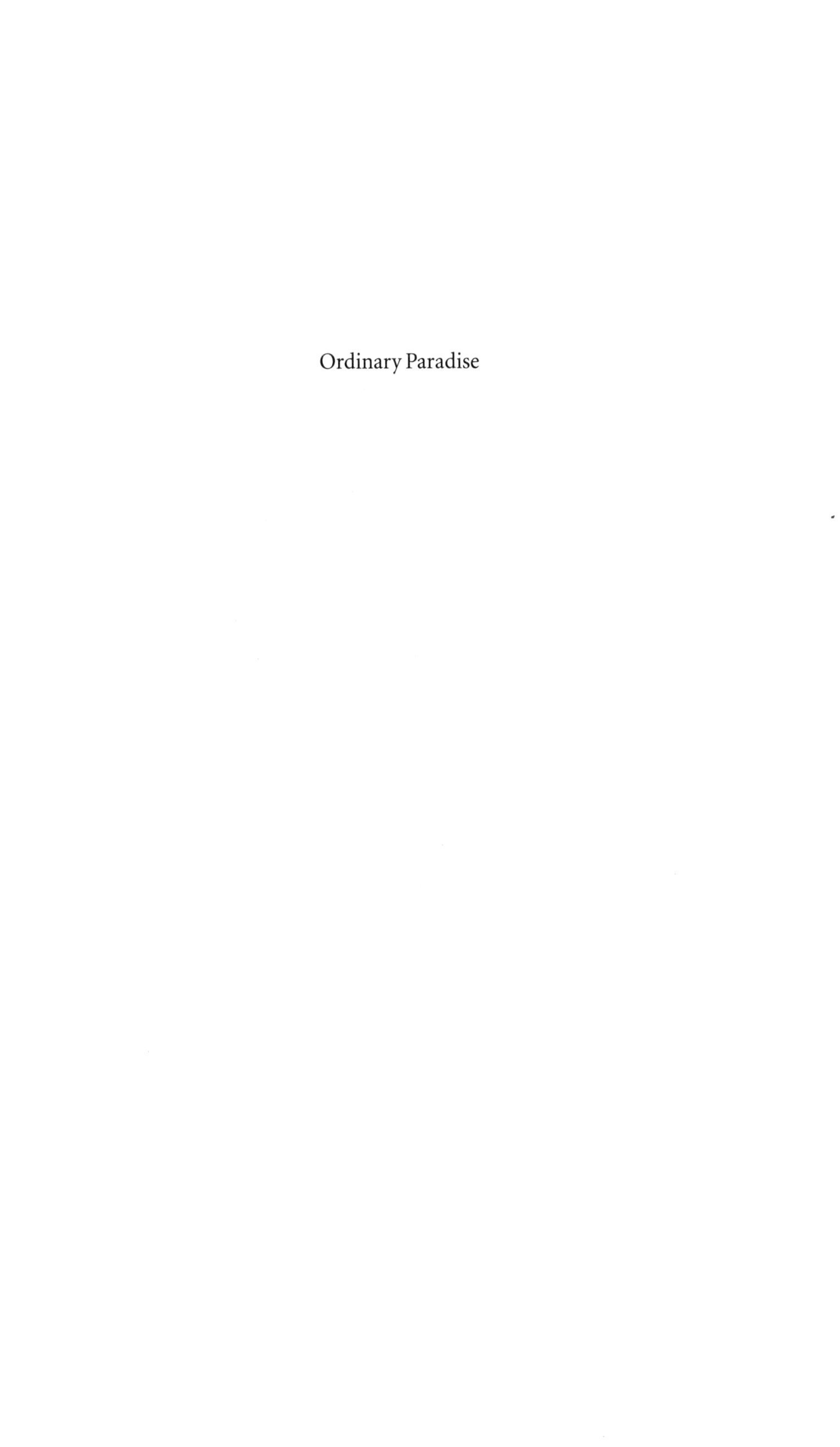

Ordinary Paradise

Also by Richard Teleky

FICTION

The Blue Hour

Winter in Hollywood

Pack Up the Moon

The Paris Years of Rosie Kamin

Goodnight, Sweetheart and Other Stories

NON-FICTION

The Dog on the Bed: A Canine Alphabet

Hungarian Rhapsodies: Essays on Ethnicity, Identity, and Culture

POETRY

The Hermit in Arcadia

The Hermit's Kiss

ANTHOLOGIES

The Exile Book of Canadian Dog Stories

The Oxford Book of French-Canadian Short Stories

Ordinary Paradise

ESSAYS ON ART AND CULTURE

Richard Teleky

The Porcupine's Quill

Library and Archives Canada Cataloguing in Publication

Teleky, Richard, 1946–, author
Ordinary paradise : essays on art and culture / Richard Teleky.

Includes bibliographical references.
ISBN 978-0-88984-409-4 (softcover)

1. Art criticism. 2. Literature—Appreciation. 3. Art appreciation. 4. Music appreciation. 5. Motion pictures—Appreciation. I. Title.

NX643.T45 2017 701'.18 C2017-905786-3

1 2 3 • 20 19 18

Published by The Porcupine's Quill, 68 Main Street, PO Box 160, Erin, Ontario NOB 1TO. http: //porcupinesquill.ca

Readied for the press by Carmine Starnino.

Represented in Canada by Canadian Manda.
Trade orders are available from University of Toronto Press.

We acknowledge the support of the Ontario Arts Council and the Canada Council for the Arts for our publishing program. The financial support of the Government of Canada is also gratefully acknowledged.

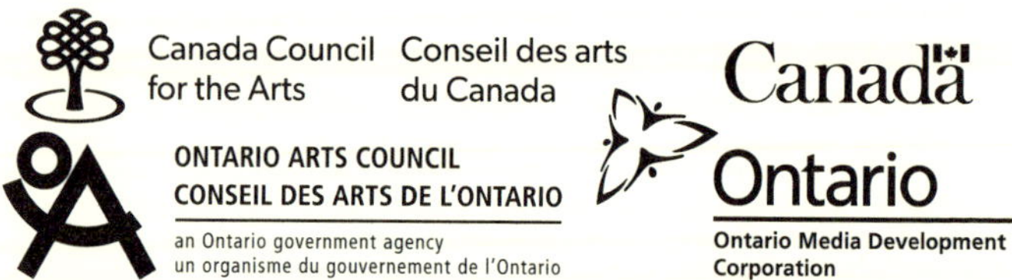

For Bill Toye,
old friend and editor

Contents

Preface

Almost an oxymoron, the words *ordinary* and *paradise* do not usually fit together, yet when I first read the phrase 'ordinary paradise' it made perfect sense to me. I came across it in A. S. Byatt's elegiac novel *Ragnarok: The End of the Gods*, the story of a young girl who, during the years of the Second World War, is evacuated to the English countryside, where she tests her experiences against a book that recounts the demise of the Norse gods. 'She grew up in the ordinary paradise of the English countryside,' Byatt wrote on her novel's first page. It's a resonant phrase for anyone who has spent years studying English literature. From earliest days to our own, this fabled countryside appears again and again, and not simply as a geographical place but also as part of the geography of the human imagination, like its older sister, the pastoral. When Andrew Marvell wrote his much-quoted line 'To a green thought in a green shade' in 'The Garden'—probably in the early 1650s—he summed up centuries of a tradition.

This collection of essays is not, however, about the English countryside, the pastoral or any facet of gardening. Rather, Byatt's phrase struck me as an ideal description or image of works of art—of novels and poems and paintings and musical compositions. Whether we are aware of it or not, they surround us everywhere: in our homes, in libraries, in stores and online, as well as in art galleries, museums and concert halls. While representing the best of human endeavour, works of art have become ordinary features of our lives, familiar and reliably present. They are, however, extraordinary. So extraordinary, in fact, that in themselves they are a kind of paradise.

What, then, is this paradise like? And how do we understand it? The word *paradise* derives from the Persian *pairidaeza*, which means an enclosed space. In the ancient Greek and Hebrew Biblical usage, the term took on the quality of a sanctified space, and a garden (Eden). The word *ordinary*, on the other hand, comes from the Latin, and has many meanings that include not only something common or familiar, but also human figures such as a bishop or judge, and the jurisdiction that belongs to each. Protected areas, in effect. Books with covers, paintings with frames, printed musical compositions, all live in enclosed spaces; they're cut off from the rest of the material world, separated by their physicality, somehow protected. This protection, however, is always tentative. All works of art are fragile, and vulnerable to the exigencies of time. They can be destroyed by misunderstanding, neglect, or censorship just as easily as by fire and water. We owe them their lives because, in an essential way, we owe them ours.

Ordinary Paradise begins with one question—'The Impossible Work of Translation?', and ends with another, 'The End of Beauty?'. In between, more questions will be raised than answered. But works of art do that, and I want to be true to my subject. Our English word *essay*, after all, comes from the French *essai* by way of the Renaissance writer Michel de Montaigne, a humanist who set out to explore facets of a subject rather than attain a final word on them. Final words can be a temptation, a puzzle, even a dead end.

The essays included in this collection appear for the most part as they were first written and previously published. They convey my thoughts about a subject that once caught my attention and held my interest (as it still does). A few additions, emendations or revisions were occasionally made, but I haven't wanted to introduce new or later thoughts. For example, 'Rereading *Doctor Zhivago*' was written to mark the fiftieth anniversary of Boris Pasternak's classic novel. Since then, a new translation by Richard Pevear and Larissa Volokhonsky has been published, as well as several studies of the book's history and impact (the most interesting is *The Zhivago Affair: The Kremlin, the CIA, and the Battle Over a Forbidden Book* by Peter Finn and Petra Couvée), and, in the spring of 2015, a lavish Broadway musical based on Pasternak's story closed after just forty-nine performances. But none of these developments changed my thoughts about the novel or its significance, so I mention them here only in passing. There are, however, a few exceptions to my thoughts about revision. I added a coda to one essay ('Getting to Know Her: Fact and Fiction') after an unexpected personal encounter that was in keeping with the original piece and seemed to be of interest. 'A Matter of Descent', about the novelist David Plante, combines several previously published articles. In other instances I've sometimes restored a few details that, for reasons of length, were cut from a previous version. In the end, however, each essay must speak for itself. Together they convey some of my long-standing concerns about the nature of reading, as well as about the way we engage with the creative accomplishments that surround us.

Acknowledgements

Many libraries were essential to the research and reading I did for these essays, but I must give special thanks to the extraordinary collection, and librarians, of the Cleveland Public Library, Main Branch. As well, the much smaller collection of the Lakewood Public Library in Lakewood, Ohio, and its helpful staff, were often consulted. My research on Diana Thorne also led me to the American Kennel Club Museum of the Dog, St. Louis; the Art Gallery of Toronto Library; the Boston Museum of Fine Arts Library; the Boston Public Library, Main Branch; the Chicago Public Library, Main Branch; the Cleveland Museum of Art Library; the Free Library of Philadelphia; the Frick Reference Library; the Kerlan Collection, University of Minnesota; the Library and Archives of Canada; the Library of Congress; the Metropolitan Museum of Art Library, New York; the Montreal Museum of Fine Arts Library; the National Gallery of Canada Library; the New York Public Library; the Osborne Collection, Toronto Public Library; the Smithsonian American Museum and Archives; the Winnipeg Art Gallery Library; and the William Secord Gallery in Manhattan.

In addition to books read, I interviewed many people about various aspects of my subjects, and wish to thank Barry Callaghan, Sheila Fischman, Suzanne Hively, David Plante, William Secord and Agnes Whitfield for their comments and time; Peter Perenyi welcomed me into his Stonington, Connecticut, home and answered endless questions about his mother and grandmother; and Phyllis Wilson kindly arranged for me to consult letters (many that I'd written) in the archives of Oxford University Press Canada. Several graduate assistants, including Jennifer Caraccioli, Jennifer Hann, Concetta Principe, and Simran Saini, did helpful detective work, as did Marc Tyndel, who saved me from some puzzling computer glitches, along with the always helpful eServices Office staff of York University. Special thanks go to the friends and colleagues who read some of these essays (or parts of them) in initial drafts, or offered their special expertise: Carole Carpenter, Christopher Doda, Doug Freake, Jason Guriel, Audrey King, Nora Shulman, Teresa Stratas, Mark Tapia, Penelope Tzougros, Priscila Uppal, Scott Wilson and Betty Jane Wylie. As well, over several decades the questions and comments of my students—too many to name—have contributed to the way I've come to think about some of the issues raised in these essays. Any omissions and errors are, of course, my own.

I'm particularly grateful to Boris Castel, publisher of *Queen's Quarterly*, for enthusiastically encouraging me to keep writing essays for the journal; to David Yezzi of *The Hopkins Review* (and previously of *New Criterion*), for his comments and suggestions; and to the editors and copy editors at the journals that first published my work, particularly Stephen Anderson of *Queen's Quarterly.* Carmine Starnino, my editor at Porcupine's Quill, welcomed *Ordinary Paradise* to the press and supported the project, and Tim Inkster, a unique publisher and book designer, made this book happen happily. As well, Elke Inkster was instrumental in the book's production, and Chandra Wohleber gave my manuscript the meticulous care of an ideal copy-editor. Finally, special thanks to Bill Toye—editorial colleague and friend since the Oxford years—who lent his attention and goodwill to these essays, earning the dedication many times over.

* * *

I'm grateful to the following journals, which first published some of the essays in this collection:

Aloud: 'Almost Quebecois: David Plante's Fiction'
Brick: 'Glenn Gould and the Mouse'
Canadian Literature: 'Editing "Old" Ladies: Margaret Avison, P.K. Page, Miriam Waddington, Suzanne Rosenberg, and Jane Jacobs'
CineAction: 'Anatomy of *Anatomy of a Murder*'
ELQ/Exile: 'Late Style, Last Works'
The Gay and Lesbian Review: 'After Reading Wendy Moffat's *A Great Unrecorded History: A New Life of E.M. Forster*'
The Globe and Mail: 'Accident of faith may not be dead end'

The Hopkins Review: 'Revisiting Stonington: Eleanor Perényi and Grace Zaring Stone'

The Little Sisters' LSB Review: 'Getting to Know Her: Fact and Fiction'

MELUS: '"Entering the Silence": Voice, Ethnicity, and the Pedagogy of Creative Writing'

New Criterion: 'On Solitude: Re-reading May Sarton's Journals'

Partisan: 'A Year at the Piano'

Queen's Quarterly: 'All Waltzed Out: Listening for World War I'; 'The Cyborgs Next Door: Thinking About Posthuman Studies'; 'Don Quixote and the End of Life'; 'The Impossible Work of Translation?'; 'In Search of Diana Thorne'; 'Introducing Emma Bovary'; 'The Life of Inanimate Objects'; 'My Viennese Vice'; 'Re-reading *Doctor Zhivago*'; 'Post-Heroism?'; 'The Road to Kamouraska'; 'The Taste for Fiction: Re-reading Novels, Reading the Self'; and 'Which Paris?'

Quill & Quire: 'The Wisdom of Age'

As well, 'Don Quixote and the End of Life' was anthologized in *The Best of Canadian Essays 2017*, edited by Marina Nemat and Christopher Doda (Tightrope Books, 2017), and 'The Taste for Fiction: Re-reading Novels, Reading the Self' was included in *The Best of Canadian Essays 2014*, edited by Natalie Zina Walschots and Christopher Doda (Tightrope Books, 2015); 'On *Deaf to the City*' originally appeared as the introduction to a reprint of Marie-Claire Blais's novel (Exile Editions, 2006); and a shorter version of 'In Search of Diana Thorne' appeared in my book *The Dog on the Bed: A Canine Alphabet* (Fitzhenry & Whiteside, 2011) and in *Queen's Quarterly*.

The Impossible Work of Translation?

On May 31, 2004, Oprah Winfrey made history again. Not, this time, for losing fifty pounds, or winning a new media award, but rather, translation history. That morning, the summer selection of Oprah's Book Club was announced: Leo Tolstoy's novel *Anna Karenina*. What's important here is that the club stipulated a specific translation, one published in 2001 by Richard Pevear and Larissa Volokhonsky. Penguin Books, which had brought out the paperback of their *Anna* in 2002, immediately planned a press run of 800,000 copies, an astonishing figure, since in a good year the translators—and Penguin—were glad to sell 20,000 copies worldwide.

Of course Oprah isn't a connoisseur of translation. In fact she had never read *Anna Karenina*, and said as much in an interview about the choice: 'I've never, ever chosen a novel that I had not personally read. It's been on my list for years, but I didn't do it because I was scared.' Then she cautioned her TV audience, 'Look for the Oprah's Book Club little sticker there because there's lots of different editions. This is an award-winning translation, so you're really going to get scared if it's not translated well, okay?' Oprah was well advised, and she chose the finest—and most expensive—translation. By Monday, June 7th, the Pevear-Volokhonsky version topped Amazon's online bestseller list, and Penguin had to return to press twice to print a total of 900,000 copies. Why is this important? I'd like to start to answer that question by referring to Oprah one last time, because she did warn her readers that they were 'going to get scared' if they used an edition of *Anna Karenina* that wasn't 'translated well'. She accepted the fact that we are dependent on translations, and on the talents and goodwill of translators, although we tend to take them for granted.

Anyone who has been reading recent academic articles knows that today's scholars are fascinated by all the *trans*-words, or words with *trans* as a prefix. Think of *trans*formative, *trans*gressive and *trans*cultural, usually written as if the author is advocating radical social change. The words *trans*lation and *trans*late are encountered less often, though in 2004 there was a call for papers for a conference at Laurentian University called 'The Canadian Cultural Exchange: Translation and Transculturation'. The prefix *trans* has an almost alchemical draw. The prefix itself is an Indo-European one (also seen in Sanskrit), meaning 'to pass over' and 'through'; it has spatial implications and suggests movement. As the *Oxford English Dictionary* shows, early-English uses of the word *translate*, dating back to 1300, suggest the actual physical movement of a person, place or object. Subsequent usage retains an element of motion in a process that involves change of some kind, whether alteration or adaptation.

At present, foreign-language requirements for undergraduates in most North American universities have gone the way of the bustle and the Model T. As well, in Canada, which likes to think of itself as bilingual (at least officially), few anglophones have even rudimentary French-language skills. In other words, we're more dependent on translators and translations than we've ever been. This means we're also dependent on a small number of books like *The Oxford Guide to Literature in English Translation*, edited by Peter France. Published in 2000, the 656-page volume follows a tradition of short, sensible literary assessments, and is a fine starting point if you want to know what has been available. Yet the *Guide* was out-of-date the day it was published, and needs yearly updating, although the economics of publishing make this unlikely.

And like it or not, translations are in part about money. This is why publishers have historically favoured a small number of languages—French, German and Russian, and sometimes Spanish and Italian. These are languages associated not only with significant books but also with power, trade and tourism. Translations from Danish, say, or Hungarian, are far fewer. Publishers have on occasion recognized this, and for some years, for example, Penguin brought out a literary series devoted to what was then referred to as Eastern Europe, edited by American novelist Philip Roth. Most of the books in this series are long out of print, though a few have been taken up by university presses that want to broaden their trade lists. Meanwhile, translations of the Turkish novelist Orhan Pamuk have caught the public eye, in part, I suspect, because of growing wartime concern about the Middle East. Pamuk is published by Knopf, one of the leading American houses, and his translated novels have had various translators. The point I want to stress is that we are dependent not only on translators' interests but also on the economics of the publishing world. And as long as governments insist on taxing publishers on unsold stock, publishers will prune their backlists, emphasize short-term sales and forgo translations.

This has not always been the case. As André Schiffrin wrote in *The Business of Books*, the American publishing industry has changed radically since the end of World War II. Our access to translations is a part of this change. When media corporations buy smaller publishing houses, and influence their lists with their own agendas, small-run books move to the sidelines, if they are given a place at all. New York City, still the American publishing centre, was at one time populated by Eurocentric editors who, given their own language skills, often had considerable sympathy for translation, producing not only canonical works but translations of unfamiliar writers. The decline in this pattern, accompanied by the reading public's shift of interest to popular culture and how-to books, means a smaller market for translations at a time when market size relates to potential print runs. The 'bestseller' mentality of today's publishing conglomerates determines the titles we're likely to see on bookstore shelves—where shelf life, in the chain stores that have come to dominate bookselling, is seldom more than half a year. According to an article by Motoko Rich in the *New York Times*, on October 18, 2008: '... 330 works of foreign literature—or a little more than 2 percent of the estimated total of 15,000 titles released—have been published in the United States so far this year.'

Looking abroad, for many years before the collapse of Soviet communism, both Hungary and Russia had excellent state-subsidized publishing houses that regularly brought out classics of national literature in English translation for the international market. Corvina, in Hungary, excelled in such books, and Progress Publishers, in Russia, published a wide range of second-rank Russian classics—Vladimir Korolenko's short stories, for example—that would otherwise have been unavailable to anyone but Russian speakers. Naturally such publishing ventures have collapsed or been cut back under the spread of the market economy, the euphemism we prefer for capitalism. Where does the marketplace leave us? To cite a personal example, in the graduate course I recently taught, Inventing Modernism, we had to use Donald Revell's flat translation of Guillaume Apollinaire's seminal book *Alcools* because it was the only translation available. A much finer translation by William Meredith, available thirty years ago, is long out of print, as is an excellent translation by Oliver Bernard. Revell's translation, by the way, is published by Wesleyan University Press, while only thirty years ago Meredith's was available from Anchor, a commercial press. We're left, then, relying on unreliable publishers, and their sporadic forays into translation, at a time when foreign-language training is on the decline. In a sense, we're left closing ourselves off from much of the world and its history.

The political implications of this situation are serious. Early in 2004, Adam Liptak reported in the *New York Times* that the American Treasury Department had written to publishers about 'criminal editing of the enemy'. Advisory letters '... warned publishers they may face grave legal consequences for editing manuscripts from Iran and other disfavored nations, on the ground that such tinkering amounts to trading with the enemy. Anyone who publishes material from a country under a trade embargo is forbidden to reorder paragraphs or sentences, correct syntax or grammar, or replace "inappropriate words" ...' Which countries under embargo were involved? Iran? Cuba? Libya, North Korea and Sudan? Trade with all of them, among others, was prohibited without government license. But while trade laws had long been enforced for oil, wheat and nuclear reactors, this was the first time such laws were applied to language.

All general, scholarly and scientific publishers were affected by this warning. Esther Allen, chair of the PEN American Center's translation committee, suggested that the rules 'appear to ban translations'. Of course publishers could print manuscripts in poor English, with a disclaimer. Leon Friedman, a law professor at Hofstra University who represented PEN, called the regulations censorship. Eventually a suit was filed against the Treasury Secretary and the Office of Foreign Assets of the Treasury Department by a group of publishers, including the Association of American University Presses and the PEN American Center. They argued that the ruling violated federal law. An editorial about the lawsuit in the *New York Times* concluded: 'Most of the countries under trade sanctions enjoy extremely limited freedoms. One of the most effective things America can do when it comes to spreading our principles is to offer the exercise of real intellectual freedom to authors from sanctioned countries.' In time the matter was resolved in a manner favourable to translation, but the episode itself symbolized the constricted nature of life in post-9/11 America.

In his introduction to *The Plough and the Pen: Writings from Hungary, 1930–1956*, an anthology edited by Ilona Duczyńska and Karl Polanyi that was published in 1963, the poet W.H. Auden wrote that a writer's only political duty is to translate the work of other writers. His admonition is taken seriously by few writers, since most are concerned with creating their own work. Because of the time constraints involved in writing extended narratives, fiction writers are less free than poets to work on translations, while poets can often find a literary journal interested in a few pages of work by an unfamiliar poet. Auden's injunction was indirectly expanded by the Mexican poet Octavio Paz in his 1990 Nobel Prize lecture:

> Languages are vast realities that transcend those political and historical entities we call nations. The European languages we speak in the Americas illustrate this. The special position of our literatures when compared to those of England, Spain, Portugal and France depends precisely on this fundamental fact: they are literatures written in transplanted tongues. Languages are born and grow from the native soil, nourished by a common history. The European languages were rooted out from their native soil and their own tradition, and then planted in an unknown and unnamed world; they took root in the new lands and, as they grew within the societies of America, they were transformed. They are the same plant yet also a different plant. Our literatures did not passively accept the changing fortunes of the transplanted languages, they participated in the process and even accelerated it. They very soon ceased to be mere transatlantic reflections: at times they have been the negation of the literatures of Europe; more often, they have been a reply.

Paz's point is worth keeping in mind; in order to make it he used several *trans*-words—*trans*cend, *trans*formed, *trans*planted and *trans*atlantic. The weight of the Spanish language is a crucial concern in Paz's poetry. But in their struggle to create, all writers can experience their own language as a kind of 'foreign' language. Translation itself can be seen as a kind of 'reply' to a work in another language that has made an impression on a writer.

How are such replies made? Gregory Rabassa, who was well known for his translations of Latin American novelists, said of his memoir, *If This Be Treason: Translation and Its Discontents*: 'My thesis in the book is that translation is impossible. People expect reproduction, but you can't turn a baby chick into a duckling. The best you can do is get close to it.' Coming from as fine a translator as Rabassa, this is worth noting, and I've taken the title of my essay from his remark. Exact 'reproduction' is of course an absurd expectation, as if one language could mirror another. Walter Benjamin addressed this issue in his essay 'The Task of the Translator' when he wrote: 'If the kinship of languages manifests itself in translations, this is not accomplished through a vague alikeness between adaptation and original. It stands to reason that kinship does not necessarily involve likeness.' For Benjamin, translation is a 'mode' that involves translatability, an essential quality of certain works. In *After Babel: Aspects of Language and Translation*, George Steiner links Benjamin's essay, and his views, to the 'Kabbalistic and gnostic traditions' and also uses the term *mystic* for Benjamin's emphasis on pure language. Years after Benjamin's essay was originally published in German, in 1923, its rediscovery, according to Steiner, helped bring about:

> ... almost metaphysical inquiries into translation and interpretation. Much of the confidence in the scope of mechanical translation, which marked the 1950s and early sixties, has ebbed. The developments of transformational generative grammars has brought the argument between 'universalist' and 'relativist' positions back into the forefront of linguistic thought ... translation offers a critical ground on which to test the issues. Even more than in the 1950s, the study of the theory and practice of translation has become a point of contact between established and newly evolving disciplines.

Much could be said about this subject since Steiner wrote these words, published in 1975. At the very least it's fair to conclude that translation is not simply a linguistic act but also an interpretative one. (By the way, the German word for 'translator' is 'übersetzer', one of those compound words that uses as its prefix the word 'über', which, like the English 'trans' also suggests movement. In German it's attached to the noun 'Setzer', which means typesetter or compositor. A translator, then, is someone who can move through type.)

Issues of 'mechanical translation', as Steiner called them, are not to be easily dismissed. In this context, the poet as translator has a long history, and an especially interesting one when poets work with languages they don't know—William Butler Yeats's lack of Greek didn't prevent him from translating Sophocles, Auden and Pound worked with poems in languages they couldn't read, and many contemporary poets have followed the practice. Robert Lowell raised many of the crucial issues about second-hand translation in his preface to *Imitations*, his volume of translations of Western poetry from Homer to Pasternak. 'I have been restless with literal meaning,' he said, 'and labored hard to get the tone. Most often *a* tone, for *the* tone is something that will always more or less escape transference to another language and cultural moment.' Like other poets who want to translate an unfamiliar language, he had to seek assistance. Speaking of Pasternak, he wrote, 'I have rashly tried to improve on other translations, and have been helped by exact prose versions given me by Russian readers.' He called this, correctly, 'an old practice' that yields new poems twice removed from the originals.

Some years ago I was curious about how this practice worked, and I interviewed Margaret Avison, arguably Canada's finest modern poet, about her translations from the Hungarian, which appeared in *The Plough and the Pen*. The poems she translated by Attila József, Gyula Illyés and Ferenc Juhász—three major twentieth-century Hungarian poets—are demanding ones, while Hungarian itself is a notoriously difficult language. Yet Avison's translations are exemplary. Avison told me that she was given the Hungarian texts, marked with the metrical stresses of the verse as well as notations of 'rhyme and assonance patterns, number of syllables and rhythmic pictures'. Literal translations accompanied each poem, with the corresponding English word under the Hungarian original, so that she could recognize each word and gauge its weight in the original poem. There were also exact prose translations—just as Lowell used—although the editors urged Avison not to work with them. Finally, tapes were made of the poems so that Avison could hear the sounds. She said, 'And I played the tapes and played the tapes and played the tapes, and once I got to know what the words literally meant, I tried to see if I could get an English one that was at all able to echo it.' Each translation went through more than twenty drafts, and the process ran over a period of four years. These figures alone may suggest why great translations are rare.

Not all translators are as talented and meticulous as Avison and Lowell. Before we trust the *tone* of a translation, we want to assume a translation's verbal accuracy. In the early 1980s I edited *The Oxford Book of French Canadian Short Stories*. After the selection was made I commissioned a number of new translations because of the problems in existing published translations. One of my favourite errors comes from a story called 'The Carnation' by Louise Maheux-Forcier. In the English-language version, an elderly woman sits down to a restaurant meal of steak and apples. This sounded odd so I checked the French original and saw that the translator had mistaken potatoes for apples, confusing *pomme* and *pomme de terre*—the most basic of errors. It matters, first of all, because it's wrong, and for its time a very *un*French meal results; it's wrong, as well, in this story—a light surrealist account of an elderly woman who has no appetite for her dinner but chooses to eat the fresh carnation from a vase on her table—because the effect of the mistranslation is jarring before we're intended to be jarred.

The stakes may seem greater when the book has influenced several generations of readers—for example, Simone de Beauvoir's *The Second Sex*, published in France in 1949 and in English translation in 1953. Scholars have now examined the translation, commissioned by Alfred Knopf, and shown how it distorts de Beauvoir's argument and tone. How did this happen? Howard Madison Parshley, the translator, was a retired professor of zoology who had written a book about human reproduction, knew French from high school and university, and had reviewed books about sex for the *New York Herald Tribune*. His errors have been examined in a collection of essays edited by Emily R. Grosholz. One contributor, Toril Moi, cited a passage where de Beauvoir appeared to criticize women who did not take advantage of organized day nurseries, but in the original French de Beauvoir actually lamented the lack of child-care assistance. The accuracy of a translation is not, however, only a matter of correct words and tone but also one of omission. Parshley's translation deleted nearly fifteen percent of the original text, about 145 pages. Sections on women's history and literature were some of the biggest omissions. Discussing the possibility of a new translation, Sarah Glazer wrote in the *New York Times* that 'unless Knopf changes its mind, American readers will have to wait until 2056, when *The Second Sex* goes into the public domain, to find out what Beauvoir really meant'. (Fortunately one was permitted—by Constance Borde and Sheila Malovany-Chevallier—and published in 2010.)

Other forms of omission are less obvious but just as grave. Most translations of modern European poetry ignore the fact that the originals were often rhymed, preferring not to produce poetry that to the eye and ear of English speakers might seem hopelessly outdated. This sacrifice means that a great part of a poet's creativity and achievement is lost, even for writers whose influence has been felt outside their own linguistic and national tradition. For example, the best translations of 19th-century French poets Charles Baudelaire and Arthur Rimbaud are in free verse. This means that English-language readers are given only a generalized sense of the writers' thematics, precisely what Walter Benjamin dismissed when he wrote, 'Yet any translation which intends to perform a transmitting function cannot transmit anything but information—hence, something inessential.' A reader of unrhymed Rimbaud would find his verse cut off from the French tradition of poetics, prosody and aesthetics.

Earlier I mentioned Donald Revell's translation of Apollinaire's *Alcools*. It was published in 1995 with a blurb from the critic Marjorie Perloff, a specialist in the American avant-garde; she praised Revell's work as 'imaginative' and wrote, 'This modernized (or perhaps post-modernized) Apollinaire deserves to have a wide audience in late 20th century America.' I'm surprised to read that Apollinaire, a central figure in European modernism, needed modernizing, or post-modernizing. Perloff's unstated assumptions are worth noting. Not only does she seem to undervalue the complex task of translation, but she also appears to undervalue reading itself. We don't read only to look at ourselves in a mirror. The desire to turn all great poetry of the past into modern English poems is an absurd one that assumes that the modern, free-verse poem is the pinnacle of literary evolution, and not simply a manifestation of a moment in literary history.

There are as many reasons for errors and omissions as there are translators, but as readers we don't want explanations; we want to be able to trust the texts we read. When Penguin Press announced in 2000 that it would undertake a new, multivolume translation of Freud, it faced a crucial decision: who would be the series editor? In selecting Adam Phillips it found a lively and controversial figure, a much-published British scholar and practising analyst. The choice—whoever it was—would inevitably raise a few eyebrows. Penguin's choice is of interest here because Phillips neither reads nor speaks German. One of the reasons for a major re-translation is to clear out cobwebs, in this context cobwebs with a prissy Edwardian feel to them, as well as to correct mistranslations. Some of the early volumes in the series are excellent, and the translation by David McLintock of *Civilization and Its Discontents* in particular offers a less Olympian Freud, one with a subtle and ironic sense of humour. The *tone*, to use Lowell's term again, seems trustworthy. Penguin will probably continue to produce worthy 21st-century translations, but a question remains: How necessary is it to know a language—and know it well—to judge a translation and re-translation? I am perhaps rephrasing Benjamin's question, 'Is a translation meant for readers who do not understand the original?' Our culture has a tendency to over-trust people we call experts—in this case, translators—so that we can avoid making a mess of things ourselves. Still, I can't help wondering why Penguin didn't select a series editor who knew German.

Translation, finally, deserves study in and of itself. As a historical aside, it's worth remembering that the city of Alexandria, founded in 331 B.C. by Alexander the Great, was a centre of humanistic studies that affirmed the value of translation in the collection of its fabled library. Margaret Anne Doody discussed this in her monumental *The True Story of the Novel*, providing one of the best definitions of *translation* I know: 'Alexandria believed in *translation*—that strange activity acknowledging that there may be some good in somebody else's culture, or indeed that a number of cultures could combine without losing identity.' In a sense translation is about a respect for otherness while, at the same time, it helps us deconstruct it; the translator is translated—or changed—by the translation. We're back to that *trans* prefix, and *trans*mission is a word the Benjamin has used as well. It suggests not only motion and change but also, in the word *mission* (which makes up half of it) the qualities of urgency and intent. And here, as my final point, is the challenge offered by the prefix *trans*: if we truly value not only translations and translators but reading itself, we will want to learn as many languages as we can—and put in the onerous work to accomplish this—so that we can be our own translators, producing the best translations we can, and in the process discovering ourselves in unexpected ways.

Rereading *Doctor Zhivago*

At a library book sale some years ago I spotted a hardbound copy of Boris Pasternak's novel *Doctor Zhivago*. The book, which turned out to be a first edition, was in excellent condition and wore its original dust jacket. Since the novel hadn't been de-accessioned from the library's collection, it must have come from one of the boxes of books donated to the sale. I paid the two-dollar asking price, brought *Zhivago* home and started rereading it, for the first time in over forty years, an image of the luminous Julie Christie as Pasternak's heroine in the back of my mind. I was surprised by the narrator's wry sense of humour, which I hadn't remembered, and the story kept my attention. Later I found the paperback edition from my high school years, its communist-red cover proclaiming it 'The Novel That Made World History'.

The fall of 2008 marked the fiftieth anniversary of the book's publication in English in 1958, a moment in time when a novel could draw the attention of readers around the world, with word of mouth spreading about a manuscript smuggled out of Russia. It's easy to forget the fear that shadowed the Cold War era. Just two years before *Zhivago* arrived in American bookstores, Soviet tanks drove into Budapest and ended the Hungarian uprising; two years after its arrival, Nikita Khrushchev pounded his right shoe on a podium at the United Nations and threatened to bury the West.

Begun in 1948 and originally planned for serial publication in Russia in 1956, *Zhivago* did not pass the censors. Pasternak had also given his manuscript to an agent of the Italian publisher Feltrinelli in the spring of that year, saying, 'You've invited me to my own execution.' The Italian translation appeared in the fall of 1957 and a Russian-language version followed, also in Milan; both were published at considerable risk to Pasternak and those closest to him. An English translation from the Russian, by Max Hayward and Manya Harari, appeared a year later, in September (from Collins in Canada and Great Britain and Pantheon in the United States) and on October 23, 1958, the second anniversary of the start of the abortive Hungarian revolution, Pasternak was awarded the Nobel Prize for Literature.

Doctor Zhivago quickly rose to first place on the bestseller lists, bypassing a book by another Russian writer—the émigré Vladimir Nabokov's *Lolita.* Perhaps *Zhivago* better suited the Cold War atmosphere, reassuring people that, despite communism, Russians could love just like any one else—reassurance no one was likely to find in the controversial *Lolita.* Naturally Nabokov despised Pasternak's novel. Stacy Schiff's biography *Véra (Mrs Vladimir Nabokov)* records the couple's dislike and distress. Nabokov considered *Zhivago* 'clumsey and melodramatic, with stock situations', while Véra maintained that 'the communists' had pushed it 'into the "Nobel prize winner" club—merely by pretending that it had been "smuggled" out of the USSR!' (According to Brian Boyd, Nabokov's biographer, Pasternak had rejected the suggestion that Nabokov was the ideal English translator for his novel, saying, 'That won't work; he's too jealous of my wretched position in this country to do it properly.')

The only other Russian writer to have received a Nobel Prize was Ivan Bunin, in 1933. This point is important, since Nobel Prizes for literature inevitably contain a political element. Russian authorities quickly saw the Nobel committee's decision as an anti-Soviet statement, and five days after accepting the prize, Pasternak declined it. As Orlando Figes wrote in *Natasha's Dance: A Cultural History of Russia*, émigrés from the Russian revolution considered Bunin's work to be proof that the realist tradition of Tolstoy and Turgenev was alive in the diaspora: 'As Bunin himself put it in a celebrated speech of 1924, it was "The Mission of Emigration" to act for the "True Russia" by protecting this inheritance from the modernist corruptions of left-wing and Soviet art.' When it suits them, governments have long memories. Pasternak was even persuaded to sign a letter renouncing his creation, an act he regretted for the rest of his life.

The Nabokovs' view of *Zhivago*'s literary merits aside, they misjudged its political situation during a time of tension in the Soviet system between rigid censorship and an impulse towards liberalization. In this context, *Zhivago* became a moral as well as a literary success. Edmund Wilson, writing in the *New Yorker*, called the book 'One of the great events in man's literary and moral history', and similar international praise greeted its subsequent translations. But global politics alone can't account for the novel's success. It's said that everyone loves a love story, and this may help explain *Zhivago*'s popularity. Several years after reading the novel and corresponding with Pasternak, the Trappist monk and poet Thomas Merton, of *Seven Storey Mountain* fame, remained so overwhelmed by its love story that he began an affair with an attractive nurse. He probably wasn't alone in his response. Even today one sees remnants of the novel's impact (and more likely that of David Lean's film version, released in 1965) in young women named Lara. A student of mine once sighed while explaining that she was named after Pasternak's heroine—she'd yet to read the novel. It's worth noting that this Lara was born in the mid-'80s, decades after the novel's publication and the film's release, which must say something about Pasternak's staying power.

As a romantic couple, Zhivago and Lara are closer to Petrarch and his muse, Laura, than to the troubled adulterers of nineteenth-century fiction, from *Madame Bovary* to *Anna Karenina*. Readers who believed that the novel's love story matched events of Pasternak's life couldn't have been further from the truth. Pasternak's affair with Olga Ivinskaya, his model for Lara, was in fact a May-December alliance, with twenty-two years between them and all that such a difference entails. The couple met in 1946, when the beautiful, twice-married Olga was an editor at *Novy Mir*. Then fifty-six, Pasternak was inspired to concentrate again on original work rather than the translations into Russian that had preoccupied him. Revered for his lyric poetry, he had been tolerated by the Soviet regime, which remained suspicious of his work. The love affair lasted until Pasternak died, in 1960, although it was interrupted in 1949 when Ivinskaya was arrested and sentenced to prison. Released in 1953, she was again sentenced to the gulag after his death, where she served four years of an eight-year sentence, punishment for her association with Pasternak, as she wrote in her memoir *A Captive of Time: My Years With Pasternak*. Whatever rumours Nabokov may have heard of that relationship, he was living safely in Ithaca, New York, and teaching at Cornell University. But safety didn't breed generosity, as Stacy Schiff showed: 'Among the insults he [Nabokov] hurled at the book was the accusation that Pasternak's mistress had written the novel for him, the worst that could be said, not because Pasternak might have delegated the responsibility, but because the thing *read* as if written by a woman.'

Movies shape our memories and even change them. As I reread

Zhivago, I often found myself recalling scenes from the film. The novel's powerful opening, like the movie's, is the funeral of young Yurii Zhivago's mother, although Lean adds a follow-up scene in which the child is given his mother's beloved balalaika. Nothing of this sort happens in Pasternak, but Hollywood perhaps needed an event to justify the balalaika orchestra that dominates Maurice Jarre's soundtrack, as cloying as a glass of Russian tea over-sweetened with preserves. When I reached the point in the novel where Lara and Zhivago finally admit their love, my mind, alas, switched on 'Lara's Theme' from the movie. (By the mid-'60s, 'Lara's Theme'—also known as 'Somewhere My Love' in popular recordings by the Ray Conniff Singers and Andy Williams—played endlessly on the radio, in cocktail lounges, and at weddings, as if it were an antidote to the Beatles. In his foreword to the brochure for the 30th-anniversary CD of his soundtrack, Jarre wrote, 'I've heard a guitar player on a gondola in Venice playing "Lara's Theme". I've heard street musicians with primitive instruments in Central Africa playing "Lara's Theme".')

And what of the novel itself? Spanning half a century, *Doctor Zhivago* incorporates war, revolution, famine, collectivization and emigration into an epic plot fuelled by implausible coincidences and reversals. Across the vast Russian landscape, quickly sketched characters bump into each other as if they lived in the same apartment building: the lawyer who drove Zhivago's father to suicide also seduced the young Lara; without comment, Zhivago's mysterious half-brother shadows him like a guardian angel, always ready with money or the things money can buy; eventually the wicked lawyer comes to the rescue of Lara and Zhivago's unborn child; and Lara's once meek husband, now turned infamous revolutionary, reappears after several reported deaths only to commit suicide after talking with Zhivago about her—to name just a few of the more spectacular contrivances. Strangely, though, these events take on a cumulative power and implausibility ceases to matter. It's as if Pasternak ascribed to a simple narrative aesthetic: if an incident would be unbelievable in life, then it belongs in a novel. Perhaps he felt that life often refuses the narrative niceties expected of fiction. In this sense Pasternak, who inherited the tradition of nineteenth-century realism, is closer to his (and Zhivago's) beloved Pushkin, and his sometimes surreal stories, than to Tolstoy.

Pasternak's characters are aware that something like fate propels them, and they often discuss the contorted turns in their lives. Zhivago and Lara would appear insufferable, like all lovers who mythologize themselves, if it weren't for the terrible hardships they endure. While David Lean's film removed many of the novel's more eccentric improbabilities by cutting back on its numerous minor characters, his adaptation maintained the curious blend of doom and optimism that animates *Zhivago*. Yet there are some significant surprises for anyone rereading the novel with the film hovering in mind. In the novel, after Lara and Zhivago separate at the wintry country home Varykino, which had once belonged to his wife's family, Zhivago ends up living in Moscow with a new 'wife', Marina, and he becomes the father of two daughters; Lean's screenwriters kept the Lara-Zhivago love story in conventional focus by skipping over Marina. Instead, a decade after the lovers separate, Zhivago is riding a Moscow streetcar when he looks out the window and sees Lara walking alongside; he flees the crowded tram and has a fatal heart attack while trying to call out to his lost love. This kind of Hollywood contrivance would never have interested Pasternak—while *his* Zhivago also has a heart attack after leaving a streetcar, the only person with a connection to the hero walking alongside it is an old French governess. But Pasternak had another, less sentimental, plot turn in store. Later, once Zhivago's body has been laid out in a coffin in his rented room, Lara happens to amble down the street, remember a room that had once played a role in her life, and wander up to discover her lost lover's body. At this point even Lara remarks on the piling up of improbabilities: 'What an extraordinary coincidence—like predestination!' Though moments like this are shaped by Pasternak's fascination with the mystical strain in Russian Orthodoxy, they also recall literary devices favoured by Pearl Buck and Sinclair Lewis, two other Nobel Prize winners infrequently read today.

Yet literary conventions endure because they contain psychological truth. And Pasternak, who frequently spoke of truth, was writing a novel, not a memoir. He knew that people sometimes want to turn the clock back, but he refused the devices of ghosts or spirits to transcend time, though Russian literature has its share of them. Lasting fiction reflects deep psychic needs, and Pasternak surely would agree with his protagonist that 'art has two constant, two unending concerns: it always meditates on death and thus always creates life'. If this credo sounds like a poet's, well, Pasternak was one of Russia's leading modern poets. The 36 pages of verse that conclude his novel as 'The Poems of Yurii Zhivago' are some of the book's most intense. The cycle of seasons running through them is reminiscent of the way the seasons shape the novel itself, nature a recurring motif that dwarfs human activity like an omniscient, impersonal deity. The love of the natural world that dominates *Zhivago*, the awe before all living things and their fragility, is rare in modern fiction. It may even seem old-fashioned, a quaint pastoral, unless one pays close attention to the devastation that nature also brings as *Zhivago* unfolds. There are pretty fields of golden daffodils in David Lean's film, not in Pasternak's novel.

Pasternak's critique of Soviet bureaucracy and, by implication, inhumane bureaucracy of any kind, will strike a chord with contemporary readers. Although Zhivago and Lara are obviously foils to the novel's villainous revolutionaries, it is only because Pasternak presents them as superior people—self-evidently finer, brighter, exceptional. At the same time, in his affection for Russian Orthodoxy, he may have associated the rituals of the Russian church with a less violent, pre-revolutionary world, as if the Christian socialism propounded by Tolstoy might have averted the revolution. Pasternak was born to an assimilated Jewish family, and as *Zhivago* makes clear, he had little sympathy for Judaism because it does not accept Jesus as the Messiah. At best, this strain of the novel came as a surprise. The quasi-religious, prophetic tone that runs through *Zhivago* reminds me of a remark in *Tightrope Walking*, the memoir by Pasternak's younger sister Josephine. Recalling a summer when her brother, then twenty-three, chose the family's vacation home, she wrote, 'As usual, Boris spoke in that specific voice of his, the voice of someone imparting to the world at large an esoteric experience.'

The world at large no longer listens to Pasternak, and Nabokov would perhaps feel vindicated by time. *Lolita* is commonly taught in university courses and played a significant role in Azar Nafisi's memoir *Reading 'Lolita' in Tehran*, while *Doctor Zhivago* has lost its claim to much public following, except through Lean's film, which regularly crops up on the Turner Classic Movies channel. In an informal telephone survey I conducted, bookstores in Boston, Cleveland, Los Angeles and Toronto all had *Lolita* in stock; none had *Zhivago*. (Lean's film, on DVD, is still popular, as is Stanley Kubrick's adaptation of Nabokov's novel. Both books have also received more recent film versions—*Lolita*, directed by Adrian Lyne, in 1998, and a BBC series of *Zhivago*, shown on PBS's *Masterpiece Theatre* in 2004.) Does sex sell better than war and revolution? Is Nabokov's novel the better book? The answer depends on the reader.

Rereading is a curious act, one of memory and reassessment; it can even be a mirror to another self—in a sense, it resembles a coincidence out of Pasternak, where one comes across a once-known place decades later, like looking at old photographs. Orlando Figes quoted a pertinent remark by Igor Stravinsky, who told his friend Robert Craft that he was rereading books he'd first read in Russia, like Gorky's *Mother*: 'I read it when it was first published [in 1906] and am trying again now, probably because I want to go back into myself.' The self one finds in rereading of course depends on one's age at the first reading. Finally, though, one puts aside a revisited book to see not just the self but the world anew. Despite the often plodding earnestness of *Doctor Zhivago*, its strength and power come from the decency of Pasternak's desire both to bear witness to the weight of history and to affirm the value of individual conscience. Thus, the novel offers readers a challenge that is still compelling: in Zhivago's place, in Lara's place, at that moment in time, in the face of all of those terrors, what might we have done? And then, what do we do today?

Introducing Emma Bovary

The western literary canon includes a small number of characters who embody the tensions in our culture and help define the way we think about ourselves. Odysseus, Hamlet, Don Quixote and Faust top the list, with only a few comparable female characters. Emma Bovary, one of the best known, has sometimes been called a 'female Quixote' because of her larger-than-life delusional fantasies. Any new translation of Gustave Flaubert's novel *Madame Bovary* (1857), which gave life to her, is a significant event. But a translation, and its reception, may also be troubling. New translations can, however, make us take a fresh look at the lasting power of Emma Bovary.

In 1849 a young Norman woman named Delphine Delamare died by her own hand, of poison. Her suicide was the subject of much gossip, and a friend of the writer Gustave Flaubert drew his attention to it. Flaubert, then thirty, had settled into his family's country home, outside Rouen, to concentrate on fiction writing. We can only guess why Delphine's grim story caught his imagination. Unhappily married to a country doctor, she had continued her search for love, run into debt and, finally, chose death to end her troubles. This story of adulterous sex and money—natural tabloid companions—became the core of the novel we know as *Madame Bovary*, a book that Flaubert spent five years writing. One might fairly say that Flaubert was Emma Bovary's first translator, turning, as he did, aspects of Delphine's life into fiction.

Iconic characters cannot be separated from their stories. Flaubert's plot is deceptively simple—a domestic odyssey gone wrong. Young Emma Rouault, who lives with her self-absorbed father on a small Normandy farm, agrees to marry Charles Bovary, the sincere but doltish local medical officer. With little aptitude for marriage or homemaking, she moves into his house, where his mother rules, and soon drifts into dreams of romance and a more glamorous life. An affair with the handsome viscount Rodolphe—an unrepentant rake—only exacerbates her fantasies, and, inevitably, he ends their dalliance. Disappointed by her husband's lack of ambition, and unable to make a bond with her baby daughter, Emma falls into another affair, this time with a passive but not unattractive clerk, Léon Dupuis. As her daily life flattens out, her longings flourish, and Emma turns to shopping as an escape from ennui. Borrowing money, she nearly bankrupts her family. After swallowing arsenic, she dies a hideous death, leaving a trail of suffering behind her, with the repellent local pharmacist, Monsieur Homais (a bourgeois Everyman) about to receive the Legion of Honour for his public career. What makes Emma's story more than a commonplace tale of adultery are the subtle irony and wealth of detail with which Flaubert conveys Emma's confining world and psyche.

It's often noted that Flaubert said of his heroine *'La Bovary, c'est moi.'* Readers and writers have been saying much the same ever since, even when Emma's troubles seem a little too close for comfort. Along with numerous translations of her story into more languages than I can count, there have been several movie versions—also translations, into the conventions of film. Hollywood took on Emma in Vincente Minnelli's lavish but banal black-and-white *Madame Bovary* (1949), starring Jennifer Jones, with a cameo by James Mason as Flaubert. (In order to circumvent postwar censorship, the screenwriters gave their movie a preachy frame, where Flaubert/Mason defends his choice of subject matter as moral.) The late French director Claude Chabrol filmed his version in 1991, starring a miscast, laconic Isabelle Huppert, who doesn't quite suggest Emma's desperate energy—Isabelle Adjani, with her frantic dark eyes, would have been ideal. Flaubert also defeated Sophie Barthes, who directed the pretty but dull adaptation of 2015. Finally, a curious Russian version, *Save and Protect* (1989), directed by Aleksandr Sokurov, with a coarse, middle-aged, Siberian Emma, has been played in art houses and university film courses; oddly, it best captures the novel's hovering gloom.

And Emma has inspired a wide range of writers. From Woody Allen, in his 1977 magic-realist short story 'The Kugelmass Episode' (about a nebbishy young man who encounters Emma outside of Flaubert's book, in a rented suite in Manhattan's Plaza Hotel, and soon tires of her complaints), to Mario Vargas Llosa, the Nobel Prize–winning Peruvian novelist, whose study of Flaubert's heroine, *The Perpetual Orgy*, is a gallant love letter, *'La Bovary, c'est nous.'* There's even a witty British graphic novel, *Gemma Bovery* (2001), by Posy Simmonds, that updates Emma's story to contemporary Normandy, and Anne Fontaine's film of it (2014).

Madame Bovary is a book I know like an old friend, yet I'm amazed by each rereading. For the last decade I've taught it in a second-year university course about the imagination, in a fourth-year seminar about concepts of love, and in a graduate course about modernism. A study of the destructive nature of romantic obsession as well as a critique of self-serving bourgeois values, the novel has a power to disturb students like none other I know. A product of her unique moment in time, yet a universal figure, Emma is too much like all of us for students to ignore. They may dismiss her as 'a bad mother' or 'a sleaze bag' (their most common objections) while feeling superior to her self-deceptions, but they still want to believe that erotic love will shape their own lives for the better, and after discussing the book they come to understand—if not identify with—Emma's longings. I often think that *Madame Bovary* may be the most important book I teach, so I approach any new translation with hope and caution.

Lydia Davis brings an impressive resumé to her work. A MacArthur Fellow with an award from the French-American Translation Foundation for her version of Marcel Proust's *Swann's Way*, and a Chevalier of the Order of Arts and Letters from the French government, Davis is also the author of several short story collections, republished as *The Collected Stories of Lydia Davis* (2009). Her stories often focus on dissatisfied middle-aged women who might be the great-great-granddaughters of Emma Bovary. But unlike her sad, sour heroines, she is a celebrity of the first rank in today's literary firmament. When Davis's translation of *Madame Bovary* was brought out in England, the publisher announced a '3-City Author Tour', as if Flaubert had come back from the grave.

Most reviewers of the new *Madame Bovary* treated Davis with awe. The American novelist Jane Smiley, known as a satirist, wrote a much-reprinted review, explaining that she'd previously read other translations of *Madame Bovary* but was 'not terribly moved'. Emma, she claimed, is a man's idea of a woman, and 'not that illuminating to actual women', though almost miraculously a female translator had saved her from Flaubert and 'returned Emma Bovary to us' as a character who merits attention. The *New York Times* assigned Davis's translation to Kathyrn Harrison, a novelist best known for her memoir about an incestuous love affair with her father. Under the title 'Desperate Housewife' Harrison wrote mainly a plot summary, comparing Emma to Anna Karenina; without mentioning other translations, she concluded: 'It's a shame Flaubert will never read Davis's translation of *Madame Bovary*. Even he would have to agree his masterwork has been given the English translation it deserves.' Not to be outdone, *New York Magazine* ran a 3-page feature about Davis under the title 'Knee-Deep in "Bovary": Flaubert's obsessive masterpiece finally gets the obsessive translation it deserves' (note the addition of 'finally' to the praise). Of course Davis's publisher placed a large advertisement in the *TLS*, quoting Kathryn Harrison. A month later its reviewer, Tadzio Koelb, called the translation 'very good', but one that 'falls a touch on the literal side'. More thoughtful and apt, the novelist and critic Jonathan Raban discussed Davis's translation in an essay for the *New York Review of Books* titled 'Flaubert, Imperfect': 'It's likely to be remembered as the version in which the translator tried to out-Flaubert Flaubert in her coolness toward her raw material.'

Why does a book's reception matter? First, it tells us something about the reviewing culture of our day. While no classic translation should prevent another translator from the challenge of Flaubert's original, anyone reviewing a new translation—Davis claims to be the twentieth translator—ought to know something about previous versions. Francis Steegmuller, one of the great twentieth-century translators, produced a *Madame Bovary* (1957) that has yet to be surpassed. He also translated the definitive two-volume edition of Flaubert's letters, and, like Lydia Davis, wrote fiction (his short stories often appeared in the pages of the *New Yorker*). His study *Flaubert and Madame Bovary: A Double Portrait* (1939, with later revisions), remains one of the best places to begin reading about Flaubert, along with Frederick Brown's biography *Flaubert* (2006). There may be a small irony here. In *Fragments* (2010), a collection of poems, notes and letters by Marilyn Monroe (yes, Marilyn Monroe), one of the final pages is a photograph of four books from her personal collection, including Steegmuller's *Madame Bovary*, with the phrase 'In a new and definitive translation' printed across the bottom, and Steegmuller's name in large capital letters. While it's the job of publishers to sell books, that's not the job of reviewers, who ought to be responsible to their readers.

Apart from Smiley's casual anti-male remarks, and Harrison's unsupported panegyric, their reviews suggest a careless reading of *any* translation of *Madame Bovary*. As I point out to my students, Flaubert's presentation of his heroine—from the start—is not unsympathetic. He titled his novel *Madame Bovary*, not *Emma Bovary*, and Emma is in fact the third Madame Bovary in the book (the other two are her husband's mother and his first wife, an elderly widow). Flaubert shows that Emma is caught in the conventions of her time (in Steegmuller's translation, the subtitle of the book is *Patterns of Provincial Life*). A version of the Cinderella figure, Flaubert's motherless Emma is not an empty vessel but rather someone who has absorbed the sentimental pieties and junk culture of her era; and, like most people, she had little choice. Flaubert's first description of her focuses on her hands—a kitchen maid's rough hands—but her suitor Charles also notices her fine fingernails: 'They were almond-shaped, tapering, as polished and shining as Dieppe ivories.' The conflict in her life is therefore established. And when Charles looks at her eyes, he sees that 'she had an open gaze that met yours with fearless candor'. Emma's desire to escape her harsh country life should capture any reader's sympathy. After she marries Charles, and arrives at his home from their wedding festivities, she finds the dried bridal bouquet of his deceased first wife still on the bedroom bureau, and there's no doubt that Flaubert recognizes Emma's plight; one might even think of him as a proto-feminist. Perhaps Jane Smiley overlooked such passages on her previous readings of the novel.

And the translation itself? Avoiding modern slang, Davis wisely keeps to Flaubert's language and time. English, however, has a different sound and syntax than French, and her precision can fall flat. Davis's rigid adherence to Flaubert's use of the imperfect tense (the *imparfait*) peppers the text with *would* and seems unnatural in English, even pedantic. While Flaubert showed little interest in metaphor or lyrical prose, he didn't write choppy sentences. And too often Davis's rendering of dialogue is awkward, if literal. When Emma, her husband and Monsieur Homais compare country life and food with that of the city, the sentence in Davis is, '"Because of the change in regimen," agreed the pharmacist, "and the resulting perturbation of the whole system."' Steegmuller wrote, simply, '"Because of the change of diet," agreed the pharmacist, "and the way it upsets the entire system."' The first version makes the reader pause unnecessarily, the second doesn't. Dull passages like this are common in Davis's Flaubert.

Yet in her interview for *New York Magazine* Davis dismissed other translations of *Madame Bovary*: 'Two of the most popular, Steegmuller and Hopkins—they're not bad books. They're well written in their own way. But they're not close to what Flaubert did.' This remark raises questions about what a translation can achieve—about what, in fact, it is. Any book needs to inhabit the language it's translated into, and that language has its own agenda. (Jonathan Raban rightly saw 'a deliberately postmodernist spirit' in Davis's translation.) Davis has also admitted that she dislikes Emma, and has even referred to the novel itself as 'a great book—so called'. Such reservations might have been a warning to her. A related matter may be Davis's own fiction. In an essay for the *New York Review of Books*, the poet and critic Dan Chiasson praised Davis's *Collected Stories* but admitted that she is often thought of as 'a cold writer', noting that 'her stories can seem like impersonal, even cruel personal ads', and are 'more forensic than empathic'—spot-on criticism. Davis may have forgotten her debt to Flaubert's irony (a debt shared by many modernist and postmodernist fiction writers), or want to disavow it.

In Davis's *Madame Bovary* I miss the sardonic lilt of Steegmuller's prose. Yet when her translation appears in paperback—with some of the glowing endorsements I've quoted—it is likely to be the edition that most bookstores order and keep on their shelves. University courses, where *Madame Bovary* has much of its life and sales, may go on introducing students to Emma with already familiar translations, but other readers meeting her through Davis won't know what they're missing. I wish I had a sweeter conclusion, but reviews and promotion do matter. Fortunately, for now, Steegmuller's translation of *Madame Bovary* remains in print.

The Road to Kamouraska

On the south shore of the Saint Lawrence River, in eastern Quebec, Kamouraska—having a population of 589 people in 2011—can be reached from Montreal by Autoroute 20, and then Route 132, which takes you directly into a village founded in the late seventeenth century. Or, simply open the pages of Anne Hébert's acclaimed novel *Kamouraska*, published in French in 1970, and in an evocative English translation by Norman Shapiro in 1973. If the book and author are no longer familiar names, we've come to the first of several troubling roadblocks.

The see-saw of literary reputation may reflect the merits of an individual writer's work, but it can also be shaped by the state of a literary culture and a reading community's social values. A case in point is Anne Hébert, one of the three or four most important Québécois fiction writers of the last century. Shortly before her death in January 2000, at the age of eighty-four, and after living in Paris for more than forty years, Hébert returned to Canada and settled in a Montreal apartment. During her long, rich, creative life, she received all the important prizes her country had to offer—three Governor General's Awards, an Order of Canada, the Molton prize and Quebec's Prix David, among others—as well as France's Prix Fémina. But once a writer is no longer around to keep the sales pump primed with new work, interviews and promotional tours, a fog-like neglect can set in. Even the posthumous publication of journals and letters, or reissued masterworks, or a well-researched biography, offer no guarantee of longevity.

Though it is seldom mentioned today, *Kamouraska* has all the ingredients of a national classic, an essential novel. According to the staff of its English-Canadian publisher, House of Anansi, 520 copies of the translation were sold in 2012, including course adoptions, with a subsequent decline. Based on a scandalous crime of passion—the murder in 1839 of Achille Taché, seigneur of Kamouraska, by an American doctor who was having an affair with Taché's wife—the novel recreates a vanished world through a story that reflects ancient fault lines in the Canadian body politic. Several years after *Kamouraska*'s publication, and seven translations of it (into Italian, Spanish and Japanese, etc.), the novel became the basis of a sumptuous two-hour film (1973) by Claude Jutra, with a mesmerizing performance by Geneviève Bujold. (Jutra and Hébert collaborated on the screenplay.) Unfortunately the film has never been available on DVD, was briefly released on VHS in 1998 and, alas, must now be seen, without subtitles, in a blurry, three-hour director's cut on YouTube. It says a great deal about our cultural moment when Quebec's humble poutine has become a fashionable dish in chic Manhattan restaurants, and is celebrated at an annual festival in Chicago, but *Kamouraska*—both novel and film—are largely forgotten outside Quebec. How did this happen?

For some decades now I've noticed a puzzling decline in new English translations of novels and short story collections by Québécois writers. In the years after Canada's centenary celebrations and Montreal's Expo '67, translations of French-Canadian fiction appeared frequently and were reviewed in daily newspapers. The tremendous early popularity of Pierre Elliott Trudeau probably contributed to that era's enthusiasm for francophone writers, at a time when Quebec may have seemed like an exotic *other*, offering a foreign culture to be explored. The province was not yet seen as the tinderbox it later appeared to be, at least to its detractors. (A popular joke of the day: Who is the most ardent Quebec separatist? An American draft dodger living in Toronto.) As the seventies morphed into the eighties, and another decade passed, Quebec's politics received more media coverage than its literature. Current statistics about translation are spotty, but my impression was confirmed by Dr Agnes Whitfied, who studies trends in Canadian translation activity and, since 2002, has commented on them for the annual Letters in Canada issue of the *University of Toronto Quarterly*. In a recent e-mail she suggested that the decease began in the late 1990s, with a brief stall sometime in the 2000s, and then further decline.

The reasons for this change likely include the ascent of official multiculturalism, with its focus on diversity; the fluctuating political mood in Quebec itself, which one conservative commentator, Rex Murphy, suggests has fostered a climate of 'separation fatigue'; a declining readership for all literary fiction, along with the corresponding decrease in newspaper pages devoted to book reviews; and the inadequate attention paid in secondary schools to bilingualism and Canadian history. Several years ago, for example, when I brought the great Québécois writer Marie-Claire Blais to speak at the Toronto campus where I teach, less than five percent of over 150 students in my class had heard of the Quiet Revolution, and most told me that the last time they'd studied New France was in the sixth grade.

Inevitably Canadian publishers have had to face a wall of anglophone indifference. Barry Callaghan—himself a poet and fiction writer, as well as an advocate for francophone literature as a translator and publisher of Exile Editions—lamented, simply, 'The bloom is off the rose.' While agreeing with him, Sheila Fischman, who translated many of Hébert's novels into English (though not *Kamouraska*, as several internet sites suggest), offered some hope for the future. One of her 'great pleasures' is finding new writers to translate, including Christine Eddie, Marie Hélène Poitras, Gaétan Soucy and Larry Tremblay. However, she did say that Canadian publishers who took a chance on Quebec writing have ended up with books they couldn't sell, adding that literary translation wouldn't survive without subsidies from the Canada Council and SODEC (Société de développement des entreprises culturelles). And we agreed that while francophone writers with established reputations still get published, their books are now issued by small literary presses, also dependent on grant money.

But what of *Kamouraska* the novel? Does it continue to claim our attention? Or help us understand the gap between Canada's 'two solitudes', novelist Hugh MacLennan's term for the national psyche? *Kamouraska*'s English translation is, fortunately, still available in paperback, and also as an e-book. Grounded in period detail, and told in a hallucinatory blend of poetic realism and stream-of-consciousness monologue, the novel is not the flat-footed narrative of much historical fiction but rather a profound study of human passions deeply embedded in a particular time and place. During one long June night in 1857, Madame Rolland, formerly known as Elisabeth d'Aulnières, then Elisabeth d'Aulnières-Tassy, watches over her dying second husband, Jérôme Rolland, the notary who supposedly saved her honour with a marriage offer after she was accused of the murder of her brutal first husband. Elisabeth's odyssey into the past is a woman's quest to shape her own future: in her freedom after Jérôme's death, will this mother of eleven finally try to 'Find my love, at the end of the earth'—Dr George Nelson, who fled to safety in the United States, to Burlington, Vermont, eighteen years before?

It would be too simple to see Hébert's novel as only the poetic account of an *amour fou*, a mad love, although Ben-Z. Shek has noted, in *French-Canadian and Québécois Novels* (1991), that 'Anagrammatically one could read the entire novel's narrative programme—passionate love and violent murder—in "Kamouraska", for *amour* is clearly enclosed with it, leaving *K...aska (Qu'est ce que [l] amour?* What is love?).' While part of the novel's power comes from its echoes of the distinctively French tradition of the *conte*, the moral tale of a tragic love affair associated with short novels by L'Abbé Prévost, Benjamin Constant and André Gide, *Kamouraska* might better be seen as a *conte canadien*, with the peculiarities of a subjugated people at its core.

The tensions between Canada's French and English underlie Elisabeth's story. As a child she was taught English by her maiden aunts; and the governor of Lower Canada, with 'his oh-so-British air', once commended her for speaking 'such elegant English'. Her comfortable house on Quebec City's Rue du Parloir is filled with English furniture; her two eldest sons study at Oxford University; fascinated by Queen Victoria and her family, she reads the popular novels of Sir Walter Scott (especially his tragic *Bride of Lammermoor*), and consults a copy of the *Boston Ladies' Needlework Magazine.* When Elisabeth recalls the charges against her—'the indictment, writ in the Queen's own English, by the masters of this land'—she thinks:

Out of the mouths of fools. How true. The Queen, against Elisabeth d'Aulnières? Absurd. Who would dare accuse me of offending the Queen? When it's obvious I look just like her, enough to be her sister, with all my brood around me. I look like the Queen of England. I act like the Queen of England. I'm fascinated by the image of Victoria and her children. Perfect imitation. Who could find my doing anything wrong?

Yet she has been flagrantly carrying on with Dr Nelson, often taking her young children to their assignations, where she leaves them with a sinister maid. But as she later reflects:

The Queen! Always the Queen! Couldn't you just die laughing! As if it makes the slightest difference to our dear Victoria-beyond-the sea! What does she care if there's a little adultery, a little murder, way out there on a few acres of snowy waste that England once took away from France?

The quasi-attraction Elisabeth feels for some English things is matched by her impatience with the stifling Catholic order of Quebec and its local oppressors.

Raised by pious aunts in a world of rosaries and priestly talk of sin, Elisabeth can only break from patriarchal constraints through an adulterous love, even if it threatens to destroy her. And the lover she finds, in a blinding moment of recognition, is another rebellious outsider. A dark, brooding American intellectual and dedicated doctor, George Nelson had been sent by his parents to Quebec as a child, to avoid what they saw as the pernicious influence of their Yankee compatriots, and in the hope that he would maintain Loyalist ties. As a fiction writer Hébert could have altered the facts behind her story, but her doctor remains American, not a Québécois or an Englishman. During his schooldays, Nelson had known Elisabeth's husband, and he is appalled by the debauched nature of his boyhood friend and by the bruises he sees on his lovely wife. If the novel here rings of a fairy tale, don't most love stories, at least in the beginning? Hébert knows this. Elisabeth and George are like orphans in a storm, clinging to each other, besotted. Gradually Hébert reveals their story, moving back and forth in time (often in the same paragraph) from Elisabeth's deathwatch to events of the affair and the murder, almost courting her readers until we become sympathetic to the lovers' plight, even complicit in their plan. But unlike her nineteenth-century literary sisters Emma Bovary and Anna Karenina, Elisabeth d'Aulnières refuses to die. Hébert also knows that her readers don't want that. I won't reveal the novel's surprises, though happy union rarely emerges from tragedy.

In a touching short memoir that served as the introduction to *Anne Hébert: Collected Later Novels* (2003), Mavis Gallant—Hébert's friend for more than forty years, when each made Paris her home—reminisced about their lives away from Quebec, almost as exiles, and Hébert's complicated relationships with Canada. ('Her mind was on the move to Montreal: it seemed still to be yes, no, yes, no.') Describing a collection of Hébert's poetry from 1953, Gallant called it 'elegant, haunting, and filled with death—the Quebec imagination of that period'. The same imagination characterizes *Kamouraska*, and may belong to the lasting shadow cast by centuries of unwanted cohabitation. Perhaps English Canada, tied to its long-ago victory over the French, can never feel quite comfortable with itself, or freed from the past. *Let's look away, not read, or translate, or think about them anymore.* Indifference seems okay.

Of course it isn't. *Je me souviens*, declare the licence plates on Autoroute 20. And if it weren't for Anne Hébert, the prototypes of her characters would be forgotten, or only a footnote in a distant true-crime story, a tidbit of very old gossip. Historical memory matters, and great books—what we like to call literature—help keep it alive. *Kamouraska* mustn't become a footnote as well, it's too passionate for that. All you have to do is turn to its opening lines, with their hint of foreboding, and you're in the hands of a remarkably clear-eyed storyteller: 'The summer went by from beginning to end. Unlike other years, Madame Rolland didn't leave her home in Rue du Parloir. It was very fair, very warm. But neither Madame nor the children went to the country that summer ...'

Don Quixote and the End of Life

On May 19, 1934, the Nobel laureate German writer Thomas Mann set out on his first ocean voyage across the Atlantic to America. With his sixtieth birthday in the next year looming, thoughts of old age were on his mind. For companionship during the ten-day crossing he brought along a four-volume German translation of *The Ingenious Gentleman Don Quixote of La Mancha*, generally known as *Don Quixote*, by Miguel de Cervantes (1547–1616). Mann had also decided to keep an account of his reading, jotting down reflections about the celebrated novel in a short diary that was later published as an essay called 'Voyage with Don Quixote'.

Cervantes's novel, and Mann's essay, have recently been much in my thoughts. As the year 2016 marks the 400th anniversary of Cervantes's death, I gave a senior seminar on his novel. *Don Quixote* was originally published in two parts—Part I in 1605 and Part II in 1615—so another 400th anniversary had just passed. Unlike Mann, however, I was able to look back on my sixth decade, which made Cervantes's thoughts about the end of life all the more compelling. When Part II appeared, Cervantes was approaching his seventieth year (a considerable age for the time), and the novel summed up his experience of the world. I knew that its daunting length—940 pages in Edith Grossman's lively translation—would challenge my students, but welcomed the opportunity to work slowly through the book with them, chapter by chapter. And I'm glad to say that the seminar was a happy experience for all of us, except for one thing. My students objected to the end of the book: they didn't want Don Quixote to die, and they disliked the way Cervantes handled his death. They may have been right to object. But first, a few words about the book itself.

One of the most influential novels of the so-called Western canon, *Don Quixote* has been translated into almost as many languages as the Bible, and any good summary of its influence would require a book in itself. Even people who have never opened a page of the novel are familiar with famous moments from it (the battle with giants, in the form of windmills, for example), or with popular images of this by Picasso and Dali, or cartoon and opera and ballet versions, films in several languages and theatrical adaptations such as the Broadway musical of 1965, *Man of La Mancha*. The book has even entered our consciousness with the word *quixotic* and the phrase *tilting at windmills*. You might say that Don Quixote and his sidekick, Sancho Panza, are a ubiquitous part of our culture. So what about that death scene?

With a nod to T.S. Eliot's admonition 'in my beginning is my end', I need to start earlier. Don Quixote's story is told by a narrator who claims to be 'recounting' the Castilian translation of an Arabic novel written by Cide Hamete Benengeli. With a huge cast of Spanish Christians, Moors and Jews, it's as multicultural as any work of fiction could prove to be. In the first chapter we learn very little about the man who becomes Don Quixote, and this is an essential part of Cervantes's genius. 'Somewhere in La Mancha,' he wrote, 'in a place whose name I do not care to remember, a gentleman lived not long ago, one of those who has a lance and ancient shield on a shelf and keeps a skinny nag and a greyhound for racing.' This gentleman, named Alonso Quixano, is an Everyman figure. He's unmarried, without family except for a sometimes intrusive niece and a few friendly neighbours, but he has a large library of chivalric romances that have driven him mad ('With these words and phrases the poor gentleman lost his mind'). We're also told that he is 'approximately fifty years old'. He takes the name 'Don Quixote' when he decides to right his world's wrongs, heading out on a quest that is simultaneously comic and tragic. We often think of Don Quixote and his sidekick, Sancho Panza, as classic doubles, a pair of opposites, or odd couple, who make up some kind of whole. But the first and perhaps most essential doubling in the novel is that of the meek Alonso Quixano with the bold Don Quixote in an act of self-invention, a change in identity that is transformative.

The American critic Harold Bloom, who has made a specialty of 'wisdom literature', naturally turned to Don Quixote's quest and why it has captured the imagination of so many readers for four centuries. Speaking of the Knight of the Sorrowful Countenance, as Don Quixote was dubbed by one of the novel's characters, Bloom wrote: 'He is at war with Freud's reality principle, which accepts the necessity of dying. But he is neither a fool nor a madman, and his vision always is at least double: he sees what we see, yet he sees something else also, a possible glory that he desires to appropriate or at least share.' *The necessity of dying*. Why, after all, must one die? Yes, it's written in the stars, or whatever metaphor you like, but something about death always seems wrong. It's too easy to say that death is the price of life. In an age of constant warfare and uncontrollable plagues, Cervantes understood the deep human aversion to death. The core of his novel, therefore, is a desire for transcendence from the limitations of the human condition. Immortality? Perhaps. Hard to say, exactly—which is part of the pleasure to be had from the novel. But one thing is clear. After following Don Quixote in his adventures and mis-adventures (which often touch on death, including suicide), Sancho Panza, that advocate of common sense and material reality, becomes a convert to his master's role as a knight errant and to his vision, as do the novel's readers. We don't want Don Quixote to die.

Most literary quests are circular, with the protagonist (usually a youth) returning home in the end. As an old man abandoning a routine, unlived life to recapture the bygone age of chivalry through adventures associated with young heroes, Don Quixote makes several returns home. After first setting out, he learns that knights need to be self-sufficient, and briefly seeks the money that will help him succeed (that reality principle, again). At the end of Part I, which Cervantes probably saw as a complete novel, Don Quixote is returned to La Mancha, initially caged as a madman. At home, 'Don Quixote's housekeeper and niece welcomed him, and undressed him, and put him in his old bed. He stared at them, his eyes transfixed, and did not understand where he was.' At this point the novel's narrator pulls back from his story, or 'history' as he calls it, suggesting that he does not know precisely what happened next. This open ending eschews the traditional storyteller's solutions of marriage, death and the like. Don Quixote, not Alonso Quixano, is asleep in an unfamiliar bed. Life goes on.

What then happened to Cervantes matters here. *Don Quixote* became, almost overnight, a success, and was soon read across the continent, in translation. The story was so appealing that another writer (whose identity is still debated) wrote a sequel to it, and Cervantes had to return to his tale to confirm ownership. He brought out Part II ten years after the novel's publication. And those must have been difficult years for Cervantes. He'd had a hard life, been a soldier, lost the use of one hand at the Battle of Lepanto (1571), been captured by pirates and imprisoned for five years, had even been cheated by his publisher and lived in near poverty. Aging and in ill health, he could not allow another writer to claim his characters, so Don Quixote, mad as ever, sallies forth to new adventures, accompanied again by Sancho Panza. If there's a message here, it's simply 'Keep working'. As perhaps befits an older protagonist, the adventures of Part II have less to do with courtly love, chivalric romance and pastoral couples than those of Part I. Cervantes now focuses mainly on encounters that question and challenge the nature of reality.

The death scene that closes Part II is painful because it seems, at first, to be a repudiation of the novel's fantasy. This may be what my students objected to. In their early twenties, they were like the young protagonists of traditional epic quests, at the beginning of what they hoped would be eventful long lives. What Don Quixote offers as his final answer won't encourage any young adventurer. He is defeated in his last battle by the Knight of the White Moon, a mirror-like reflection of himself; reality triumphs. By then Don Quixote the character has supposedly read Cervantes's account of his adventures as well as the false Part II; he now rejects the chivalric way of life and, calmly approaching his village, says to Sancho, 'Let us get off to a good start in our village, where we shall exercise our imaginations and plan the pastoral life we intend to lead.' The pastoral, of course, is a sophisticated dream of urbanites, and has little to do with the hardships of any shepherd's existence. It's a dream of simplicity, more befitting an old man than the desire for knightly exploits. Once Don Quixote confesses his defeats, and explains that he would like to be called 'Shepherd Quixotiz', he heads to bed for a long rest. He wants to be at peace with himself and his past, shedding the madness of all life's noble scrambles.

Reality, however, seems to have been too much for him. He is fragile, broken, but touchingly human in his weaknesses and failure. The final chapter of Part II opens with this:

> Since human affairs, particularly the lives of men, are not eternal and are always in a state of decline from their beginnings until they reach their final end, and since the life of Don Quixote had no privilege from heaven to stop its natural course, it reached its end and conclusion when he least expected it, for whether it was due to the melancholy caused by his defeat or simply the will of heaven, he succumbed to a fever that kept him in bed for six days, during which time he was often visited by his friends the priest, the bachelor, and the barber, while Sancho Panza, his good squire, never left his side.

On waking from the fever, he announces, 'Good news, Señores! I am no longer Don Quixote of la Mancha but Alonso Quixano, once called *the Good* because of my virtuous life.' He renounces his knight errantry 'by God's mercy', writes his will, receives absolution and, as the narrator remarks, 'gave up the ghost, I mean to say, he died'. There seems to be a shift in tone here from the satire and parody of the bulk of the book to a more elegiac vision. Yet a subtle irony underscores the death scene. Soon we learn that the death certificate of Cervantes's 'Ingenious Gentleman' does not name the town where he died, 'so that all the villages of La Mancha might contend themselves to claim him as their own, as the seven cities in Greece contended to claim Homer.' Later, the narrator writes, 'For me alone was Don Quixote born, and I for him; he knew how to act, and I to write.' But who is that 'I'? The narrator or Cide Hamete Benengeli? Both of them, in a sense, but mostly Cervantes, who transforms Don Quixote's death from a Christian bedside re-conversion back into the novel's more secular religion of the imagination.

Of course people are uncomfortable looking at the end of life. Today's well-intentioned social workers and gerontologists, psychologists and confessors, lifestyle journalists and marketers, all warn us to stay active, exercise mind and body, socialize, get involved, think young. 'Who needs a *memento mori*?' they seem to ask. But why shy away from a confrontation? Who defeats death? That, of course, was Cervantes's great subject. His answer: no one. And we'd better accept it.

Don Quixote's death scene arouses an experience of my own. Anyone who has been with an elderly parent while he or she dies will understand its painful privilege. On the January night when my mother died in her eighty-eighth year, I sat by her bedside, aware that she was 'at the end', in the words of one nurse. This took place in the most caring of nursing homes, with my four-year-old pug Rennie—my shadow—at the foot of Mother's bed, his head resting against her ankle. When Mother took her last breath at four a.m., the nurses suggested I leave the room while they prepared her body for the undertaker. I called to Rennie. He looked me in the eye and refused to budge. So I left the room with the door ajar, assuming he would follow. But he didn't. After ten minutes the nurses called me back. Rennie was still on the bed, at Mother's feet, staring up at me. One nurse said that he'd growled when she first touched my mother's arm. Since Rennie was the gentlest of dogs, and I'd never heard him growl, I was puzzled. Apparently the presence of death hadn't frightened him;

indeed, it seemed to cause him to remain with my mother, almost guarding her. I've mentioned this story to doctors, veterinarians, dog trainers, philosophers, even one priest, and no one could offer an explanation that satisfied me—a fact that is oddly comforting.

And what of Thomas Mann's ocean-voyage journal? Like my students, Mann was bothered by Don Quixote's death, which he saw as an inevitable plot device to protect the character's creator. More important, though, was this objection: 'Certainly it was imperative to save Don Quixote's soul to sanity before he died. But in order that this salvation might be after our hearts, the author should have made his unreason less lovable.' On the last morning of his voyage Mann recalled his dream of the previous night. He'd spoken with Don Quixote, found him 'very tactful and courteous', and was filled with 'pain, love, pity and boundless reverence' because, in Cervantes's words, 'both while he was plain Alonso Quixano and while he was Don Quixote de La Mancha, he was ever of an amiable disposition and affable behaviour, and was therefore beloved, not only by those of his own family, but by all that knew him'. Mann was too grandly solemn here, disregarding the pages that followed Quixote's death. Considering his love of the book's humour and its gentle satire—the light, forgiving touch that could make life's difficulties seem bearable—he might have included another quotation that deserves repeating: 'For me alone was Don Quixote born, and I for him; he knew how to act, and I to write.' That's clearly the right epitaph for both Don Quixote and Cervantes.

In Search of Diana Thorne

Who was Diana Thorne? On first asking this question, I had no idea where it might lead me, and that answering it would threaten to become a life's work. A notable dog painter, illustrator and author during the late 1920s through the '40s, Thorne—who claimed to have been born in Winnipeg—had more than thirty books to her credit (many for children). As well, she held numerous solo exhibitions of her oil paintings, pastels, watercolours and etchings in leading art galleries across North America. Her classic *Drawing Dogs* (1940) went through several reprintings in the United States and England. Thorne painted a portrait of Franklin Delano Roosevelt's beloved Scottish terrier Fala in addition to those of dogs owned by many celebrities of her time, including Gary Cooper and Katharine Cornell. Then, around 1950 or so, she seems to have vanished. Puzzled by this, I didn't guess that my research would lead in unexpected directions, to subjects like Russian-Jewish immigration, wartime internment and contrived identities, or that I would end up questioning the practices of many contemporary libraries and archives.

The story began one August afternoon in 2008. While browsing in an antiques mall near Shaker Heights, Ohio, I came across a tattered oversized book titled *Puppy Stories*, with colour illustrations by Diana Thorne, that had been published in 1934. Now I'm a sucker for old books about dogs, an interest that grew out of my research for a study of the human/dog bond, as well as from my reading for an anthology of dog stories I was editing. That summer I hoped to find a good cover subject for it. Flipping through *Puppy Stories* I was struck by a pastel drawing of a Boston terrier, a breed my family had enjoyed since the 1920s.

When my anthology's publisher approved the image, I set out to clear permission for its use, beginning with an Internet search for the Saalfield Publishing Company of Akron, Ohio, which had brought out the book. A once-prominent publisher of children's books, Saalfield closed its offices in 1977, when its papers were deposited in the Kent State

University Archives. However, nothing there addressed my concerns, and I began searching for Thorne's birth and death years. This ought to have been a simple task, considering our fine libraries and sophisticated technology. After all, I wasn't researching the death date of an obscure 13th-century monk/illustrator. Or so I thought.

After contacting many of North America's best public and museum libraries, I found that only a few were able to do more than check Internet sites. Standard reference books—such as *Who Was Who in American Art 1564–1975*, *Biographical Index of Artists in Canada*, *Dictionary of Women Artists* and *Illustrators of Children's Books 1744–1945*—were also unhelpful; too many reference writers have been content to repeat, without questioning, 'facts' in previous studies, thus perpetuating errors. I also learned that most libraries have discarded their old vertical files of clippings from newspapers and magazines, as if the entire world of print, or at least what matters, has been scanned and digitalized. This reminded me of the novelist Nicholson Baker's book *Double Fold: Libraries and the Assault on Paper*, a lament about the microfilming of old newspapers, the end of the card-catalogue system, and the loss of the information they had contained. Baker's book may have seemed like the reflections of an eccentric Luddite to some readers but I thought otherwise. The loss of the material that was once kept in vertical files, now discarded, is a serious one. As well, I soon learned that public archives like the Bureau of Vital Records of New York's Department of Health were unable to offer assistance because concerns about identity theft have solidified policies that prevent them from releasing birth or death records (if they have them) to anyone but family members. But I'm getting ahead of my story.

Thorne's year and place of birth, according to reference books and most websites, were 1895 and Winnipeg, Manitoba; oddly, none of these sources included a death year. However, Thorne's biography on DogsCo.com, which deals with dog art and collectibles, suggested that she was actually born Ann Woursell on October 7, 1895, in Odessa, Russia. While I'm skeptical about much Internet information—and Frank J. Leskovitz, who was responsible for the site, did not respond to my queries—the reference to 'Ann Woursell' had to be followed. Were Thorne and Woursell one and the same? I would need to go back to as many original documents as I could find.

Newspaper articles related to Thorne—announcements of exhibitions, subsequent reviews and profiles—tell only a part of her story. The earliest reference to her in the *New York Times* comes from an advertisement she ran on July 19, 1925, for 'hand-painted' dresses:

> Smart women are wearing and will wear during the coming season hand-painted frocks for all occasions. Mine are different from anything you have seen. Each frock is an individual creation. NO *duplicates.* Wear one and be distinct! Your own ideas of color-scheme and design. *Write for further information* DIANA THORNE, 211 West 11th Street, New York, N.Y., Telephone *Penn*—0015.

The Greenwich Village address caught my eye, but more significant is that the name 'Diana Thorne' was being used by 1925. While New York's garment industry has long been associated with Jewish immigration to the United States, and the rich culture that grew from it, this advertisement appears to be Thorne's only connection to the 'rag' trade. (A technique common in Chinese and Japanese clothing design for centuries, painting on silk probably accompanied the popular Oriental revival in the 1920s. Similar to silkscreen, the procedure would be familiar to someone who had studied printmaking.) The advertisement shows Thorne's entrepreneurial streak, yet she may not have made a success of the venture. I suggest this because her next appearance in the *Times* was in an article from March 6, 1928, titled 'Dog Quits Modeling To Lead Her Own Life; Pat, Posing Terrier, Jumps Out of Taxicab in Union Square and Disappears'. Pat, the wire-haired terrier in question, belonged to Thorne, whom the article refers to as 'the etcher, of 47 West Fifty-second Street', also noting that the missing dog was one of Thorne's regular subjects (Pat's image had already appeared in the Book Review section of the *Times*). The article goes on to say that Thorne was using Pat 'as the principal model in a book of etchings she is preparing', indicating that in less than three years Thorne had changed the focus of her endeavours and gained enough status in the Manhattan arts community to merit a human-interest article of this sort.

Here is where a library's vertical files first came into the story. One winter morning I had the good fortune to visit the library of the Cleveland Museum of Art, which had several thick files devoted to Thorne's work. After an hour at the photocopier, taking care not to damage any of the fragile newspaper clippings, I understood the treasure trove at hand. One item interested me in particular: a copy of the invitation to Thorne's first New York exhibition, of drypoints and drawings, at the

Schwartz Galleries on Madison Avenue, from April 8–27, 1929. It wasn't the invitation itself—but rather the brief artist's biography it included—that mattered to me:

> Born in Winnipeg in 1895, Diana Thorne of an early age went to Europe, where she received her education at the Imperial Academy in Munich, and the Charlottenburg Technical College in Berlin, where she worked at Anatomy and Design. Caught in the war-net, she escaped with her five younger sisters to England, where she began an adventurous career as vicar-mother, newspaper reporter, librarian, scenario writer, fiction writer and what-have-you; in the meantime, drawing and etching as opportunity offered, and studying under the late William Strang whose sound techniques formed the safe ground work for her individual experiment in Etching. To America in 1917, and in 1926 the opportunity offered for the publication of her plate 'Rollin' Home', which met with a success pleasant but unexpected and which thence narrowed her work to this direction.
>
> Fine Prints of the Year and the Fifty Best Prints of the Year selected her 'Pan of Puck's Hill'. She was then elected member of the Chicago Society of Etchers, California Print-Makers, and acclaimed by the late Haldane MacHall, doyen of the British Critics of Fine Art as likeable only to Kate Greenaway in Whimsical Humor and understanding of Dog and Child. Miss Thorne in this, her first showing in New York, is at the outset of a career of an astonishing promise justified by her attainment.

Since Thorne surely would have approved this biography, she must have also supplied Winnipeg as her birthplace; over time it became part of her official biography. Gradually Thorne appears to have elaborated on this 'fact', blending details of her actual history with a preferred version of her self. If it hadn't been for a well-kept vertical file, this single piece of paper folded in quarters—a seemingly valueless old invitation—would not have come to my attention.

Thorne's first exhibition in New York must have been a success because shortly after it her work was shown by galleries across the United States—during the early years of the Depression, a difficult time for artists. Enthusiastic reviews appeared along with interviews. *Arts Digest,* the *Boston Post,* the *Chicago Tribune,* the *Christian Science Monitor,* the *Cincinnati Post,* the *Detroit News,* the *New York Times,* and Canada's *Saturday Night* all devoted space to Thorne and her work. As well, illustrations by Thorne began to appear regularly in their pages, and soon in popular magazines, from the *American Magazine* and *Nature Magazine* to the *Woman's Home Companion.*

In interview after interview Thorne maintained the 'fact' of her Winnipeg birth, spoke of her father as 'a wealthy Canadian rancher' and suggested a background of privilege, with a governess and tutors. But something didn't add up. While in some interviews her family consisted of five sisters, in others there were four sisters and a brother. In 1930 she told the *Cincinnati Post* that she became interested in painting while visiting Germany with her mother, and that 'she was forced to support her family when her father lost his wealth during the war'. But in a 1929 *Saturday Night* profile, she spoke of an idyllic childhood: 'What did I do in Winnipeg? Oh, I read Shelley and took rides on horses.' She also mentioned that she had been 'a strange, silent child who spent half of her leisure reading Hegel and Kant and the other half devouring the adventures of Robin Hood'. Thorne recalled joining her father on his visits to various Alberta ranchers, noting that he made a great contribution to her intellectual and emotional development: 'A long dissertation on the immortality of the soul was as likely as not to be followed by a fishing trip to the nearest pond.'

In a *Chicago Daily Times* interview from 1930, Thorne claimed that after her cattle-ranch childhood she 'went to Munich and Berlin to study art, and was caught there during the war and taken for a spy'. She also noted that after escaping to London she ran a bicycle shop while studying etching. *Who Was Who in American Art* quotes her as saying that she was 'sent to France and Germany, and later to Scotland to study etching'. In the *Christian Science Monitor* she claims that at the age of eighteen she was left with the smaller children of her family to support, and that she escaped to England 'after being suspected as a spy'. For the *New York Times* she claimed to have escaped from Germany to England with her younger sister, 'with just a few pounds between them and starvation'; that she worked as a typewriter repairwoman; and that upon arriving in America after the armistice she 'became a publicity director for several actresses who rewarded her with magnificent evening gowns' (the vertical file that included this interview did not have a date marked on it—a frequent occurrence with many old newspaper clippings). In another undated interview, from the *Christian Science Monitor,* Thorne was asked how she first came to paint animals: 'It probably all began because I had a wonderful Scotsman for a father, and was born on a farm ranch in Winnipeg, Manitoba.' The interviewer, Barbara E. Scott Fisher, concludes: 'This artist didn't begin modelling animals in mud back in Winnipeg for nothing, nor did her far-sighted father make any mistake when he consulted the great French sculptor Rodin about a little colt that the child had modeled while playing in the paddock.' As late as 1940, in the *Detroit News Pictorial*, Thorne recalled that at an early age 'she went to work to support five younger sisters because of her father's illness'. Was Thorne a fantasist? A habitual liar?

Six months after I began my research I hired an assistant, a former student, Jennifer Hann, who has a rare interest in history and exceptional computer skills. We began compiling a collection of public documents related to Thorne and her family from such sources as the records of Ellis Island; the United Kingdom Incoming Passenger Lists, 1878–1968; the Census of Manitoba, 1906; the Census of Canada, 1911; the American Petition for Citizenship; the World War II Draft Registration; and the Social Security Death Index. The Kerlan Collection, an archive devoted to figures connected to children's books, had a file of letters related to Thorne, and photocopies were ordered. I was now flooded with paper.

Then, one May morning, while I was marking exams in my campus office, the telephone rang. Persistent queries had finally located one of Thorne's relatives, a great-niece. By now I'd speculated about a sad end to Thorne's life, and felt protective of her. After all, most people who've had a career of note in the arts don't disappear without a trace. That telephone call led to others, and soon I spoke with the daughter of Thorne's sister Paula, as well as this niece's husband, and later their daughter, an artist in her own right. The puzzle began to come together.

Thorne's father, Chaim (Charles) Woursell, first visited Winnipeg in 1903, at the age of 33, bringing with him $2,500; he described himself as a 'married cattle dealer'. Liking the prospects offered by the city, which had a growing community of Russian-Jewish immigrants, he returned in 1906 with his family, this time in possession of $9,500. The family included his wife, Rosa, 32, and six children: Anna, 11; Abraham, 9; Paulina, 6; Ida, 4; Samuel, 2; and Geta, 7 months. Ellis Island records note 'Hebrew' alongside their names. Over the years, records of the names of the children vary: Anna is once registered as Emma; Ida becomes Ada and later Edith; Geta becomes Kitty and later Lola. As well, the last name is spelled variously in different documents—mostly as 'Woursell' but sometimes as 'Woursel', 'Wourcell' and even 'Weursell'. The name itself made me wonder if it was a variant on the German 'Würzel' (the word means 'root'); some German-Jewish families had settled in Odessa in the mid-nineteenth century. Thorne's last surviving niece recalled that her mother, Paula (Paulina), thought 'Woursell' may have been taken from the name 'Varsa'. She believed that her grandfather had attended university in Russia and been a political progressive who'd shared sympathies with the early Zionists; he had taken his patrimony to Canada, along with an attractive wife who was not of the same social class. At any rate, the Woursell family was living in Winnipeg during the 1906 census, and for business reasons Chaim soon moved it Calgary, where a seventeen-year-old female Roman Catholic 'domestic' from Galicia (hardly a governess or tutor) lived with them.

Around 1912 Chaim became ill with a serious lung problem (perhaps tuberculosis) and moved the family to Berlin, Germany, where doctors specialized in his condition. The family had a more than comfortable lifestyle until the outbreak of war, when their money was confiscated. Thorne's brother Abraham, nearing draft age, was interned, and the family—perhaps without Chaim—moved to Bristol, England (where Paula went to boarding school), and then to London. Chaim was reputed to be a charming fellow, attractive to the ladies. Here, of course, the story depends on memory, and memories of old retellings. Abraham was eventually released to his family, and in 1920 the Woursells settled in New York City. Chaim arrived first, from Le Havre, on March 13th, followed by his son Abraham, on September 17th, also from Le Havre, and then by the rest of the family, on September 29th, on the same ship from Liverpool. (In the 1911 census Chaim had listed his son Abraham as a 'cattle dealer', and he may have been helping to set him up with the business connections he'd previously made in New York's meat-packing industry.) That year Chaim made three trips between England and the United States, returning to Europe without his family and then seemingly vanishing. Abraham settled in New York, along with his mother and siblings, and became a successful businessman.

Out of this history Thorne fashioned a public persona, and like many artists who devote some of their creative powers to self-invention, she played loose with the facts of her life. She must have had a forceful personality in order to put her stories across. Various interviewers described her with these phrases: 'that bundle of human energy known as Diana Thorne'; 'the little black-eyed artist'; 'her dynamo energy'; 'casual and dynamic all at the same time'; and my favourite, 'Her dark eyes seemed to penetrate to the bottom of things at a glance. She had the quick light step of the walker, small wiry hands—and strong—and an engaging smile.' Clearly an attractive person, which always helps in building any career in the arts, Thorne had a keen awareness of herself as a public figure. She complained of 'autograph hunters' and 'photograph hunters' who should prefer a photograph of a painting to one of the painter, and to one interviewer she said, in a Garboesque fashion, 'Like most public persons, I am frequently misquoted.' 'Too much publicity,' she told a *Detroit News* interviewer in 1930, 'is no better for dogs than for humans.' (In the same interview she went on to speak of a Boston family who took down one of their family portraits by Sargent to make room for her portrait of their old collie.)

Drawing on public records, I can conclude that Thorne was born in 1894 (a date that appears on some census records), despite her stories. Her brother Abraham, the second of the six siblings, was born on April 25, 1896, according not only to immigration records but also the U.S. World War II Draft Registry. Counting backwards, it's unlikely that Thorne's birth date could have been October 7, 1895, especially in light of the medical conditions of that era. Newspaper obituaries, when accurate, can also be informative. I was puzzled not to find one for a person of Thorne's renown, but she did appear as 'Diana Thorne' in the *New York Times* obituary for her mother in 1954, and several years later, in 1957, as 'Ann Woursell North' in the *Times* obituary for Abraham. This was the best proof that Diana Thorne and Ann Woursell were one.

The letters from the Kerlan Collection make up almost 200 pages and include a correspondence from 1930 to 1940 between Thorne and Dr C.C. Young of Lansing, Michigan, who was the Director of the Division of Laboratories of the Michigan Department of Health, as well as various letters regarding Thorne's work from gallery owners and publishers. An admirer of Thorne, Young hoped to collect examples of everything she had completed—from individual pieces to books—for an annotated bibliography, with the help of his colleague and wife, Minna Crooks Young, who also became an epistolary confidante of Thorne's. The letters are a candid look at the travails of an artist's life, but while reading them I often felt like an intruder, since they were not meant for my eyes. On April 27, 1936, Thorne wrote to Crooks: 'But look here seriously, those letters of mine are pretty sketchy affairs. They shouldn't be kept as records.

Really.' She was wrong. If letters like these had covered Thorne's entire life it would be possible to construct a detailed biography, allowing for the secrets she kept from even those closest to her.

Thorne's private life is something of a mystery. Reference books and websites claim that she was married to a Mr Arthur North of Philadelphia, and that she made her home there. (No records can be found to corroborate this, and none suggest that she ever lived in Pennsylvania.) It's even been claimed that Ann Woursell took the name Diana Thorne as an anagram of North. Certainly the name (which she was using in 1925, if not earlier), has an anglophile ring to it that would appeal to a woman who called her father 'a wonderful Scotsman' when she knew this to be untrue. The casual and often official anti-Semitism of public life during the years Thorne was making her way as an artist are not to be ignored. Many immigrants altered their names in an attempt to pass as part of the American WASP mainstream rather than face the prejudice that was commonplace, and Jewish immigrants faced additional animosity.

Several sources suggest that Thorne may have had a second marriage, to Carton Moore-Park (1877–1956), a fellow artist. Her niece believes that her aunt never married, but that she had a long-term relationship with an older married man, and I've come to agree with her. Moore-Park is thought to have been born in either New Brunswick or the Hebrides. Often referred to as a Scots-Canadian artist, he was an illustrator and portraitist who studied in Glasgow and settled in New York City around 1910. My suspicion is that North and Moore-Park were one and the same, another fiction that may have been a public cover for an illicit relationship. In her letters Thorne often spoke of her husband, Arthur, a sickly and aging portrait artist she doted on. (She wrote to Dr Young in the fall of 1930: 'Mr North was at one time one of England's ablest portrait painters—he is now practically retired—never touches a portrait.'). Thorne also mentioned a young man named Howard, whose identity and relationship with 'the Norths' is unclear. Moore-Park did have a son named Howard (1907–1983), who donated paintings by his father to museums in the United States and Britain, and such a coincidence seems unlikely. (Moore-Park's wife, Annette, had followed him to America in 1913, with Howard. According to the *New York Times* of May 25, 1923, she was held on $100 bail before a trial for sending harassing letters to a woman—not Thorne—she'd accused of alienating her husband's affections.) Another puzzle: a copy of a photograph dated '1928', from a vertical file in the Boston Public Library, shows 'Diana Thorne' sitting between her sister 'Kitty' and her husband 'Carton Moore Park'. Even more curious, shipping records from 1935 note that Thorne and Moore-Park travelled together to England that summer under the names 'Ann Woursell' and 'Carton Woursell', at a time when Thorne was signing letters 'Mrs Arthur North'. Both falsely gave Canada as their 'last country of permanent residence', and they remained together in England until the following summer. I should add that Moore-Park and Thorne never became naturalized American citizens, although most of Thorne's family did. Finally, in a letter of 1969 to Howard 'Moorepark' from one of Thorne's publishers, regarding her estate—a letter sent to me by a great-niece—'Mrs Diana Thorne North' was referred to as 'your step-mother'.

Some of the family's remarks about Thorne were startling. 'They were a strange family, they were all liars,' one person observed. Thorne's niece, who remembers meeting her aunt only several times, said, 'She was an incredible liar.' She went on to describe a luncheon Thorne gave for twelve guests, at a hotel in Manhattan's Murray Hill neighbourhood, in 1945. The niece, then seventeen, arrived on time but only three other guests appeared. Thorne greeted her and without further attention turned back to the male guests—'boy is she strange,' her niece recalled thinking. 'There was a great tradition of fabrication in the family,' one grand-niece said, 'and when they didn't like the truth, they changed it.' I prefer the word 'fabulist' for someone like Thorne, who emerges from her letters as a hard-working person, and who seems to have embellished situations with no apparent reason (for example, her remarks about five younger sisters rather than three sisters and two brothers). It's fair to speculate that as the eldest child she may have felt responsible for her mother and her siblings, and had also been aware that she wasn't able to provide for them as she might have wished. In interviews she spoke of her father with love and admiration, and his absence from the family must have been painful. Since women of Thorne's time were expected to confine their interests to the domestic sphere, an identification with her father may have been crucial to Thorne's efforts to make a career for herself. That she ended up living with an ailing artist seventeen years her senior is almost too Freudian to ponder.

The financial life of all but the most successful artists is precarious. In New York City's competitive art world, where new talent was arriving annually from art schools across the country, opportunities for profitable work must have been frustrating, especially with the passing years. Gradually I saw that many of Thorne's fabrications were a kind of self-advertising, born of her particular situation. In order to receive the lucrative commissions she needed, Thorne had to present herself to the monied establishment in a way that made them comfortable with her. That her clients would have valued status and appearances, and may have been anti-Semitic, should be kept in mind. Thorne was smart enough to realize that even during the hard years of the Depression, this clientele had disposable income that could be used to commemorate their purebred pets, for purebred dogs had become one of the favoured luxuries of that era. When it was convenient, Thorne presented herself as British. Interviewers have described her as 'a young Englishwoman', but Eleanor Jewett wrote in the *Chicago Daily Tribune*, in 1930: 'Diana Thorne is not in the least the typical Englishwoman. She acknowledges she was born in Canada and that explains much of the irrelevance of her appearance and manner. She has a great deal more of the French than the British in her. She is dark, sparkling, animated and speaks with a slight accent.' (Suspicious of journalists, Thorne had written to Young, on August 9, 1930: 'Newspaper people have very little imagination; they always want to know what someone else has written.')

Thorne needed to travel frequently for work, moving her studio for months at a time to different cities (Boston, Chicago, Detroit) to acquire and paint her commissions. She told one interviewer, 'Artists do not make money by trying to do so. It makes itself for them when they do not seek it. At least, this was my experience.' Not exactly, but the right persona mattered. In 1930, a journalist in the *Cincinnati Post* observed: 'A report that Miss Thorne is to make portraits of favourite dogs owned by Henry Ford and his son was gently set aside, neither denied nor confirmed, by the woman artist.' (This was a time when the word 'woman' was often attached to the word 'artist' as if there was something unusual, to say the least, about a woman making art.) When she was able to stay in one place for longer periods, despite her 'restless spirit' as she called it in a letter from 1936, Thorne always thrived on private hours of creation. After Young's first visit to her Chicago studio in June 1930, she wrote: 'It is heavenly today to be at work quietly on my etching with not a soul to disturb the work (I have "padlocked" the telephone and the doorbell.).' Thorne had this to say about her working methods, in an article for the *Christian Science Monitor* in 1936:

Dogs have been shipped to my New York studio from all parts of the country—from Maine and Arizona, from Florida and from California. If for one reason or another I cannot leave the city at the time the commission is placed in my hands, the owners send their dog to me for a week or two. He lives in my studio with me under my personal care and becomes my friend for life. I enjoy the visits; so do the dogs.

There's every reason to believe she meant these words.

The Depression and its effect on the art market also became a recurring theme in Thorne's letters. After a painting stint in Chicago, she wrote to Dr Young, on December 18, 1930: 'I found conditions in the East extremely depressing—New York is in mourning. Really seriously. I never saw anything like it since the war.' By August 3, 1931, she could write: 'There's no money in fine art these days—nothing but expense and irritation.' The Depression forced her to concentrate on book and magazine illustrations. 'Prints don't sell, so naturally one has to do something else,' she wrote to Young several months later. 'I have had my nerves on edge all the time from irritation caused by dealing with these stupid and sometimes also cheerfully crooked institutions and individuals,' she wrote in July 1932. Yet despite economic insecurity and the steady scramble for commissions, Thorne described an existence that included winter trips to Key West and Havana, fishing holidays in Maine, polo matches on Long Island, horse races at Saratoga—her husband's health, work opportunities and potential exhibitions were often cited as reasons for the constant travel. Meanwhile, she moved from one good Manhattan rental to another. In 1934 she created a short-lived American Authors and Artists Agency, then decided to visit England. On August 4, 1935, she wrote to Young: 'I gave up our apartment, chucked a lot of stuff into storage and decided to get a change or die in the effort!' The year abroad did not bring the commissions she'd hoped for, but rejuvenated by the trip, the couple returned to New York and Thorne's American contacts. Soon she was pursuing work while publishers were busy remaindering overstock. She now had to work for royalties, not advances—slow money.

Given the financial pressures Thorne faced, it wasn't a surprise to hear from her relatives that she often borrowed money from her brothers, and that they didn't expect it to be returned. One Sunday morning in December 1948 she appeared at a relation's Manhattan apartment, looking for fifty dollars while explaining that she'd been with Harry

S. Truman's entourage on the night that he won the presidency. Was this true? It hardly matters now, but the mention of Truman does suggest Thorne's political values, as well as her continuing desire to appear as a person of social standing. (According to Thorne's letters, she also borrowed money from Dr Young and regularly from 'another friend, my lawyer'.) Another family story suggests that she wasn't particularly good at managing money. Thorne's niece remembered a complaint from her grandmother about her aunt, who had once received a commission from the Dupont family to repair the hand-painted Chinese wallpaper in the dining-room of one of their homes, near Washington, D.C. The task suited Thorne, who bought herself a diamond ring with her payment.

Thorne mentioned her childhood only once in the Kerlan letters, during a cold spell in January 1940: 'I hate cold and always have considering that I had to put up with it as a steady diet in Canada as a kid.' Her mother is the only family member she spoke of, and again only once. From England, Thorne wrote on March 14, 1936: 'I put some money on a horse the other day and won! Although only a few shekels I want to salt it away into some American stock. What shall I buy? General Motors or what? Its [*sic*] going to be a present for my mother at Xmas.' If an individual's reaction to current events reflects something of her own situation, then this remark from 1937 is telling: 'Everyone here seems to be agog over the famous coronation which we are not being a little bit pro-Edward and Simpson and luke warm on the new outfit. We think he had a lot of guts to do what he did and not that he was weak in falling for a fallen woman, as most people I talk to seem to think.' Thorne often mentioned 'North's' precarious health, and it's evident that she was the sole family breadwinner. A heavy smoker, he seemed to go from one bout of bronchitis to another; his few letters suggest a man with a wry sense of humour, but one who was definitely high maintenance. Thorne wrote, also in 1937: 'I sometimes wonder why and how I manage to keep him going.' Perhaps she found a curious kind of strength in caring for a difficult partner, something that spurred her on to face the changing fashions in the art world.

Hard times continued. 'Sometimes I wonder if its [*sic*] worth being a creative worker,' Thorne wrote in a Christmas letter to the Youngs in 1937. 'If I've had one "Famous Americans" annual or famous women or what have you writing me this year for my biography, there have been a half dozen. At the rate my fame is growing one would think I was coining money—but fame and cash have nothing to do with one another it seems.' Throughout the war years Thorne continued to illustrate books for children, some with wartime settings. She even tried to revive her former artists' agency. The death of her kind supporter Dr Young (1887–1944) must have been a shock. But Minna Crooks Young had created the Torchlight Book Exchange, out of Michigan, as a supplier of Throne's art and books; it brought in small amounts of needed cash.

Carton Moore-Park died in 1956. Whatever the official status of their relationship, his death must have been a great loss for Thorne. I have no idea how she spent her remaining years, and the nature of her subsequent illness is not clear. By the age of seventy or so her mother was living in what was then called an old-age home, and she did not recognize her own children. Alzheimer's? Early dementia? A similar fate was suffered by Thorne's sister Paula. Sometime in September 1962 Thorne was committed to Manhattan's Bellevue Hospital as 'mentally ill' (records are kept for only twenty-five years for mental-health patients). According to cremation documents and surrogate court papers, Thorne died, intestate, at the City Hospital on Welfare Island (now Roosevelt Island), one of New York City's hospitals for the poor, in July 1963.

Artists who devote their talent to dogs have often been marginalized, as if a dog is a less worthy subject—somehow less serious—than a bowl of fruit, a vase of flowers, or a stand of trees. The reasons for this are complex and fall beyond the scope of my essay. Even the few exceptions—Rosa Bonheur, Sir Edwin Landseer, George Stubbs—do not have the following of many less interesting and less skillful painters. Add to this ambivalence about dog paintings the fact that Thorne was a successful illustrator and we might begin to see why her work is no longer known, or valued as more than well-drawn studies from a bygone era. Like most freelance artists, Thorne developed a variety of styles to suit the publications that bought her work. 'You know what the average magazine editor wants—' she wrote to Minna Crooks on February 20, 1936, 'saccarine and more saccarine [*sic*]'. Yet her formal oil portraits and best line drawings, pastels and etchings do not cross the line into sentimentality. Whether she was producing illustrations for children's books or Sunday-magazine cover art, which had to appeal to a popular taste for illustrators like Norman Rockwell, Thorne took her audience into account—no fault there. Recent books have revived interest in the work and 1920s milieu of commercial artists like J.C. Leyendecker, known for his stylized Arrow Collar Man. Thorne's achievement, though less iconic, deserves attention as well.

Strong, lively drawing was the core of Thorne's versatility. While I don't want to make exaggerated claims about her art, here is some of the critical reaction it once received. From her first exhibition on, Thorne was praised, especially for the quality of her technical skills: 'A workman of exceptional skills' (*Chicago Evening Post*); 'In painting portraits of dogs in oils, Miss Thorne stands practically alone. Extremely few artists have followed her into this field.' (*Chicago Tribune*); Thorne is 'a skilled craftsman and her work ranks high among artists' (*Chicago Tribune*); and, 'an artist of gorgeously diversified talents', with 'a touch of Daumier in some of her work; the sardonic humor of Toulouse-Lautrec shines through other of it' (*Chicago Examiner*). In the *Christian Science Monitor* Barbara E. Scott Fisher called Thorne 'the modern Rosa Bonheur'. If that remark seems over the top, the etcher Berthe Jaques had this to say about Thorne: 'Her wit is effervescent and her treatment spontaneous. Balance and composition, which make or unmake all design, are so cleverly handled as to appear unstudied.' And in language typical of its time, Canadian journalist Dora Albert wrote in *Saturday Night*: 'Canada is therefore all the more fortunate in being able to claim one of the most successful women etchers, Diana Thorne, whose work can easily stand on its own merits without any consideration of whether the producer is a man or woman.' Thorne collaborated several times with Albert Payson Terhune (1872–1942), a popular American writer of much-loved novels about his favourite breed, the collie, and he described her work as 'vibrant with spirit, with mischief, with intelligence'.

Thorne was serious about her art—as serious as anyone can be while trying to make a living from it. In her 1936 article 'Look Doggish, If You Please!' for the *Christian Science Monitor Magazine*, she described the pressures she felt as a painter:

> Each portrait, even after all my years of practice (and I have had a score of them), still presents a new problem and challenges all my powers to their limit of capacity. Will I succeed in capturing a good likeness? And will the thing also be a good piece of painting? These two achievements seldom go hand in hand.

Thorne always emphasized the importance of a good model, and when she didn't have a live one she often consulted photographs. In a letter of March 14, 1936, she wrote, 'I can't draw anything unless it is in front of me. If there is nothing in front, there's just a blank sheet of paper.' She discussed the need for close observation as a special requirement of animal art in *Drawing Dogs*: 'The *all-important* things to remember are form, bone structure, and individual character.' When the variety of dog breeds is considered, the canine skeleton is actually more varied than the human skeleton, and any artist attempting to convey not only movement but a particular dog's position during modeling (sitting, standing, running) needs to think of its skeleton, its essential form. A distillation of Thorne's experience, *Drawing Dogs* is both a gracefully-written guide and an apologia for an artist's life.

In the end, what matters most about Thorne is the talent and attention she lavished on dogs. Her work is important in the context of the changing status of dogs in North American society. Following the founding of the American Society for the Prevention of Cruelty to Animals in 1866, and the American Kennel Club, with its emphasis on purebred dogs, in 1884, a massive cultural shift in pet-keeping had begun. No longer kept mainly for their work—for hunting, herding, and other agrarian practices—purebred dogs, and even beloved mutts, now slept indoors, by the fireplace, or on the living-room sofa. Thorne insisted that she did not focus on specific breeds, claiming, 'It's not so much the breed but the individual dog which arouses my enthusiasm.' But her portraits of wire-haired terriers and Scotties, dachshunds and spaniels, collies and German shepherds almost belie her words. Thorne's work, for both commercial consumption and private commissions, assisted this cultural shift, making dogs a true part of the modern human family. As a dog lover I can only be grateful to her, whoever she was.

What is the truth of an individual's life, and how do we research it? What roles does the material world play in our research? One might even ask if it really matters that Thorne changed her place of birth by a continent and her year of birth by twelve months. In the grand scheme of things, probably not. But—and this is a sizeable 'but'—we don't live our lives only in the grand scheme of things. Was Thorne a bohemian artist, a liberated woman who had no use for conventions, a self-denying Jew? None of these entirely, yet perhaps a little of each. Above all, she was an artist, and that's why I kept trying to follow her story. And I began to understand that my search for Diana Thorne was actually a shadow of her own search for this creature she called Diana Thorne.

Late Style, Last Works

What do you do while waiting to die? Most of us prefer to ignore the question, or defer it as long as we can. After all, we're only human. But the death of Canadian printmaker and sculptor Claire Weissman Wilks (1933–2017) sent me to my bookshelves with that question in mind. Not for a catalogue of her haunting and haunted images, though there are several of those, but for a collection of essays by the influential late critic Edward Said, who is best known for his study *Orientalism.* Said had taught a course at Columbia University called Last Works/Late Style, and after his death, in 2003, several colleagues and his widow collected his writings about the subject in the book *On Late Style: Music and Literature Against the Grain* (2006). What about a visual artist like Claire, I wondered—where did she fit into the scheme?

At the 'shwake' (a combined shiva and wake) for Claire in her Toronto home, her partner of forty-seven years, the poet and fiction writer Barry Callaghan, had set out a number of framed and unframed works on the second floor. As I climbed the stairs to see them I remembered how many previous times I'd visited Claire's bright studio on the top floor, where she showed me her latest monoprints and drawings. This was an enchanted space, and I enjoyed talking with her there as I looked and looked.

The concept of 'late style' didn't originate with Said. The Frankfurt School musicologist-*cum*-philosopher Theodor W. Adorno had already used the term in an essay, written in 1937, about Beethoven's late quartets and their notable dissonances. He saw the great deaf composer's late style as one of profound alienation, which Said described as a kind of 'revaluation': 'There is heroism in it but also intransigence.' The twists and turns of Adorno's text are irrelevant here, except that they enabled Said (who suffered from leukemia in his last years) to understand the quality of 'unearthly serenity' that only a few creators achieve in their last works. Think of Shakespeare's late romances or Rembrandt's final self-portraits, and the mysterious authority, and transparency, they represent—their calm, their anger, their near elegiac protest in the face of death.

Claire Weissman Wilks is a figurative artist: she drew the naked human body over and over again, from every angle, conveying a multitude of experiences. Bodies were her enduring subject. Chosen or given? It's hard to say. I'm almost tempted to write that it doesn't matter—artists somehow manage to find their subjects—but in writing about Claire I think it does matter. Her own body may have provided her subject. At the age of seventeen she was diagnosed with tuberculosis, and she had to spend three long years in a sanatorium which she described as an 'internment camp' in Weston, on the outskirts of Toronto, to recover. Consider as well that she had only recently watched her body transform itself from a girl's to a young woman's, with all the attendant associations, conflicts, and desires, and it's little surprise that the female body became a permanent subject, allowing her to express what she knew to be true. Claire once called women's bodies her 'chosen landscape', but she did not consider this a political statement: 'The female form is my line, the form lives in the brain of my finger.' If there is any debt in this (and for most artists there are always a few, even if unacknowledged), it's not to the soft portrait work of Mary Cassatt, or the sleek pastels of Helen Frankenthaler's lyrical abstractions, but to the stark, strong lines of the German Expressionist printmaker Käthe Kollwitz and the Austrian painter Egon Schiele.

The bodies in Weissman Wilks's work *move*—they cradle themselves (and sometimes other bodies, as well), they bend, crouch, writhe, lull about, curl up, they expose, protect and even hide themselves. And why not? Unlike sedentary writers with their pens and computers, many visual artists embrace movement as an essential part of a work. We see its most extreme example in the action paintings associated with Abstract Expressionism, which may also have influenced Claire. (Why did we never talk about this? We did, however, discuss that great colourist Joan Mitchell, and Claire spoke about her enthusiastically.)

In 'What the Hand Sees', a thoughtful essay from the catalogue for *The Etty Drawings*, a 2015 exhibition of Weissman Wilks's work, novelist Anne Michaels wrote that 'In her drawings the body is not a symbol. Abstractions find form in these bodies yet their flesh is always powerfully real. How much longing, fear, passion, self-knowledge, tenderness, joy, abysmal loneliness, grief, resignation, despair is in the position of a foot, the weight of a limb or breast, the folding or grasp of a hand, bodies so full they are empty, so empty they are full?' The figures that Michaels described were inspired by *The Interrupted Life*, the diaries of Etty Hillesum, a Dutch-Jewish woman who died in Auschwitz, in 1943, at the age of twenty-nine. Claire had read the diaries in the 1980s, shortly after their publication in an English translation, and her response was the Etty series of drawings—though as a teenager after the Second World War she would have learned of the Nazi death camps, along with her fellow North Americans who were also struggling to assimilate the knowledge of those horrors. This happened, of course, during the late 1940s, when anti-Semitism was a barely concealed aspect of Toronto's civic life. The first photographic images of the death camps may have taken root in Claire's visual imagination.

Although live models had once been important to Weissman Wilks—models that she carefully posed, sometimes in awkward, even uncomfortable positions—around 1980 she turned inward for inspiration, and 'internal' bodies pressed themselves on her imagination; they almost called out to her, beckoning for attention, needing to be freed from her mind by whatever medium she chose to use. Yet the naked human figure never seems naked in these drawings, but rather clothed in shifts of emotion conveyed partly through a subtle use of colour, especially earth tones. These figures are not realistic life studies, but rather images that have been pared down and become primal. While they belong to the instinctive world of Freud's id, death seldom seems distant from them, even in their moments of joy, erotic bliss or deep communion.

Claire Weissman Wilks was diagnosed with leukemia in March 2015, and for almost two years faced the daunting knowledge that each week could be her last. When she had strength enough to draw, she did, and when she couldn't, she longed to be back in her studio working. During the ensuing courses of chemotherapy and blood transfusions she made thirty-one drawings and prints. Imminent death, we're often told, can clarify and sharpen the mind. The concept 'late style' does not mean a break or rupture with an artist's accustomed approach, but rather an extension or refinement of it. Nor does the term suggest the embrace of hard-won wisdom or dramatic revelation or a grand detachment. For Said, late style meant 'difficulty and unresolved contradictions'. Struggling with his own mortality, he praised a 'defiant' stance in the face of illness and death. In this sense he and Claire shared a mutual bond.

Claire's last drawings understandably focus on the body alone, in physical and psychic isolation. While she had often worked on a large scale, after the first year of intensive treatments she lamented that 'I want to do something big, but I don't have the strength.' She drew now only with Conté crayons (a blend of powdered graphite and wax or clay), experimenting with new Conté colours. The sometimes delicate cross-hatched lines of earlier ink wash sketches gave way to a heavier black line—almost foreboding—that seems to vibrate, even glisten, with mystery. In the drawing she made shortly after her diagnosis Claire revels in the murkiest blend of khaki grey-green, its pool of sour colour perhaps a protest. Her subject, in profile, appears to have fallen onto her back, in a vulnerable fetal position. While making this figure, did it matter to Claire that exhibitions of her work had once opened to glowing reviews in museums and galleries in Stockholm and Jerusalem, in Venice and Zagreb and Mexico City? Or that she had been championed in these cities by writers such as Tomas Tranströmer, Yehuda Amichai and D.M. Thomas? I doubt it. No—her work is too defiantly life driven, as she confronts cancer and death, for past praise to matter.

Six of the drawings are portraits. Their striking faces are not simply androgynous but almost simian, with near snout-like features that forsake human consciousness: they represent flesh-and-blood animal life—mammal energy—wanting to defeat death. Most striking is a small, plaintive head (an 8-inch square) of an ageless but childlike face, whose full life has been wiped away. Seven other drawings are narrow rectangles (roughly 30 by 7 inches) resembling coffins. Their confined figures appear to be struggling to break free but are in fact doing battle with death—these drawings are not a memento mori but the decisive final condition itself. And death, here, will not come gently. These coffin drawings also evoke the slab-like berths in the Holocaust's death camps, linking the artist's late work with earlier concerns.

Claire's final drawing, made two weeks before her death, is still attached to its 8 1/2-by-11-inch spiral pad. The solemn, strong-thighed figure, kneeling in profile with her head bowed, is too powerful to be a supplicant, beseeching help or consolation; it reminds me of one of William Blake's monumental angels. The image is simplicity itself, direct and immediate. The figure looks away from the viewer, as if she has said her last goodbye to the world and no longer needs it; she knows, and accepts, where she's going. This may be what Adorno had in mind when he wrote, 'The power of subjectivity in the late works of art is the irascible gesture with which it takes leave of the works themselves.' Claire's final figure is almost stiff, fixed, no longer capable of movement. She possesses a secret, and as we wonder what she knows, she keeps the knowledge from us. Death doesn't have the last word, *she* does, silently.

On a personal, lighter note, I want to mention a fact that may, at first, seem irrelevant. Claire and I shared a love of dogs, so it didn't surprise me to hear that when she was asked who she might want to see in the afterlife, if there is such a place, she mentioned only her four dogs, and especially Be-Bop, the golden retriever who had died during her illness. Over the years I'd often urged Claire to paint one of her dogs, perhaps with a nude human figure, as Lucian Freud did so movingly. But it was the human body Claire favoured, as if it were inexhaustible. In a sense her studies were both concrete and spiritual: *What else, what more,* she seemed to ask, *are our bodies capable of?* Still, I kept hoping for the appearance of one of her dogs, and whenever I visited I always brought along my own pug or spaniel. Claire welcomed them heartily, gave them the fuss they craved, and said she was finally going to 'make that sketch'. It never happened, yet what splendid dogs she would have drawn.

We always want more from our artists than time allows them to give us, and Claire Weissman Wilks is no exception. Perhaps it's best to be grateful for what we have, for what remains. What else can we do? Her family and friends will mourn; others can look at—and reflect on—the art she left behind.

The Life of Inanimate Objects

Two recent books, one museum exhibition, and a purchase of my own have caused me to spend time thinking about objects—not only about what they mean to us symbolically or otherwise, but about the life of inanimate things. Old objects, especially, appear to have a hidden life of their own, and they can evoke complex responses in us that are beyond matters of taste, personal associations and even projections. Objects, of course, vary in age, size, shape and quality, and their value depends on a range of concerns, from rarity to history to our private memories. Antiques, collectibles, *objets d'art*, tchotchkes, whatever we call the stuff of our lives, some things seem to make claims on our attention and allegiance. Ever since the Public Broadcasting Service (PBS) began its series *Antiques Roadshow* in 1997, with specialists visiting cities across North America to assess the objects people bring in for consideration, the life of objects has become a popular, even commonplace, subject. Yet too often an old object is assigned a monetary value, as if that is its essence, and the thing itself almost disappears. Or we may feel that by touching it we're reaching through time to touch the past—an illusion, because our physical contact is with the thing in the present (once again the thing vanishes).

Every object merits attention for its thing-ness, which is hard to define. Along with their history and the materials that went into their production, our objects have a separate existence from ourselves. Erica E. Hirshler, a senior curator at Boston's Museum of Fine Arts, has written a curious book called *Sargent's Daughters: The Biography of a Painting* (2009), which, because of its subtitle, offers a good place to begin examining some of my preoccupations. The book is a detailed account of one of the museum's most celebrated objects—a painting, *The Daughters of Edward Darley Boit.* Yes, a painting is an object, like a porcelain bowl or a fine chair. It's not a utilitarian object, but many objects aren't utilitarian or necessities. (We tend to think of paintings as a special class of objects, as fine art, because they're usually signed by an individual.) Made by the American painter John Singer Sargent when he was just twenty-six, the Boit portrait was first exhibited in the Paris Salon in 1883. An imposing work, it is slightly larger than seven feet square. Having admired it for more than three decades, I read Hirshler's study hoping to learn about the material nature of the painting. But her account of the work is mainly a rich piece of social history, telling the story of a wealthy nomadic family, travelling back and forth between Boston and Paris with their painting, and of the eventual lives of the four Boit girls. The study is not a true 'biography' of a painting.

Any painting exists in a context of other paintings if one thinks in art historical terms. It's curious that Hirshler doesn't mention another work by Sargent, *The Breakfast Table*, housed only four miles from the MFA, in the Harvard Art Museum. Painted in 1883–4, though on a smaller scale than the Boit girls (21 by 18 inches), this oil on canvas—a study of Sargent's younger sister, Violet—bears a striking resemblance in tone and style to his more famous bravura work. After spending hours before both paintings, I'm left with a set of questions about their production and materials: Did Sargent mix his own oils or use commercial paints? Where did he purchase his canvas, and did he stretch it himself? How much varnish did he mix with his oils to achieve the mirror-like effect of the floor in the Boits' foyer? These are only the first of many such questions. Sargent is admired for his *alla prima* manner, often using a single layer of paint rather than building up several layers, and it's exciting to stand close to his Boit group portrait and see the images disappear into brushwork, into gestures at vast dark space. Hirshler simply writes, 'The paint seems almost effortlessly applied: each girl is defined by thick, confident strokes made with a fairly large brush and a palette knife, while the background and the floor are suggested with extremely thin, broad washes of color', and leaves it at that.

Instead of concentrating on the physical nature of Sargent's painting—and its existence apart from the aesthetic and psychological responses it evokes—Hirshler emphasizes human relations, explaining, for example, that the artist regarded the Boit girls almost as nieces. Does this account for the familiar quality of the two paintings? The enigmatic, even evasive expressions of the subjects in both works makes me ask if Sargent was consciously painting the self that any model hides. And more important, how did he use paint to achieve his effects? We learn a great deal about the Japanese vases in the Boit portrait, which hangs in the MFA with those same tall vases standing on either side, almost like a surreal trick: from a distance they appear to have jumped off the canvas. While the Boit family also travelled with their vases, this tidbit from Hirshler does not bring us closer to the painting, just as we would connect no better with Sargent's *Breakfast Table* if the whereabouts of its silver teapot were known.

Such questions about a painting's materiality, bypassed for social history, remind me of similar questions left after reading Edmund de Waal's popular family memoir, *The Hare with Amber Eyes: A Family's Century of Art and Loss* (2010). A noted British ceramicist, he ties his chronicle to a collection of 264 netsuke, small Japanese button-like figures carved from various materials, including ivory and boxwood. Early on de Waal promises his readers, and himself, that he will avoid nostalgia. Maybe he will help clarify my thoughts. The story he tells of his Russian-Jewish forebears, the Ephrussi, who, along with the Rothchilds, were one of the wealthiest families of 19th-century Europe, inevitably evokes an era of bygone luxury. Along with anecdotes about family connections to prominent figures such as Marcel Proust and Edgar Degas, de Waal also records the growing horrors of European anti-Semitism, and the Holocaust that eventually destroyed his forebears. We follow the netsuke collection from its first owner in the 1870s, Charles Ephrussi, a Parisian connoisseur (and model for Proust's aesthete Swann), to his nephew Viktor in Vienna, in 1899, and then to the family maid, Anna, who kept the objects hidden under a straw mattress to protect them from the Nazis.

Like Hirshler, de Waal focuses on people, and not the netsuke. Yet near the end of his book, while visiting an ancestral home in Odessa, he decides to skip the journey to Berdichev, a shtetl in eastern Ukraine where the saga began: 'I want to see what the sky looks like in Berdichev, but I have to go home.' The book closes with this evasion, for de Waal has lost himself in nostalgia; nothing about a shtetl will be 'worldly', one of his favoured adjectives. And what of the netsuke? Part of a 19th-century European craze for Japonica, like the Boits' vases, they remain only sketched. The book contains photographs of the Ephrussi and their mansions but, oddly, none of the netsuke, the ostensible reason for the book and the source of its title. 'Objects have always been carried, sold, bartered, stolen, retrieved and lost,' de Waal admits. 'It's how you tell their story that matters.' But their story includes more than owners and barterers, fascinating as they may be. While objects don't exhibit consciousness, they wear their histories in marks of ware. I expected that a ceramic artist like de Waal, whose work appears in museum collections around the globe, would be curious about the craftsmanship and condition of the netsuke. Still, I'm sympathetic to him, and to Hirshler, because I've also known the limitations that passing time can impose on a writer when one's subject is an object.

Several years ago, while travelling in northeast Ohio, I stopped at a high-end antiques shop for my annual visit to its treasures. I had my last pug dog with me (carried under one arm) and the proprietor, who recognized us, immediately remarked, 'I have something you'll want to see.' Soon a miniature bronze sculpture of a pug sat in my right palm—one of the famous Vienna bronzes, just three inches long and an inch and a half high. More than a century old, the piece is cold painted (after the bronze was fired), with much of its paint still intact. I asked the price tentatively. The piece had just arrived at the shop, and the owners knew it would sell quickly.

The European tradition of bronze sculptures of dogs is a long and venerable one, with notable artists from Jean-Baptiste Carpeaux in the 18th century to Alberto Giacometti in the 20th contributing to it. Good miniature bronzes, however, are rare. The Franz Bergmann Studio produced some of the finest, and I'd just been holding one. An hour after leaving the antiques shop I telephoned the proprietor, we settled on a price and the next day the bronze belonged to me. The shop's owners knew little of this pug's history. Its previous owner, an elderly antiques collector in Massillon, Ohio, was breaking up a collection and had recently sold the piece; beyond that, nothing. How had the little pug crossed the ocean? With a wealthy tourist or emigrant? It had been treated with care, so someone knew its value. Was it once a family heirloom, preserved for sentimental reasons? All possibilities. After a while you have to make peace with the fact that you'll never know that history.

And I didn't want to see the object only through its owners' stories. I read about the Franz Bergmann Studio—its founding in 1860, the anonymous sculptors who worked there, the new foundry opened in 1900, its designs in the Vienna Secession style (Austria's Art Nouveau), and its closing during the Depression—but that didn't satisfy my curiosity. Nothing in my life had compelled me to purchase the figure—my choice seemed to be made by the appeal of the piece itself. Yet when I write 'the bronze belonged to me' I should add the words 'for now', because I'm only its caretaker; the sculpture will, I trust, have a life after mine. This is not something I write easily, yet I *am* glad to ensure that this artful object will have an opportunity to move into a future that I won't know. We're caretakers at best, whether we like to admit it or not.

The difficult notion of caretaking struck me during a visit, in the fall of 2011, to an exhibition called *The Tsar's Cabinet: Two Hundred Years of Russian Decorative Arts Under the Romanovs* at Toronto's Gardiner Museum of Ceramic Art. I say 'difficult' because objects can make us admit our human limitations. Passing case after case of imperial soup tureens and gilded tea sets, I listened as other visitors remarked on the pieces they'd like to take home. 'For the cottage', one well-dressed dowager said, about a porcelain service for the Tsar's yacht (a yacht is, after all, an object too—just a very big one). Wall posters told of royal owners long dead, and the combination of contemporary desire or acquisitiveness with the tragedies of history made me relieved to depart.

The emotion I felt was not unlike one I've sometimes known in antiques malls, where aisle after aisle of old objects soon began to trouble me. At first there's a pleasing air of visiting Grandma's attic, but eventually I'm struck by the forlorn appearance of the objects on sale, or on display (a strange word, *display*, combining the element of fun with the prefix *dis*, its negation). Cut off from their original owner's choice—separated from that place of desire—they seem to cry out for their past, which they wear in worn spots. I don't mean this to sound mystical, or to suggest that I hear cries from the objects. But inanimate objects are made up of atoms, they're not dead things. I don't need to raise issues like subatomic particles, quantum mechanics or string theory and the like to suggest that it's wrong to regard inanimate matter as dead matter. Objects have a kind of 'persistence', as Verlyn Klinkenborg once wisely wrote in an editorial for the *New York Times*. Without our quite recognizing this quality, persistence may be one reason why we stand in line at art museums, preserve family heirlooms or shop for the objects that help define us in our homes. When we don't want to be alone, objects make us feel less alone with our mortality.

The theory of object relations, as psychologists call it, suggests that one measure of human development is the formation of bonds with inanimate objects: a child needs to relate to a blanket or to a stuffed animal in order to begin claiming a place in the world. This theory may help explain why most people see themselves as the focus of their relations with objects. Is there an ambivalence here about the objects themselves? Yes, because objects evoke emotions in us even if *they* don't have emotions, or so we believe. Apart from our caretaking (we can damage objects, or preserve them to their betterment), our relations with objects aren't, in a basic way, reciprocal; they do need us, however, in order to survive, or persist. It's a paradox that while we live in a world of consumerism, which advocates personal fulfillment in shopping and collecting material goods, we may feel embarrassed by our own need for things.

Can one learn to accept the otherness of objects, and their essential mystery? James Joyce offers assistance in his novel *Stephen Hero* when he speaks of the way objects can reveal themselves to us in moments of epiphany. Discussing how we 'focus' on things, Joyce writes: 'First we recognize that the object is *one* integral thing, then we recognize that it is an organized composite structure, a *thing* in fact: finally, when the relation of the parts is exquisite, when the parts are adjusted to the special point, we recognize that it is *that* thing which it is. Its soul, its whatness, leaps to us from the vestment of its appearance. The soul of the commonest object, the structure of which is so adjusted, seems to us radiant. The object achieves its epiphany.' I trust that most people have experienced something of this sort, unless they would be happy to live in near-empty rooms. When the Boit family travelled on a transatlantic steamship with Sargent's portrait, when Edmund de Waal admired the family netsuke at his uncle's home in Tokyo, when curators at the Gardiner Museum decided to show the Romanov collection and when I tried to reconstruct some of the history of my Viennese bronze pug, we were all making connections that took us outside of ourselves, if only for a brief time, with an object we couldn't fully know. We were, momentarily, relating to a thing itself, and we were probably the better for it. I'd like to think that the objects of our attention, of our study and desire and admiration, were better off too.

On Solitude: Rereading May Sarton's Journals

On January 1, 1975, May Sarton, the American diarist, poet and novelist, went up to the third-floor study of her house in York, Maine, and glanced out the window at its ocean view. She had just one daily task ahead—walking the dog at noon. When she opened a new calendar, the 'only connect' epigraph from E. M. Forster's *Howard's End* caught her eye. Sarton began an entry in her journal by recording this moment, and soon fell into a riff about solitude and detachment, one of the 'mini-essays', as she called them, that appear in her journals. The context of her thoughts that morning was the recent Christmas holidays and her sense of release after the departure of welcomed guests, an overload of preparations and the annual visit from Judy Matlock, Sarton's former companion, a retired professor of English who was then lost in the early stages of Alzheimer's. Sarton's entry moves deftly, with a kind of free association. From Forster's admonition she proceeds to Sybille Bedford's biography of Aldous Huxley, which she had been reading, commenting on his vision of life ('he was able to *create* only a fragmented world'), and then recalling an afternoon in London, during the previous fall, with her friends Julian and Juliette Huxley (Aldous and Julian were brothers), whom she found to be 'old now, old and self-absorbed', set against happier memories of their youthful generosity during the years before the Second World War. Thoughts of friendship lead her to her latest novel, *Kinds of Love*, which had brought her new readers who even showed up at her door with gifts—one young man offered a bunch of roses from his grandmother and a Belgian cake to honour her forebears. Sarton ends the passage with a nod to solitude's freedom: 'Let it all begin once more, the step-by-step joyful effort to lift a poem out.' This entry, running three pages, appeared in *The House by the Sea* (1977), and is as familiar to me as a comfortable old sweater.

May Sarton is not a great poet or novelist. There, I've said it. Why, then, this essay? Because she is an exemplary diarist. Every January, for over two decades, I begin my reading of the new year with one of her journals. It's become a tradition, a ritual of sorts, and it embodies the desire to see my world with a fresh eye. You might say that I reread one of Sarton's journals instead of making any new year's resolutions. There are a total of eight journals, which means that I've read all of them at least twice. And I'll admit that several times in the past decades I've taken out a specific volume and looked for a marked passage that seemed relevant to something troubling my own life: the death of a parent, a difficult move, the loss of a beloved pet, the end of a friendship. Sarton, who lived alone for thirty-seven years (until her death at the age of eighty-three, in 1995), often makes a great deal of sense about living alone.

The subject of solitude is a difficult one because it can mean so many different things. While May Sarton's poetry is often predictable, and her novels sometimes hastily written (among several exceptions: *Faithful Are the Wounds*, *As We Are Now* and *Mrs Stevens Hears the Mermaids Singing*), she kept some of the most interesting journals of the last quarter of the 20th century. Her publisher, Norton, treated her like a cash cow, bringing out a new book almost yearly and barely editing them for repetition, flaccid writing, and banal imagery. In the journals, however, Sarton rose above her limitations both as a writer and a cult figure to the feminist and gay and lesbian movements in the 1970s and 1980s. She recorded her thoughts, her wishes, her problems and fears, but most of all the dailiness of living: planting spring bulbs, organizing her desk before a writing session, grooming one of her cats, making *Carbonnades à la Flamande* (a Belgian beef-and-beer stew from her childhood), coping with a broken furnace, napping beside her sheltie Tamas, watching the sky or the ocean, listening to a favourite Mozart recording, and reading, reading, reading. Yet the comings and goings at her houses—first in Nelson, New Hampshire, in *Journal of a Solitude* (1973), and then near York, Maine, in the subsequent journals—are always shadowed by aging, illness and depression. My interest in Sarton was piqued by her first journal, and the title itself may help explain why. Instead of calling the book *Journal of Solitude*, Sarton added the article *a*, giving the noun 'solitude' a double meaning as both a place, state or space, and a person, figure or psychological type. This blurring of literal sense is crucial.

Beyond Sarton's use of the word *solitude* is the core of the word itself. Think not only of *solo* but of *sol*, 'sun' in Latin. In the deepest recesses of our minds most people believe that the world revolves around them, whether we like to admit it or not. But solitude isn't the same as being alone (though that's a big part of it) or loneliness, yet it can flip into a lonely state and is its most intense when an individual lives alone. Solitude describes a state of mind as well as a person's living arrangement. For Sarton, isolation was an important part of solitude, yet the word *isolation* carries a forlorn aspect that the gentler and more capacious *solitude* lacks, though the later word echoes *solitary*, a negative term for some. Sarton's solitude welcomes a generous chunk of isolation from other human beings, although she did live with various cats, her sheltie, a green parrot named Punch and, for one summer, a donkey called Esmeralda. As she wrote, 'Solitude shared with animals has a special quality, and rarely turns into loneliness.'

While a solitude or solitary could be a hermit, hermits aren't likely to publish a private journal. Keeping a journal for publication meant that Sarton edited herself for her readers: each journal became a public performance of sorts. She was aware of this paradox, and thought that the art of keeping a 'very personal record' for publication pivots on the writer's attitude, which Sarton summed up with an axiom from her friend Elizabeth Bowen, the Anglo-Irish novelist: 'One must regard oneself impersonally as an instrument.' About her own readers, Sarton wrote, 'From my isolation to the isolation of someone somewhere who will find my work there exists a true communion.' In an interview from 1976 with Jane S. Bakerman, she claimed that she had never kept a journal except for publication: 'I think that people who keep journals not for publication are terribly narcissistic. It's very fashionable now; people are keeping journals more and more. But I very much doubt whether they really are honest with themselves. I think often, it's just a reflective mirror in which you see yourself in the best possible light.' Along with a conversational tone, Sarton's method of journal writing, which she discussed with Bakerman, was to move beyond the personal: 'Quite a large part of my journals is really short, very short, informal essays of two or three paragraphs.' These mini-essays allowed her 'to examine experience and to relate it to universal experience. It is this reflection which *makes* a journal; it's not just telling what happened today.' *Universal* was probably the wrong word for Sarton to use—*general* might have been a better choice—since her journals record an uncommon life, though elements of it appealed to readers of disparate backgrounds.

Sarton began writing *Journal of a Solitude* because she believed that her popular memoir *Plant Dreaming Deep* (1968)—about reclaiming an eighteenth-century house in a small New England village and making a life there suited to the needs of her writing—gave a false impression of a serene life in the country, an idyll of easily produced books and effortless gardening. Known for her complaints about inviting guests for lunches of lobster salad and Pouilly-Fuissé and later wishing she had more time to herself, Sarton was brutally frank about her conflicting needs for time with people and time alone, and the price that she—and sometimes others—paid for this conflict. Far from being a recluse, Sarton required the silence at the core of solitude to balance her contacts with the world. In the thirty-minute film documentary *A World of Light: Portrait of May Sarton* (1980), by Martha Wheelock and Marita Simpson, Sarton called solitude 'my last great love'. And like many great loves, it had complications. One requirement of solitude, she argued, was 'not to get unbalanced and not let depression get hold of you. Everything becomes more intense, which is partly why it's marvellous. There's nothing to break the intensity.' Such intensity, she told Wheelock, provides an ideal ground for creation: 'The great flow from the subconscious to the conscious is the good thing about solitude; there's no barrier between consciousness and the subconscious, or much less.'

While not everyone who lives alone wants solitude, this apparent contradiction may relate to a pervasive social stigma, as if solitudes are deficient in some way. In his study *Going Solo: The Extraordinary Rise and Surprising Appeal of Living Alone* (2012), sociologist Eric Klinenberg examined the tremendous growth in people living alone over the last fifty years and concluded that the trend will continue because it satisfies many diverse desires. Statistics show that 28 percent of all Americans and Canadians live in 'households with only one occupant' (the figure is closer to 50 percent for large metropolitan areas); the national percentage is greatest in the highly developed Scandinavian countries, with 40 to 45 percent, and lowest in the poorest, with 3 percent in Pakistan. But I don't want to get lost in numbers and bypass my true subject, which is not the practical problems of living alone, or self-sufficiency, but solitude.

Though there are more than four centuries between Michel de Montaigne's classic essay 'Of Solitude' (1572–74) and British psychoanalyst Anthony Storr's much-praised study *Solitude: A Return to the Self* (1988), Sarton might have agreed with the ideas of both men. Montaigne, who had retired from court life to his father's country estate, saw solitude as something to follow experience of the world, and suiting some temperaments more than others. It was a state of being alone where 'our ordinary conversation must be between us and ourselves' (much like keeping a journal) and also a challenge: 'let us win from ourselves the power to live really alone and to live that way at our ease'. Storr saw solitude as a capacity to be alone 'linked with self-discovery'. While temperament plays a part in this 'return', as he put it, for creative individuals solitude always involves 'the search for coherence and sense'. That phrase might have come from Sarton herself; it echoes her idea of 'the whole self' and her emphasis on discovering one's true identity in solitude, and 'growing' into that self. Was she temperamentally suited to solitude? Storr noted that solitude is good for the growth of every child's 'imaginative capacity', arguing that 'Many creative adults have left accounts of childhood feelings of mystical union with Nature.' His list of examples included Wordsworth, Whitman and C.S. Lewis; Storr might have added Sarton if he'd read her journals. As an only child of creative parents whose marriage was not an easy union, she learned early on how to thrive outside of her home: solitude can be a way of caring for one's self. But what does it mean to care for oneself? Not simply pampering, it's deeper, and interior—a comprehension of life's possibilities, with a recognition of inevitable hardships and pain, perhaps clarified by solitude. While Storr emphasized the connection between interpersonal relations and maturity, as most psychoanalysts do, he admitted that 'The great introverted creators are able to define identity and achieve *self-realization* by *self-reference*, that is, by interacting with their own past work rather than by interacting with other people.' Sarton's solitude wasn't as extreme as this paradigm, but I can't help wondering what she would have thought of a recent website, www.hermitary.com, which subtitles itself 'resources and reflections on hermits and solitude'.

Sarton's attitude towards journal writing grew from her commitment to solitude. She wanted her journals to be written 'on the pulse of the moment', as she said in *The House by the Sea*, in the process showing how one might live as a solitude yet engage life fully. She further developed this idea in *At Seventy* (1984), claiming that it is 'the business of the journalist to record a mood as it comes, as exactly as possible, knowing that life is flux and that the mood must change'. Sarton recognized her own limitations, including a tumultuous temperament: 'I feel too much, sense too much, am exhausted by the reverberations after even the simplest conversation. But the deep collision is and has been with my unregenerate, tormenting, and tormented self.' In Wheelock and Simpson's documentary, Sarton explained that for journal writing she was 'not dependent on the muse', as she was for poetry. However, it was necessary to discover 'the right line between indiscretion and openness'. Journals allowed her to 'find out where I really am'. Recording dailiness mattered: 'What seems often fairly meaningless—I mean like weeding a patch in the garden—when I write about it in the journal, it sort of becomes something else.' Dailiness shapes the balance Sarton sought for her life and work: 'I think I have a kind of balance and discretion in the journals that I really don't have, unfortunately, in my life.' (In the film she paused before saying 'unfortunately' with a small laugh.) Does her statement suggest that the journals are a distortion? Not necessarily. Sarton's answer was that 'as an artist I think there's taste', which she defined as 'what you are going to talk about, and what not'.

While Sarton rarely wrote extended discussions of public affairs, and did not spend pages recollecting memories for their meanings, such topics do appear, usually in relation to the moral imagination. She often mentions her attachment to Europe, her parents (George Sarton, a Belgian historian of science, and her mother, Mabel Elwes, an English clothing designer); she speaks warmly of her New England childhood, and of numerous friendships with figures of note, from the actress Eva Le Gallienne to the Huxleys to other poets, including Louise Bogan and Muriel Rukeyser. When Sarton mentions a lover (mostly unnamed), it's the process of love that engages her imagination, not confessions about an individual. Almost inevitably the process touches on solitude and the claims that others made. Sarton had the misfortune to find an unsympathetic biographer in Margot Peters, whose *May Sarton: A Biography* (1997) includes her subject's admission that conflict had become 'the leitmotif of this journal', but Peters dismisses Sarton's self-analysis: 'A true solitary would not complain publicly about solitude, inspiring hundreds of people to relieve it. But then May was a solitary only because of her impossible temperament.' The word *relieve* here suggests that Peters misunderstood Sarton's ideas about solitude. Apparently she wanted her subject to be an iconic model of female creativity, the Wise Woman—a role that Sarton declined to play.

If one accepts Sarton's ideas about an artist's life—'How one lives as a private person is intimately bound into the work'—then her journals can be seen as a struggle to attain the balance that would let her continue writing. In *Journal of a Solitude*, she thought of herself as someone 'always split between art and life', with solitude providing a bridge between them. Never serene, she did try for something like equilibrium. The impression of continual striving—and the sheer hard work of it—is one of the most original features of her journals. As she admitted, 'It occurs to me that boredom and panic are the two devils the solitary must combat'; several times she notes the 'panic of solitude'. Though she left this 'panic' undefined, in an interview with Karla Hammond, from 1977, Sarton spoke about 'making a life out of solitude', and observed, 'Many people live alone. So there's a great interest in this, just as there's a great interest in dying. Solitude has some resemblance to dying.' Its relation to death may be what sometimes makes solitude an uneasy state, yet Sarton's journals also show that, as a place or space, solitude can bring a heightened sense of awareness of the non-human relations of one's life; this is, in part, what I mean by dailiness. It's not just that she takes the time to notice her surroundings (the bulbs, the sunsets, the snowstorms), or her rich ties to animals, but that without human companionship Sarton has the time, though never quite enough, to realize the significance of bonds that might otherwise seem insignificant. Yet the idea of death remains constant: 'I feel sure that after sixty everyone has death in the back of his or her consciousness much of the time,' she wrote in *The House by the Sea*. (Sarton was about to turn sixty-five when she made that observation.) With heightened awareness, she saw her world more sympathetically—an ideal condition for art-making, even if the art doesn't always match the vision.

May Sarton, at her best, reaffirms the importance of paying attention to the smallest details of the day, yet she often had to remind herself of this: 'I always forget how important the empty days are, how important it may be sometimes not to expect to produce anything, even a few lines in a journal.' When she gave advice about writing journals, in an interview with Lois Rosenthal in 1989, Sarton emphasized the quotidian: 'Remember to write about what you are seeing every day, and if you are going to hold the reader's interest, you must write very well. And what does writing well mean? It means seeing very well, seeing in a totally original way.' Keeping a journal is worthwhile because 'it gives a certain edge to the ordinary things in life', which makes the solitary enter a deeper relation with his or her surroundings, enjoying the full benefit of solitude. This 'edge' was a recurring motif in Sarton's various interviews, and she elaborated on the idea while talking with William Heyen and Mary Elsie Robertson in 1983, explaining that 'what's important about life is not the major calamities or joys but just living the day, just seeing the light on the wall'. Easier to say than to do.

As time passes, literary reputations go in and out of fashion. Since May Sarton's death, Norton has published three new books of hers, all selections of letters edited by Susan Sherman. I doubt that I'm the only reader still holding on to my old copies of the journals and wishing for a new one. Sarton often complained that too many readers and critics preferred her journals to her poetry, but in 1987, at the age of seventy-five, she was able to tell interviewer Connie Goldman: 'I think I have created something of a work of art with the journal, and I'm proud of that. For a long time I brushed the journals aside and said, "They're just nothing," but I don't think that now.' Sarton's readers would have agreed.

Several summers ago, while visiting a friend in Boston, I decided it was time to drive to Nelson, New Hampshire, for a literary pilgrimage. With my dog and an old friend along for the outing, I wondered if I would recognize Sarton's house, and how it might have changed in the thirty years since she'd left it for Maine. I needn't have worried. Driving past Nelson's small green common I couldn't have missed the house, set back from the road a bit and still resembling the black-and-white photographs in her books. The house was clearly occupied, but no one was home, and my friend urged me to walk up the drive and stand by the front steps for a quick photograph, as though I were one of the intruders who had interrupted Sarton's work; today I'm glad to have that picture. Later we drove to the Nelson cemetery where Sarton is buried, her grave marked by a stone sculpture of a phoenix rising from flames, the subject of many entries in her journals and once a decorative feature in her garden. Someone had left a yellow plastic mum and there were a few other tokens. I cleaned the gravesite as best I could, removing dried leaves and twigs, while my pug dog watched with a puzzled expression. He had slept by my side while I'd read one of Sarton's journals every January, and I reminded him of that, though of course he didn't take in my exact meaning—but he didn't attempt to lift his leg anywhere near the grave. May Sarton, I knew, would have understood exactly why I spoke to him. There was nothing more I could do for her but write this essay.

Editing *Old Ladies*: Margaret Avison, P.K. Page, Miriam Waddington, Suzanne Rosenberg and Jane Jacobs

Old is a curious word. In a culture where people try to convince themselves that sixty is the new forty, *old* can be problematic—harsher, say, than *senior* in *senior citizen. Ladies* I'll save for later. Editing was once my livelihood. For fifteen years, as Managing Editor of Oxford University Press Canada, I searched for, commissioned and edited a wide range of books, both trade and academic. And during that time I had the good fortune to edit some of Canada's finest writers. I want to discuss only a few of them here—the poets Margaret Avison, P.K. Page and Miriam Waddington, and prose writers Suzanne Rosenberg and Jane Jacobs—as well as some possible connections among them.

We're often told by lifestyle journalists that older North American actresses have a difficult time finding appropriate roles, and that women of a certain age dislike becoming invisible. Fortunately, women who write seem to be the exception to such limitations. They explore new subjects, publish the results of their efforts, win literary prizes and continue on in the work of their lives. The writers I want to discuss were all around seventy years old when I first met them, and were all born between 1915 and 1918, a short span of time during the First World War. A significant part of their identities, their early years and educations were shaped by parents and teachers who had come to maturity in the decades before that war, a cataclysmic event that shaped the consciousness of the next generation at a time when women were finally obtaining the right to vote in Canada and the United States. While British novelist Virginia Woolf suggested that western civilization changed dramatically in 1910, when she believed the modern age began, it probably took the First World War and women's suffrage to make such a change clear to a population broader than Bloomsbury's.

The management at Oxford University Press Canada kindly allowed me to spend an April day in 2011 looking over old files related to the writers I'll discuss here. This was a great help in refreshing my memory and shaping it with greater accuracy. It was strange to read the thin pink-tissue copies of letters I'd sent, some more than thirty years ago, and there were a few surprises.

MARGARET AVISON (1918–2007)

Margaret Avison's *Selected Poems* came to me in 1990, late in my career at Oxford, and the year before I left publishing to teach and concentrate on my own writing. Already familiar with her work, I was eager to meet the poet I considered to be Canada's finest. For reasons I can't recall, I expected her to be difficult. Something austere in her work—not the style but the vision behind it. We'd been in touch the year before when Avison had telephoned me about a young illustrator she admired, a woman named Karen Reczuch whom I'd hired to illustrate Jane Jacobs's children's book. I'd asked about Avison's future plans, we exchanged letters and by April 1990 she had signed a contract with Oxford. In a letter of April 20th to the poetry editor at McClelland & Stewart, who objected to Avison's signing with Oxford, she wrote that she liked the fact that I would make the selections for her book, and include only the poems (no introduction), and that she would only be asked to approve choices and omissions, 'without any demanding PR from me'. She also noted that I had suggested the *Selected* before anyone else thought of it, that her experience at M&S had not been happy and that when I heard about one of her former publishers' interest in the book, I deferred to any prior rights it 'may have established'.

Avison was anything but difficult. *Pure* is the right word, even if it's oddly vague and unhelpful. Our meetings took place in her small apartment in Fellowship Towers, a high-rise building several blocks north of Toronto's Bloor and Yonge intersection. Fellowship Towers is run by the Baptist church, and its residents have access to on-call medical help, as well as a dining room for those who can't, or won't, cook their own meals. Avison had been suffering for some years from lupus, a chronic nerve disease, and she couldn't always predict the state of her health. She explained this matter-of-factly, almost without interest, but I heard the subtext of her words, and understood that she wasn't going to commit to much in the way of book promotion, which most of the writers I'd worked with had enjoyed. Her apartment on the twelfth floor was a spartan affair, simply furnished with low shelves of books along one wall, but it had a fine view looking east, over the Rosedale Valley ravine, which seemed to be Avison's only luxury. She reminded me immediately of some of the older women teachers in my high school's English Department, the kind of women once called 'spinsters', a word that no longer has legs. But there was nothing spinsterish about her.

We spoke almost at once about books—what we were reading, what we liked. She recommended a novel by an unfamiliar American writer, Jane Vandenburgh's *Failure to Zigzag*. I read it eagerly, curious to understand her taste, and was surprised to find a story about a smart-mouthed teenage girl and her troubled mother—a mental patient and carnival ventriloquist. What had I expected? That she'd recommend something like Georges Bernanos's *Diary of a Country Priest*? Avison's Christianity informed her poetry, but she is not simply a religious poet, nor a mystic. She was, I came to understand, a truly worldly person, though in a way that alters the meaning of 'worldly'—*of* the world, but not *in* it. Discussing the reception of her first book, *The Dumbfounding* (1966), she recalled hearing from Norton's New York office that they were accepting her book. (It was, then, less common for Canadian poets to publish outside of Canada than it is today.) 'Like it or lump it,' she said, with a wry smile, 'recognition matters'.

Work on her book went smoothly. She considered my selections sound; we made a few additions, and that was that. (By then I'd already edited selected poems by Patrick Lane, Daryl Hine and P.K. Page.) Avison agreed to include several splendid translations of Hungarian poems that she'd made for a Canadian anthology published in 1963, and I was pleased because I'd been studying Hungarian for several years (it was the language of my grandparents, remembered from childhood). Most friends regarded these studies as an eccentricity—literary multi-culturalism was only starting to catch on in the late 1980s—but Avison said she'd loved hearing the language, it reminded her of the Tagalog spoken by Filipino friends. I saw her book through its last stages of production and then left the press to begin teaching at the start of the 1991 academic year. When I first told people that I was striking out, most warned of the risks; not Avison. She called my idea a good one and agreed to let me interview her for a book I was planning about Hungarian culture. We also spoke of caring for aging parents; Avison had lived with, and looked after, her elderly mother, and I was increasingly drawn into my father's health problems.

Avison's translations for *The Plough and the Pen*, edited by Ilona Duczyńska and Karl Polanyi, let me know her better. The anthology, introduced by W. H. Auden, is where he penned his much-quoted dictum that a writer's only political duty is to translate the work of other writers. Avison enjoyed remembering her introduction to its editors by Marshall McLuhan, in the Chinese courtyard of Toronto's Royal Ontario Museum. She was drawn especially to Ilona, and working with the couple meant a great deal to Avison (I always called her Ms Avison) in the years after the Hungarian uprising of 1956; she had passionate sympathies with oppressed people everywhere. Avison particularly liked the Hungarian poems for a quality she called 'direct utterance', though she never discussed this term, as if its meaning was self-evident. I've often thought about it since, and believe she was referring to poems where the mind and the heart (to use those almost old-fashioned terms) came together, especially in strong images. (I wrote about the technicalities of her translations in an essay called 'The Poet as Translator' for my book *Hungarian Rhapsodies.*)

When we spoke of Avison's Hungarian translations, she mentioned that Bartók's string quartets had, more than anything, keyed her to the rhythm she wanted to achieve in her versions. Avison is not often thought of as a particularly musical poet, so I was interested to find in Oxford's files a photocopy of a letter to her from Glenn Gould, dated September 14, 1962. Gould wrote to thank her for a letter regarding a recent concert, and her approving remarks about early Hindemith and William Walton. Most current Classical concertgoers have yet to catch up with Avison's sophisticated ear. (How did this letter get into Oxford's file? In 1991 I was about to serve as the press's editor for Glenn Gould's selected letters, and I must have mentioned this to Avison, who probably let me copy the letter as a possible inclusion.) Today I still keep in my top desk drawer the tape recordings I made of those afternoon conversations with her.

In subsequent years, Avison kept in touch with notes about the books I'd written. I was initially surprised, and touched, that she took the time. But she remembered the encouragement she'd given me, and took it for granted that she would write. When she won the Griffin Poetry Prize for *Concrete and Wild Carrot* in 2003, I was on holiday in Maine, but as soon as I heard the news I sent a card with congratulations, and when I returned to Toronto she telephoned with her thanks. (Occasionally she phoned with publishing questions, or about a proposed biography that she didn't want written.) 'Direct utterance' is not a technique or style, it's a way of seeing the world and relating to it. Not quite a vision, it comes from a particular slant or angle that can't be faked. It has to do with life, not lifestyle, and the belief that words can trap us and free us, so they must be used with great care, but without study, without thought for anything but the truth. Direct utterance is what I mean by the word *pure* for Ms Avison.

P.K. PAGE (1916–2010)

P.K. Page told me that her poems came to her through the top of her head, as if they'd been dictated, and all she had to do was type them up. They were complete, whole, already themselves. This fascinated me, and made a kind of sense for a poet who had written a much-anthologized early poem called 'The Stenographers'. I saw her poems only in their final typed form, and have no idea what the drafts looked like, or if there were any.

P.K. was introduced to me by a mutual friend, Rosemary Sullivan, a professor of English at the University of Toronto best known for her literary biographies. P.K. had completed a new collection of poems, which became *The Evening Dance of the Grey Flies*, and she was not happy with her previous publisher. She liked the interest of a younger generation of readers, and after our first meeting her book was mine. There were enough poems for a short collection, perhaps a chapbook—not Oxford's style—but I'd read Page's futuristic short story about a woman and her dog, 'Unless the Eye Catch Fire …', and suggested that she break the book into three parts and use the story at the centre, making a triptych. We debated—did the story seem too influenced by Doris Lessing?—and I pointed out that Elizabeth Bishop had included a prose memoir as the middle section of a recent collection. Page remembered Bishop from her time in Brazil as an ambassador's wife, and my idea now appealed to her. *Evening Dance* came out in 1981, and she was pleased enough by its reception to make Oxford her future publisher.

Like most of the poets I'd worked with, P.K. enjoyed sharing books and ideas about art; she urged me to read Julian Barnes's *Flaubert's Parrot* and Kathleen Raine's wonderful essay 'The Use of the Beautiful' in her *Defending Ancient Springs* ('It is nearly my bible,' she wrote to me on November 9, 1981), and I recommended something in return. We were both fascinated by Doris Lessing, though I had little interest in Sufism, or the version of it promulgated by Idries Shah. When Lessing came to

Toronto to read at Harbourfront, P.K. had arranged to met her (they'd corresponded, about Sufism), and I offered to drive P.K from Oxford to Lessing's hotel. When she invited me to join them I was delighted, and amazed by her generosity, since Lessing had been one of my favourite writers for at least twenty years. We met her for tea in the hotel dining room. Lessing was tempted to order a fruit salad, but decided it was too expensive; she recommended several writers to me, including an Indian mystic named Sri Aurobindo; and I was in bliss. After half an hour I excused myself so that the two women might have a private talk. Later I realized that P.K. had actually been quite nervous about meeting Lessing, and I'd been a kind of ice-breaker—my good fortune. I began to sense P.K.'s insecurities.

We next worked on a new selected poems that was ultimately called *The Glass Air: Selected Poems* (1985). P.K. had already published a *Selected* with McClelland & Stewart, in 1974, and there weren't enough new poems to justify another book. I suggested that we make her new book into an event, and include two short essays by P.K. that had appeared in *Canadian Literature*: 'Questions and Images' and 'Traveller, Conjuror, Journeyman'. As well, during a visit to P.K.'s home in Victoria, I'd seen some of the drawings she'd done while living in Brazil, and suggested that we also include a selection of her Dufy-like work (we settled on nine images) and use one of her paintings on the cover. When several of her friends objected to her proposed title, *The Glass House*, she still wanted to keep the word 'glass' so we dropped a poem called 'The Glass Air' and used its more elusive title for the collection. The visual and prose additions gave the book a comprehensive quality that P.K., and the reviewers, appreciated.

P.K. loved the literary lifestyle (the public attention from readings, interviews, book promotion), though I doubt she would have admitted it. She also liked having an entourage, and seemed to need her courtiers—all women—for second and third opinions about everything that touched her career. She encouraged their romantic dreams with stories about the great love of her life, the married Frank Scott, and continued to lament his loss. After meeting P.K.'s husband, Arthur Irwin, and watching her solicitous treatment of him, I was puzzled by the seeming disloyalty. Much of P.K.'s life (her travels, her start at painting, her elegant home and garden) came from Arthur, and if he was a stiff and conventional partner, she'd chosen him. There was a tension in P.K. between the former ambassador's wife—the gracious lady—and the wild romantic or free spirit she was afraid to become, and I saw that this wasn't the source of her poetry's strength but of its exquisite limitation. P.K. needed to be courted. She was annoyed that her work was ignored in the United States, but she didn't take the risk of submitting it and facing rejection. Her lack of confidence was almost touching. Since Rosemary and I were close friends, P.K.'s entourage was at first fine by me (Rosemary has good judgment), and I liked Arlene Lampert, but the list also included Connie Rooke. Connie insisted on being present when I made the initial mock-up of *The Glass Air* in my Oxford office, and though she had nothing to contribute, I knew she was P.K.'s envoy and had to be accommodated.

Our next books were P.K.'s fairy tale, *A Flask of Sea Water*, and a revised edition of *The Glass Air* (1991). The long debates about an illustrator for her children's book, and her dithering over the bright work of Laszlo Gal, one of Canada's prominent illustrators, seemed unhelpful. I was also troubled by her notion of a natural aristocracy of 'blue blood', as she called it, in the fairy tale. Perhaps there was something Sufi about this, but the idea reminded me of the unfortunate puzzling title of one of her poems, 'The Yellow People in Metamorphosis', which I'd previously questioned—the entourage thought it okay. When P.K. sent me a 20-page sample of the manuscript that was to become *Brazilian Journal* I was intrigued but not as enthusiastic as she might have wished The marketing department, with more Page backlist in the warehouse than they liked, took against the project from the start; I had no choice but to reject it. Not long after, I left publishing. P.K. continued to send me her new books, and I brought her to York University for a campus reading, but our relations were never the same. When I edited *The Exile Book of Canadian Dog Stories* (2009), I was glad to include P.K.'s 'Unless the Eye Catch Fire ...'—it was the last thing I could do for her. I wonder if she saw the book before she died.

MIRIAM WADDINGTON (1917–2004)

Miriam Waddington appeared in Oxford's lobby wearing a full-length dark mink coat, old jeans and black Reeboks. She'd just come from an afternoon swim and was glowing with the enthusiasm for life—coupled with endless complaints—that made up her unique style. She was curious about everything on one hand, and frustrated on the other. I felt in complete sympathy with her, and said that she looked like a Broadway actress late for rehearsal. Miriam made perfect sense to me. Later we figured out that I shared a birthday with her eldest son (not only the day, but the year) and joked that we had a special connection because of that. Maybe it was true.

Miriam had been an Oxford author long before I got to know her. Bill Toye was her poetry editor, but as he concentrated more and more on reference books, she needed a new advocate. In 1987 I suggested that she bring together her essays for an Oxford series I was developing, Studies in Canadian Literature, which went on to include books by Adele Wiseman, Robert Kroetsch, Janice Kulyk Keefer and Linda Hutcheon. Since Miriam lived not far from the office in Don Mills, in a mid-century split level on Yewfield Crescent, I fell into the habit of almost weekly Friday lunches with her. The house was filled with books and magazines, artwork gathered over her travels, some by old friends, like the wonderful Montreal painter Philip Surrey, Danish modern furniture and Mexican weavings and bibelots, all making a welcoming hodgepodge. There was usually a homemade soup, an Israeli salad, fresh challah. And endless talk—and gossip—about books and movies, mutual friends and Miriam's old times: her childhood in Winnipeg and Montreal, the Depression, the coming of World War II, the growing years of Canadian literature, her various love affairs with some prominent men, including the art critic Harold Rosenberg, an early champion of Abstract Expressionism, and a few well-known macho writers. It was the old times that won me over.

I convinced Miriam to put down some of her stories, to write about the Yiddish circle of her childhood, her immigrant parents, her years as an undergraduate. At the same time I read her published essays and newspaper articles—a portrait of the Yiddish-Canadian poet Rochl Korn, reflections on A.M. Klein and John Sutherland and accounts of her own writing. I even took several short review articles (on Anaïs Nin, Violet Leduc, Hannah Arendt and Simone de Beauvoir) and combined them into a longer essay. Miriam, who loved good talk, liked my editing, and the manuscript that became *Apartment 7: Selected Essays* grew out of those lunches. She would talk about her lovers, but I couldn't convince her to write about them—a sentiment that seems almost antediluvian today. That her book received splendid reviews was a bonus.

Oxford was known for its literary anthologies, usually a sure moneymaker, and I next urged Miriam to compile an anthology of short stories by Jewish-Canadian writers. My only stipulation was a gender balance (it turned out to be twenty stories—ten by men, ten by women) and Miriam agreed at once. But she was hesitant about including a story from her own collection *Summer at Lonely Beach* (1982)—a rare modesty in anthologists, who are usually all too eager to include their own work—so I chose Miriam's 'Breaking Bread in Jerusalem'. While we worked on these collections, she read some of my own short stories and encouraged me to concentrate on my writing. She knew of my Hungarian studies, which didn't seem odd to someone who was a gifted translator of Yiddish writers and very much interested in the act and art of translation; her enthusiasm for Central and Eastern European writers was rare among my colleagues. Sensitive to the undercurrent of anti-Semitism in the Canadian literary world, and justly so, Miriam didn't feel appreciated by the Toronto establishment (it rankled when she saw her work left out of college anthologies, while arty younger poets received attention), yet she gave a shrug to it all, and planned another of her trips. Some of the best advice she gave me about writing—advice I've since passed on to my own students—was this: 'Just do your own work and hope that taste will improve, though it probably won't.'

My final project with Miriam, before leaving the press, was her collection of poems *The Last Landscape*. It's one of her best books, and when it was published in 1992 I was pleased to find that she had dedicated it to me. Of course I continued to see her after I changed my life—lunches now became dinners—and I still remember the sad day when she announced that she was selling her house and moving to Vancouver to be closer to family. Most of her friends objected to the decision, and I think we were right to believe that Miriam would feel cut off from a world she'd taken a lifetime to create. When I learned that one day she'd stopped eating, had in effect turned her back on life, I could only admire her courage while hearing her say softly, after one of our lunches, 'My father's spirit is always with me.' I remember helping her pack before her move. For an afternoon I sat on her basement floor and tore up boxes of old bills and cheques, some dating back to the 1960s (a time before shredders). Of course we spoke on the phone after her move, but that was no substitute for meals that could meander with a life of their own. I'm not sure if Miriam's work is much read today—it deserves to be—but when I think of her, I miss those long lunches.

SUZANNE ROSENBERG (1915–1988)

One spring afternoon in 1987 I was staring out of my office window onto a large expanse of lawn when I noticed an elderly woman in a navy-blue dress, spotted with white polka dots, tentatively crossing the grass towards Oxford's drive, as if she was lost. A few minutes later my secretary came into my office with a manuscript, bound in string, which she set on the slush pile of unsolicited projects. The manuscript, it turned out, had just been dropped off by the woman in the polka-dot dress. Curious, I asked to see the manuscript. In no time I realized I had an important book in my hands.

Suzanne Rosenberg's memoir *A Soviet Odyssey*, which Oxford went on to publish in 1988, is a horrific account of her life in a totalitarian state. The Canadian connection was her youth, in Montreal, where she'd settled with her immigrant parents, and brother, before her mother decided to return to Russia with her family, in 1931, to help make a communist utopia. As if the Montreal childhood wasn't enough Canadian content, along with the fact that Suzanne was a cousin of Mordecai Richler on the maternal side of her family, her first love, in high school, turned out to have been the young Irving Layton (he wrote his own account of their bond in his memoir *Waiting for the Messiah*, 1985). But before accepting Suzanne's manuscript, I sent it to Robert Conquest, one of the leading North American specialists in the Stalin years. He encouraged publication and also wrote this jacket endorsement:

> Suzanne Rosenberg's book is one of the most remarkable autobiographies of our time. It covers the whole Soviet period, and at levels from the intellectual world to the labour camps. Above all, it is the most valuable perspective on the whole Soviet phenomenon ever to be published by someone who can rightly be described as both an extraordinary and an ordinary woman.

When Suzanne submitted her manuscript she was living in London, Ontario, and teaching Russian-language classes as part-time faculty at the University of Western Ontario. My first visit there remains clear in my mind. It was a grey autumn day, and during the cab ride from the train station to her apartment I spotted a florist's, stopped the cab for a moment and went in to buy some flowers, a dozen long-stemmed red roses. Suzanne blushed when she saw them, and said it had been a very long time since a man had last brought her flowers. To refresh me after the trip she offered a glass of old Georgian brandy from a bottle that had belonged to her last husband—a good beginning. Her small, spare apartment had only a few mementos of Russia, but its bookcase with glass doors had an old-world quality to it; the table where we worked, I recall, was a fold-up card table that suggested a temporary student dwelling. Suzanne's manuscript needed little shaping, but as we talked I encouraged her to develop several sections of it, and urged her to add more about the composer Prokofiev and other artists who had managed to continue creating under appalling conditions.

Working with Suzanne was a rare experience. I brought to it a love of Russian literature, which I'd studied at university, and Suzanne had worked as an English translator in Russia, so we had some wonderful talks about books. She was particularly proud of her translation of the short stories of Vladimir Korolenko, a nineteenth-century writer I didn't know (she gave me a copy of her translation, published by Progress Books in Moscow), and we both shared a fondness for Leo Tolstoy's *Resurrection*, a novel unmarred by some of his ideological concerns. My upbringing and education had made me Eurocentric, and Suzanne was the kind of person whose history, intellect and gracious manner appealed to my imagination. When I mentioned her to Miriam Waddington over one of our lunches, she almost jumped. It turned out that Suzanne was a friend of hers but hadn't mentioned submitting her manuscript to Oxford, although she must have heard my name from Miriam. Miriam suggested that she would have been glad to make an introduction, however I already knew enough about Suzanne to understand that she would never trade on friendship; she wanted her work to speak for itself. Which of course made me admire her all the more.

During her book's production, Suzanne was diagnosed with terminal cancer. She lived to hold her book in her hands, but when I drove her to a bookstore launch in Toronto she had to stretch out across the back seat because of the pain. The reviews of *A Soviet Odyssey*, both internationally and in Canada, were everything I'd hoped for. Oxford sold the paperback rights to Penguin, a film was discussed (films were always being discussed) and I helped arrange for a Japanese translation with Iwanami Shoten of Tokyo—it's the one book I own in Japanese.

In July 1988 I received a phone call from Suzanne's daughter, Vicki, who was teaching economics at McGill University. Following the instructions of her mother's will, she was about to mail a package to me. I wondered what it might contain, and after opening the parcel lifted out several jars of the finest Russian black caviar, which had been cold packed. That night I toasted Suzanne with vodka after vodka, and enjoyed her lavish bequest. Of all the books I brought out in my Oxford years, I'm proudest of hers.

JANE JACOBS (1916–2006)

While at my desk one summer day in 1987 I received a telephone call from Jane Jacobs. She lived in Toronto's Annex, next door to my friend Frieda Forman, a feminist researcher and also a Yiddish translator (Frieda had started up a small group of Yiddish translators who were all women, and it included Miriam Waddington—the world can sometimes seem like a small place). Jacobs was writing a children's book and wanted to talk about it. Though I wasn't a children's editor, I had been responsible for several books associated with the genre (by Joy Kogawa and P.K. Page) so Frieda made the connection. When I mentioned Jacobs's call to my colleagues they hoped that we might become her regular publisher, but I saw from the start that she was only interested in finding a home for her children's project. Still, any book by Jane Jacobs...

Of course I'd seen Jane on the front porch beside my friend's house, and knew that she presented herself as the neighbourhood eccentric. Her unkept yard would have drawn complaints had she not been the local celebrity, and large old cardboard boxes and other such rubbish often graced the porch. Jacobs, however, didn't cultivate eccentricity, it was something in her blood, almost genetic. A cult figure to city planners and environmentalists, she was admired for her influential study *The Death and Life of Great American Cities* (1961). She had immigrated to Toronto during the Vietnam War era, settled in the Annex, a neighbourhood bordering on the University of Toronto and, in her own way, held court. Stooped over, with a beaky hen's face and short greyish hair that looked like someone had set a bowl on her head and trimmed around its edges, she resembled the archetypal Granny in Hollywood movies about the Depression, someone out of *The Grapes of Wrath.* (By the way, my comment about her haircut isn't an exaggeration. Apparently that's how Jane's son cut her hair.)

After several meetings I signed up Jane's project. Intrigued by her persona, I enjoyed her stories about her background. The daughter of a well-off Yankee family—her father was a doctor—she exuded the self-assurance of someone who had long ago decided not to question her views about the world. As a child she remembered going along with her father on his house calls, and claimed that that was when she'd learned about life. Her parents had such faith in her that they left her alone. If she didn't go to school one day, and no one in the family knew where she was, her parents assumed she'd gone to the library, and weren't worried. Not exactly patrician, she reminded me of a certain generation of women, like the actress Katharine Hepburn: if she had an opinion it had to be the only right one. Jane wasn't one of the house-proud Annex types, and she had furnished her rooms with a funky style—against one wall of the dining room stood a real working telephone booth, glass doors and all, like something lifted off the street.

As usual, we talked about books other than Jane's own. Yet she spent more time praising her neighbourhood, and seemed oblivious of the fact that people sometimes refer to its inhabitants as 'Annex ethnics' because they can seem smugly insulated from many of the stresses of urban life. In Jane's case this insulation was intensified by early recognition, a long and loving marriage and a happy family life, which harmonized with what appeared to be an essentially cheerful nature. Jane wasn't caught up in her celebrity, just used to it; people were kind to her because of her fame, and in return she treated them kindly. After her death in 2006, the detached house she lived in was sold for more than a million dollars, and gutted for renovations; it now has an official memorial plaque on the front lawn.

Editing went smoothly. Jane knew that a children's book by her might cause a stir, and she didn't want any publicity until she was satisfied with the text and the illustrations. In August 1987 I asked Sheila Egoff (the Oxford author of *The Republic of Childhood*) for her general reaction to the manuscript, and she said that it suited 'ages seven to ten'. On May 5, 1988, Jane wrote to me, saying that I might notify the Toronto press about her forthcoming book: 'It's all right now, as I've been in touch with everyone I wanted to let know personally, first.' And she was enthusiastic about Karen Reczuch's illustrations, making only a minor suggestion about one of the characters, in a letter of November 12, 1988: 'Slap looks a little *too* genial.' The book appeared on the spring list of 1989, ahead of schedule.

Whenever Jane's books are mentioned, *The Girl on the Hat* is rarely included in the list. It's a 50-page novel about a girl named Ernestina who is so small she can fit inside a peanut shell. A Tom Thumb–like fantasy, it is based on stories Jane made up to entertain her children who, when grown, urged her to set them down for her grandchildren. Ernestina, who lives in a drawer, is nicknamed Peanutina, and called, for short, Tina. Her adventures lead her to find an identity in work as a photographer, and the importance of the right work—that old Yankee ethic—is the crux of the book. It's easy to see that the tall, gawky Jacobs, who may have felt like an outsider as a child, was, in part, writing about herself. Before showing the manuscript to me, she'd asked Frieda to read it for feminist content. At that time Jane had become interested in feminism, and wanted to know how her book accorded with feminist principles.

Jacobs's name is often invoked by progressive politicians and think-tank afficionados, yet when I read their remarks I recall not only the best of her writing but also one of her last books, *Dark Age Ahead* (2004), a grim but familiar lament about the sad state our civilization has fallen into and the failure of the elite class to do much about it. Jane almost seems to acknowledge some of the nonsense attributed to her, or done in her name. She was eighty-eight when that book was published—an encouraging thought.

* * *

Why do I write about these five women? I'm not a feminist looking for ancestors. I knew them mainly as an editor, someone who acted in a courtly manner they enjoyed, who cared for something about their work, someone from a younger generation who had an eye on what kept them going, on the future. In my work I represented their interests to the press, my employer, and the press's interests to them. I was a go-between, the editor's tricky balancing act, but I think they knew that their interests were what mattered the most to me. Miriam I counted as a true friend, Suzanne as a model of the moral imagination. They were all 'ladies' in a sense—women from another time, when their achievements cost in ways we barely understand today, no matter how we try. Yet their sense of themselves as women and as writers, at least as I saw it, was something they had learned to carry with grace—a grace I associate with the outmoded word *lady*.

Each one helped me understand something about the nature of a writer's life. Unlike the male writers I knew, who too often seemed, even as they aged, to concentrate their energies on sex, alcohol and sexual nostalgia—all invitations to bitterness and regret—these writers had a lively interest in the present. Their work, good or not, was partly about possibilities. Though I knew her last, Avison's emphasis on direct utterance mattered the most to me, reinforcing my values about writing and what my work in publishing had taught me: the literary life gets in the way of creation, yet many writers who admit this are addicted to it. P.K. Page and Jane Jacobs were in their own ways committed to their personas, yet despite this each continued to create. Miriam Waddington's counsel to keep writing no matter what, came from the deepest part of her sense of self, and is good advice to anyone in the arts, where disappointment is inevitable; while Suzanne Rosenberg's courage, fortitude and generosity of spirit before unimaginable suffering still amaze me, and have left me with the wish to show her my own books over some old Georgian brandy. Once I read an interview with Doris Lessing where she remarked that she and her friends, all in their eighties, were learning Russian. The idea appeals to me because that's the one language I would still like to be able to read. Maybe some day, I tell myself. Though it will be too late to speak a few words to Suzanne in the language she loved.

Glenn Gould and the Mouse

On a cold wintry Sunday three of us sat around my dining-room table finishing the sandwiches I'd set out for lunch while continuing a lively debate about which of Glenn Gould's letters would make it into the book we were preparing. For no good reason I still remember the sandwiches: rare roast beef and ham-and-cheese. We'd even played a game that I associate with musicians, identifying each other as a musical key. One of the guests, John Roberts, said that I was definitely B minor.

This working lunch took place back in 1992, not long after I left my job as Managing Editor of Oxford University Press Canada to concentrate on my writing and to return to teaching. But I had agreed to serve as the press's editor for a book I'd previously acquired: Glenn Gould's *Selected Letters*. The opportunity to work with editors from the Gould Estate was too interesting to pass up because Gould had been a hero of my musical life since I was an undergraduate and bought his extraordinary LP of Bach's *Goldberg Variations*. As well, the Art Deco apartment building where Gould lived for much of his adult life, near Toronto's Yonge and St. Clair intersection, was only a four-minute walk from my own apartment; in the 1970s I'd actually spotted him twice on the street, heading late at night towards Fran's, one of a popular chain of restaurants that kept long hours.

The Gould Estate naturally wanted a book of musical substance, which of course suited Oxford, and the editors were chosen accordingly: John P.L. Roberts was then Dean of the Faculty of Fine Arts at the University of Calgary, and a former producer at CBC in Toronto, where he'd been Head of Radio Music; he was also President of the Glenn Gould Foundation and a close friend of Gould himself. His co-editor, Ghyslaine Guertin, was a professor of philosophy at the Collège Édouard-Montpetit, an associated researcher at the Faculty of Music at the Université de Montréal and a member of the Glenn Gould Prize jury. I hoped we would see eye to eye. Fortunately the literary agent for the Estate, Lucinda

Vardey, was one of Canada's savviest, and I'd always enjoyed working with her. She saw the potential for a cult of Gould and had even selected the book's cover photograph, a sexy, James Dean-ish image of the cool young pianist, which Vardey also wanted to turn into a poster. We were all working on behalf of that creature now referred to as 'an icon'.

Before our Sunday meeting I'd read photocopies of all the letters (or at least the ones I was shown) and marked my own selection, keeping in mind Otto Friedrich's biography *Glenn Gould: A Life and Variations* (1989). A senior writer for *Time*, and the author of books about Hollywood in the 1940s and Berlin in the 1920s, Friedrich no doubt faced many obstacles in writing about Gould, which perhaps explains why his book is light on personal material. He doesn't even mention Gould's affair with Cornelia Foss, wife of the American composer Lucas Foss, though in musical circles it was a matter of common knowledge. The Gould letters I was given were mainly professional notes to colleagues, discussions of upcoming recitals, recordings and television documentaries, courteous replies to media requests (to name his favourite local restaurant, for example) and the like. Gould the man remained hidden, if not a mystery—a perfectionist who seemed to float above the messier details of ordinary human life. No matter how sexy the cover photograph of the *Selected Letters* might be, the actual book would please only Gould's most devoted admirers and other musicians. Careful selection was essential for our book to come alive.

A formal man, John Roberts showed up at my apartment in a sports coat, white shirt and tie, the perfect picture of a college dean. But the twinkle in his eyes told me that he had an artist's temperament. Ghyslaine Guertin, a trim and handsomely dressed woman around forty, with a silk scarf tied artfully about her neck, seemed more reserved, but she soon relaxed. I knew I could be direct with both of them. I explained that we might make a somewhat shorter book than originally imagined (it turned out to be 256 pages, including the preface and index) but one that would do Gould proud. Roberts had many personal stories to tell about Gould and his frequent middle-of-the-night telephone calls, though he made it clear that these stories were private. (Gould's friends had to be tremendously tolerant of his eccentricities and self-indulgence.)

We would attempt to offer as rounded a portrait as possible, and make certain that our selection of letters didn't duplicate the same information over and over. To begin, we eliminated any repetitious letters. Letters that would interest only musicologists were set aside for consideration, since the book had to have musical integrity. We considered both the recipient of each letter (notable figures such as Leonard Bernstein, Yehudi Menuhin and John Cage were given an edge) and its subject. There were only a few personal items. I was attached to one that Gould wrote to his mother when he was twenty-five years old and performing in Vienna. The letter was slight but it showed a playful side of Gould not present in his other correspondence. Dated June 3, 1957, it begins with a surprising salutation: 'Dear Mouse-Possum-Bank'. 'Mouse' refers to his mother, 'Possum' to his father, and 'Bank' to his dog Banquo. (Neither John nor Ghyslaine could explain the derivation of the first two nicknames, but 'Banquo' came from Shakespeare's *Macbeth*. Why anyone would name a family pet after a murdered nobleman remains a mystery.) Gould describes his recent travels in Germany and northern Austria, complains of a sinus infection and urges his parents to save money for a trip to Europe. For Gould this was a long and chatty letter. It even included a quick rough sketch of a possum on a dead tree trunk and a mouse chasing a hound (each with its appropriate label). We debated about the merits of the letter. John was more inclined to include it than Ghyslaine, and I remained its advocate.

Just as we were finishing the last of the coffee, there was a loud snapping noise and the sounds of a scuffle in the living room. I guessed at once what had happened. That winter the apartment building where I lived had, almost overnight, been faced with a visitation of mice. I'd seen only one scurrying across my bedroom floor, but it was more than enough, and I complained at once to the landlord. The superintendent placed a mousetrap (with a dab of peanut butter on it) behind the ficus tree by my balcony door, and exterminators were to arrive later in the week. Embarrassed, I excused myself and headed toward the commotion; the concealed mousetrap must have smacked against the tree's large Chinese pot. The armature of the trap had caught a mouse, and the poor creature (trapped, it now seemed like a poor creature) thrashed about. There were several smears of blood on the floor. John followed me and together we looked down at the dying mouse. Ghyslaine, quite elegantly, remained at the table and took up some manuscript pages. Even if the mouse could have survived, it was snowing outside and there was no place to set it free. I had no idea what to do.

'Bring a bucket of water,' John suggested. He had already taken off his sports coat and was now rolling up his shirt sleeves. I must have looked puzzled because he repeated the request, and added, 'We'll have to drown it. That's the most humane thing to do.'

I hurried to the broom closet, grabbed a plastic pail and quickly filled it with water. When I stood beside John again he reached for the wooden trap—the mouse just barely moving—and set it in the water. Nothing happened. The mouse floated.

'We need a broom,' John said, and in no time I returned with one. He took it from me calmly and pushed the mousetrap, with its captive, deeper into the water.

Ghyslaine remained at the table, eyes averted, turning pages.

I don't know how long it took for that mouse to die, but it seemed endless.

Later, after I'd wrapped the mouse in some newspaper and a plastic bag and dropped it down the garbage shoot, John and I returned to the table and to the task at hand. Then we started to laugh. Quietly, ruefully and with an odd resignation. There was no question in anyone's mind.

I was the first to speak up: 'We have to keep that letter to Mouse.'

John and Ghyslaine vigorously nodded their assent. We were all affected by the coincidence. It was as if the ghost of Mrs Gould had, for a moment, come to haunt us, inhabiting the body of a poor creature in search of a warm home and a little taste of peanut butter. Mrs Gould, or Mouse, had demanded a place in her famous son's *Selected Letters*.

Or had Gould himself intervened?

That Sunday, as the hours passed and daylight darkened, neither John, Ghyslaine nor I could have guessed that a future issue of the *New Yorker* would include George Steiner's fine essay 'Glenn Gould's Notes', with praise for our *Selected Letters* and its 'weight of ardent technicality'. While taking pleasure in this, we might also have had a sense of what Freud calls the Uncanny: 'anything to do with death, dead bodies, revenants, spirits and ghosts'. We had, after all, just shared in the death—even the murder—of a mouse.

This is sometimes how books are made.

My Viennese Vice

On Halloween night in 1963, CBC Television broadcast the Orchestre de Radio-Canada in a program called *A Viennese Evening*. The legendary German soprano Elisabeth Schwarzkopf and Austrian conductor Willi Boskovsky, known for his operetta recordings, were guest artists. I had not yet immigrated to Canada so I didn't see this concert until recently, when I came across a DVD of it, released in 2006 by Video Artists International. Although the images are somewhat grainy, the sound is more than adequate and I was pleased to make this discovery.

All right, I confess: my vice is Viennese operetta. The first strains of Schwarzkopf singing 'Wiener Blut' took me back to my childhood, and to my grandmother softly humming while making apple strudel. But my love of operetta isn't only about nostalgia. I've used the word *vice* here because, except in rare circles, operetta is seen today as old-fashioned kitsch or campy schmaltz, at best a Eurocentric phenomenon for senior citizens. Never mind that the Toronto Operetta Theatre marked its thirtieth anniversary with its 2014–15 season, or that the Ohio Light Opera Company, with its ambitious history, draws an audience not only from the American Midwest but from across the continent—operetta still evokes a quaint bygone era.

As the demographics of North America change, and the influx of Central European and German immigrants from the early part of the twentieth century are finally buried, operetta has almost been buried with them. By the time large numbers of Hungarian refugees arrived after the abortive uprising of 1956, it was probably too late to change the course of operetta history: the popular culture had moved on to rock and roll. The best book on this subject—Richard Traubner's *Operetta: A Theatrical History*, first published in 1983—has been in and out of print. But in his award-winning study *Opera in America: A Cultural History*, John Dizikes remarked that *The Merry Widow* was an important part of the growth of opera in America. In 1907, two years after its premiere in

Vienna, one hundred companies around the world were performing *The Merry Widow*. Franz Lehár's Balkan fantasy is still a money-maker for opera houses that neglect equally fine works by Emmerich Kálmán and Carl Zeller, and Johann Strauss's *Die Fledermaus* remains a draw, especially for festive New Year's Eve galas. This music cannot be easily dismissed. In a recent issue of *Opera News*, the Swedish soprano Nina Stemme, known as a gifted Wagnerian, was asked to name the most underrated piece of music, and she replied: 'Lehár operettas. Much more difficult and beautiful than most people think.'

The term *operetta* means 'little' opera. Musicologists cite French *opéras-comiques* and Jacques Offenbach's operettas as the origin of Viennese operetta. I've never fully accepted this argument, or warmed to Offenbach's music, which lacks the bittersweet combination of charm and melancholy that characterizes the best music of Lehár and Kálmán. For me the origin of Viennese operetta lies elsewhere—in an opera from Giuseppe Verdi's middle period, *La Traviata*. Recently I mentioned this notion to Teresa Stratas, the Greek-Canadian soprano who was an extraordinary Violetta in Franco Zeffirelli's film of that opera, and who has also left a notable legacy of her operetta ventures (alongside her *Salome* and *Lulu*) in several films for German television, including Lehár's *Der Zarewitsch* (The Tsarevich), available on DVD. Teresa immediately let out a laugh and chimed in with, 'Oh, yes, that oom-pah.' We joked that if Lehár or Strauss had composed an operetta based on the Camille story, its final scene—which we'd like to hear—might have been a reconciliation in heaven between Violetta and Alfredo.

I take frequent long road trips, usually travelling with a canvas bag of operetta CDs, which make excellent listening when my energy begins to flag. One of my friends refers to this bag as 'the Betty Blackhead Collection', slighting Schwarzkopf unjustly. Why is operetta so often mocked? The plots, of course, may be part of the problem, especially for contemporary audiences with a fondness for naturalism. All those tipsy aristocrats, lusty gypsies, star-crossed lovers, long-lost siblings and mistaken identities—though these are the old stuff of comedy (think of Mozart's *Così fan tutte*). No, I believe the reasons are more serious, and may have to do with a century of world wars and the changes in musical taste that ensued.

Viennese operetta flourished in the early years of the twentieth century but became unpopular in North America during World War I, along with most things German (New York's Metropolitan Opera even stopped performing Wagner's music dramas). Still, Giacomo Puccini, known for his lavish scores, was tempted by the operetta ethos, and composed an appealing late work, *La Rondine* (1917), with a nod to Vienna. During the 1920s operetta regained its audience, and composers like Sigmund Romberg and Rudolf Friml, Central European immigrants drawn to Broadway, created popular entertainments such as *The Student Prince* and *The Desert Song*. With new operettas being composed at a rapid pace, it was inevitable that the style would calcify. The British writer Paul Bailey sets his moving short novel, *Uncle Rudolf*, in this milieu, telling the story of a charismatic Romanian tenor. The narrator is his nephew:

> The voice you hear today on the Golden Age label gives just a hint of what he was about. It is bright and confident, as befits a reckless vagabond; a prince who believes he is a simple gypsy fiddler; a champagne-guzzling gambler who plays roulette with no thought of tomorrow. These were the kind of improbable men Uncle Rudolf impersonated, giving them—for as long as he could bear to—angelic expression. But the angel wanted to sing of other matters, of other, more serious, concerns, and he had already left it too late to do so by the time I arrived in his life.

Meanwhile, inspired by the genre, American composer Jerome Kern gave it an American twist in *Showboat* (1927), which Traubner rightly calls 'America's greatest operetta'. By the 1930s, operetta had gone Hollywood with the popular film team of Jeanette MacDonald and Nelson Eddy singing their way through *Naughty Marietta* and other now-risible confections.

World War II added the *coup de grâce*. After the war a de-nazification process faced German musicians like Wilhelm Furtwängler, Elisabeth Schwarzkopf and Herbert von Karajan, who had performed under the Third Reich. All were exonerated, but their public acts may have tainted the seemingly innocent nature of operetta, at least in North America. In Europe, operetta reminded people of brighter days. In his memoir *Reverberations*, the great German baritone Dietrich Fischer-Dieskau described this Berlin scene of 1947: 'And right next to some temporary stage where *The Countess Maritza* was being performed, the "rubble women" (the women who cleared the bomb sites) handed each other pails full of debris in a sort of bucket brigade.'

Along with improbable plots, operetta scores are filled with lush melodies, and in recent years the value of melody has come into question, as if the human voice must never sing a line of seductive beauty. Melody is now something to distrust. The best Viennese operetta, however, thrives on the tension between its melodies and the guttural nature of the German language itself. The heartfelt emotions that ground these melodies—longing, joy, sorrow—are seldom ironic, our style *du jour.* This unique, tuneful music is sometimes called 'light' by critics, yet Lehár's and Kálmán's works in particular are harmonically inventive and slick in the best sense. As well, the erotic style of operetta, with its underlying waltz rhythm, appears to be too sedate for the postmodern ear. We're far removed from the social norms of the nineteenth-century, when the waltz was once a controversial dance, censured for its allegedly racy nature. After Maurice Ravel wrote *La Valse* (1919–20), catching a society dancing into the oblivion of World War I, the waltz form never seemed quite the same. In 1973, Stephen Sondheim evoked a tradition of 3/4 time with his operetta-like musical *A Little Night Music*, and American opera companies have begun to include this arch crowd-pleaser as part of their repertoire. Whatever it's called, *A Little Night Music* harkens back to Lehár, but its true roots are in Friml.

Anyone who doesn't travel in Europe, where operetta is regularly performed in Vienna and Budapest (and at summer festivals in places like Austria's Mörbisch Lake), must resort to CDs. In the last few decades some fine CDs of operetta arias have been made by contemporary singers with international careers, including the late tenor Jerry Hadley, baritones Thomas Hampson, Simon Keenlyside and Bernd Weikl, soprano Barbara Bonney and mezzo-soprano Angelika Kirchschlager. Reissues of older recordings by Hilde Gueden, Schwarzkopf and Fritz Wunderlich take on new life when set beside a new generation of singers. As well, during the 1950s, Walter Legge, the famed classical producer at EMI, decided to record the great operetta repertoire with his wife, Elisabeth Schwarzkopf, and their classic versions have often been reissued, most recently by Naxos. If you've only heard 'Vilja's Song' from *The Merry Widow*, and a few other old chestnuts, a good place to begin is with Sony's *Dein Ist Mein Ganzes Herz* (My Heart Alone) with Kirchschlager and Keenlyside, made up of splendid arias and duets. Next, go on to Johann Strauss II's masterpiece *Der Zigeunerbaron* (The Gypsy Baron), with Schwarzkopf in the lead and Otto Ackermann conducting; then try my two favourite operettas, both by Emmerich Kálmán: *Die Csárdás Fürstin* (The Csardas Princess) and *Gräfin Mariza* (Countess Maritza), on the EMI label, with Anneliese Rothenberger and Nicolai Gedda.

In the last years of her life, Elisabeth Schwarzkopf often criticized the sound of transfers from vinyl recordings to CD. Yet several weeks before her death in 2006, at the age of ninety, she agreed to the DVD issue of her evening with the Orchestre de Radio-Canada. She had never performed operetta onstage, only in the recording studio. How fortunate we are to have her concert preserved rather than lost to time. Almost a master class in Viennese style, it is a unique evening in itself, and one that embodies a world that lives on only in music. Listen carefully.

All Waltzed Out: Listening for World War I

Over the weekend of June 28, 2014, newspapers around the world marked the centenary of the First World War with memorial articles, often accompanied by a blurry photograph of the bodies of Archduke Franz Ferdinand and his wife, Sophie, shot by an assassin in Sarajevo. Pundits from the right and left opined, and distinguished historians with more to say said it in op-eds. When the news coverage returned to the latest troubles in the Middle East, only a few journalists bothered to note that artificial borders drawn up after the war had led to the problems of today. A grand history lesson was done for now, or at least until another anniversary came by. But what might we have understood if we'd lingered a while longer in the early years of the last century?

Thoughts of this nature came to mind a month later when I left the Freedlander Theater, on the campus of the College of Wooster, where the Ohio Light Opera had just given a lively performance of Emmerich Kálmán's 1912 operetta *Der kleine König* (The Little King). In its thirty-sixth year, the company was continuing its annual exploration of seldom-performed operettas. Why should anyone care about the matinee of an obscure entertainment in a small college town? I left the show humming though almost waltzed out. It's a commonplace of music criticism that Maurice Ravel's *La Valse* (1920), in both its solo piano and orchestral versions, reflects on Europe's 'dance' into the First World War. That view, however, sidesteps the fact that the composition was a backward glance, affected by hindsight. Earlier music perhaps foretold the war but few were listening. I'm not thinking of the dissonances of Stravinsky or the fresh harmonies of Bartók, but rather of the hummable tunes of operetta and the plot of Kálmán's score. Operetta is too often seen as a musical *bon-bon*—sentimental, old-fashioned, irrelevant. However, *The Little King* and works like it—central to the popular culture of their day—have deepened with meaning over time, and, through their artistry, form a bridge to the past.

If Emmerich Kálmán (1882–1953) isn't a familiar name, permit a short digression. Known for bittersweet, minor-key melodies, gypsy rhythms and the harmonic shifts of his lush scores—such as *Die Csárdás Fürstin* (The Gypsy Princess, 1915) and *Gräfin Mariza* (Countess Maritza, 1924)—Kálmán is one of the most esteemed of operetta composers, the equal of Franz Lehár and Johann Strauss, musicians who helped shape the sensibility of prewar Vienna, along with Freud, Schnitzler and Klimt. Yet half a century passed after Kálmán's death before he received a full-scale biography in English with the translation from the German of Stefan Frey's *Emmerich Kálmán: Laughter Under Tears, An Operetta Biography* (2014). Frey also explores the operetta 'industry' that emerged before the First World War, when productions occurred in cosmopolitan cities across the globe soon after premiering in Vienna. After the horrors of the war, qualities of nostalgia and sentimentality came to dominate the form's evocation of a lost world of minor royals and café society. *The Little King* belongs to the prewar generation, and brings to mind 'Arms and the Man' by George Bernard Shaw (1894)—a critique of false heroics—which, in 1908, was turned into a tuneful operetta, *Der tapfere Soldat* (The Chocolate Soldier) by Oscar Straus. In fact, after that operetta became more popular than its source, Shaw forbade further musical versions of his work (*Pygmalion* from 1912 only became *My Fair Lady* in 1956 with the playwright's death).

Born in Hungary, Kálmán witnessed one of Europe's grimmest times. After studying law, and then composition, he enjoyed both artistic and commercial success by the age of twenty-five, when the Budapest triumph of his first operetta, *The Gay Hussars* (1909), led to productions across Europe and, six months later, on Broadway. From that time on his music flowed, one hit after another. When the genre evolved after the war, Kálmán upheld its Viennese roots, though with a Hungarian inflection, and incorporated elements of newly popular styles like jazz and tango. But by the 1930s Europe had darkened under the rise of Hitler, and the Jewish Kálmán, then living in Vienna, had every reason to be fearful. After he turned down the offer of honorary Aryan status, it was time to move on. Like other artists who joined the exodus to the United States, Kálmán departed for Hollywood in 1940, later settling in New York. Revivals kept him before the public, but the allure of operetta was fading as new musical styles transformed the era's musical theatre. Fashions don't endure, fortunately, and Kálmán's work has eventually been rediscovered in the last few decades. His music hasn't changed but it no longer seems mainly about nostalgia and sentiment, it can again be heard for its intrinsic worth.

Back in October 1910, revolutionaries forced the abdication of Manuel II, the twenty-year-old king of Portugal. Kálmán and his librettists took this story from their daily newspaper and turned it into the subject of popular entertainment. *The Little King* premiered in Vienna's famed Theater an der Wien on November 23, 1912—a year and a half before the Archduke's assassination—yet in his review in *Die Zeit* the following day, the critic Richard Specht commented that it embodied 'the chaos from which modern operetta is born'. He'd heard and understood the evening's message. Kálmán's plot included the coincidences and romantic entanglements of much light opera, and, for that matter, of grand opera too. With a deftly sketched background of economic inequality and social injustice, the libretto concentrates its action in the lavish rooms of a palace, but the threat of rebellion from the outside is always present, and rebels appear several times, along with servants sympathetic to the republican cause.

The story: A ballerina named Zaza arrives at the palace for an assignation with a sweet but immature young king who likes to be called Koko. Since he has just returned from a performance of *Carmen* enthralled by its prima donna, Zaza is foisted off on a newly made Baron. When the diva Anetta appears, she joins a group of rebels in their revolutionary song. Soon the king pursues her, unaware that she is the daughter of an anarchist seeking to avenge her father's murder. If Tosca and Leonora come to mind, they should—opera heroines have a traditional link with politics. As part of her plan, Anetta carries a bouquet of red roses that conceals explosives. (Operetta antics often mirrored European politics. In 1938, Stalin had Yevhen Konovalets, the Ukrainian nationalist leader, murdered by a bomb disguised in a box of chocolates.) But the King charms her, and inevitably they fall in love. Anetta sees beyond his inexperience, to a good man who could be a just leader. Like in the story of Manuel II, Koko's palace is soon surrounded by rebels, its future looks bleak and he rejects a demand for abdication; instead, he'll fight to the death. So Anetta turns to the old Field Marshal, pleading with him for Koko to abdicate: 'He's more than a King, he's a good man.' After her relation to the rebels is revealed, Koko believes she has betrayed him and heads into exile with his beloved dog. Still, there's another act. Anetta follows him to a villa on the English coast, where a few royal cronies dream of fighting the good fight. Of course the Field Marshal finally tells Koko of Anetta's devotion, and love triumphs.

In an NBC radio interview of May 5, 1940, six weeks after arriving in the United States, Kálmán explained that he collaborated actively in the writing of any libretto he set to music, and its concerns were his own. While the military men of *The Little King* give voice to a battle cry (some more grudgingly than others), it's the women who are deeply anti-war. Anetta explains that she would never kill anyone for a cause, even a just one: her grievance is personal. After she recognizes it as misguided, she makes the case for finding space for a personal life in an unstable world. Meanwhile, Zaza, though a ditzy soubrette, dismisses sabre rattling as a childish game. Neither woman mentions the inevitable casualties of war, nor does she advocate women's rights or suffrage, but it's not an exaggeration to hear the operetta's proto-feminist tone—its heroines sensibly want good lives, and if that includes love, all the better. It's also worth remembering that *The Little King*, like most classic operettas, was written long before women achieved the vote.

Perhaps the seemingly absurd plots of many operettas have caused critics to look away from the form, just as they tend to eschew 'light' music in general. Although Alex Ross does discuss the impact of the First World War in his deservedly praised *The Rest Is Noise: Listening to the Twentieth Century* (2007), he ignores operetta, never mentions Kálmán, only cites Oscar Straus for a remark he made about Alban Berg, and writes, rather patronizingly, that at the Austrian premiere of Richard Strauss's *Salome*, in 1906, Johann Strauss II's widow, in attendance, 'represented old Vienna'. Did Ross think operetta dismissible because of its popularity or its status as light music? He might have listened to the words of that fine philosopher/musicologist Theodor W. Adorno, who wrote that in the decade before the First World War, 'the true Orpheus migrated to operetta, taking possession of our underworld'.

A backward glance is easier than foresight, but works of art do sometimes see ahead, if not prescriptively. Had Europe's powers-that-be paid attention, might they have averted the Great War's bloodbath? This question may sound naive, but it shouldn't. Like Shaw and Straus, Kálmán warned of a dark future, using humour and heartfelt melody to win over his audience. It's amazing how people who value the arts can ignore their content. In perhaps a bleak moment, the Irish poet Seamus Heaney once remarked, 'It is difficult at times to repress the thought that history is about as instructive as an abattoir.' The fault, of course, is not with history, but with us. Yet if we don't learn from experience, from history, we probably won't learn from music either. What a tragedy, what a farce—and that is, precisely, the mixed mood of operetta.

A Year of the Piano

From Edmund Spenser's 'The Shepheardes Calendar' to accounts of the gardening year or memoirs like Phyllis Rose's *A Year of Reading Proust*, writing structured around a calendar always appeals to me. Music also suits this form, but where to begin? The obvious month is September, when the concert season takes off for professional musicians and concert-goers alike, and classes resume for conservatory students after the summer hiatus. Since I'm not a piano student in any formal sense, my choice is freer. Once my academic year has ended I have more time to practise, the current concert season has left its memories, and brochures arrive for the one ahead, like tempting seed catalogues in January. Spring, therefore, starts my chronicle.

MAY

This summer I want to concentrate on several pieces learned last year, bringing them back into my hands. Inevitably, the ritual of practising makes me recall piano teachers from my past.

Your first piano teacher can set up your musical life or kill your musical instincts. Mine, fortunately, was an extraordinary, fortyish woman named Susan Krausz. Born in Stuttgart, Germany, Mrs Krausz (that's how I still think of her) studied there before marrying a violist; after World War II they immigrated to America, where he became principal violist of the Cleveland Orchestra. I didn't then know that Mrs Krausz and her husband, Laszlo, had escaped the Holocaust to live in Switzerland. I did know that she claimed to understand very little English when they arrived in New York, and that she kept ordering fried eggs for breakfast because her vocabulary hadn't caught up with her appetite. Later, during the decade I studied with her, I learned that one of her teachers had been the legendary Romanian pianist Dinu Lipatti, who died at thirty-three, of leukemia. Only recently, while reading an entry about her from the Cleveland Composers Guild, did I find that she'd also studied with another legend, Edwin Fischer. Humbling thoughts.

It now amazes me that every Thursday afternoon Mrs Krausz drove to my family's house, arriving at 4:30 for a thirty-minute lesson that lasted for forty-five; that she charged $3.50 a lesson; and that this splendid musician sat patiently beside me, correcting my mistakes. She managed to have a career as a performer—I've kept the program for her 1957 performance with the Akron Symphony—compose music and eventually lecture in piano at Case Western Reserve University, while raising two sons. From her I had the first glimmering that an artist's way of life was possible. My mother and I once visited her upstairs duplex in Cleveland Heights. There was no sofa in the living room; instead, two grand pianos, bookcases of musical scores, her husband's paintings on the walls, some low benches. The room should have felt gloomy but seemed alive. (She took my mother into the kitchen to show her, with pride, two recent purchases: a stove and fridge in the avocado colour then the height of kitchen fashion.) Decades later I wasn't surprised to read that 'Susan Krausz taught privately until the day before she died'—at ninety three.

After high school I set my piano studies aside, though I attended concerts by a celebrated generation: Arthur Rubenstein, Rudolf Serkin, Lily Kraus. I didn't resume lessons until graduate school, as a distraction from my doctoral thesis. I registered at Toronto's Royal Conservatory and had the good fortune to land on Andrew Markow, another excellent teacher. Some years passed, Andrew moved to Russia for a time, and I was teacher-less. My work in publishing consumed much of my energy, but Ron Tomorelli, who gave private lessons, was for several years a good coach who overlooked my spotty preparation. By then any spare time was given over to writing, something had to go, and it was the piano. I could never sound like the splendid pianists I heard perform—Alfred Brendel, Maria João Pires, Claudio Arrau. Of course I missed the piano but didn't touch mine for over a decade. Would I ever return to it?

Several years ago, one summer afternoon, a Cleveland friend who once studied at Salzburg's Mozarteum, phoned about a piano that she'd come across in a consignment store. The Krakauer console had been well cared for but not much played. Absurdly, after several markdowns, the cost was $200. 'It's a Chopin piano,' my friend said, speaking of its warm tone. An hour later it was love at first sound, and the piano was mine.

After a good tuning, the tuner found the piano's serial number, made a quick phone call and we learned that the piano had been built in 1959, a pre-plastic era, which helped explain the rich tone for its size. Then I took out my old music and saw, with no surprise, how rusty I'd become. Oddly, it no longer mattered. I didn't have to sound like one of my idols, I just had to enjoy myself.

JUNE

With Dinu Lipatti's wonderful 1950 recording of the Chopin waltzes in my head (he made it five months before his death), I bought a fresh edition of the Schirmer's score and decided to start with the B minor waltz (Op. 69, No. 2). I learned each hand by itself and only put them together slowly, after several days, forcing myself to resist the temptation to 'play' the waltz. I didn't want to build wrong notes into my hands, causing neurological patterns that would need correction. When I mentioned this to a physician friend, he said that piano practice was a good way of keeping one's memory sharp, since it involved coordinating neurological responses in two hands doing different things, along with a foot on the pedal. To my surprise, my pug dog Rennie, who was unaccustomed to the sound of a piano in the living room, came and sat at my feet. Once I was almost comfortable with the waltz, which took longer than I'd hoped, I put a CD of Lipatti's recording on a small portable player, slipped on earphones and played along with him. Not well, but keeping up. It took a while to find the gentle rolling movement for my left hand that makes the simple three-beats sound expressive rather than mechanical.

I leaf through old scores, deciding against the Bach inventions I once loved, or long pieces. There isn't enough practice time for sonatas, and I don't want to frustrate myself. I'm tempted by music played before, like a visit to friends one hasn't seen for years, but choose Chopin's posthumous Mazurka Op. 67, No. 4, which I loved on a CD by the young Polish pianist Rafal Blechacz, who won the Chopin Competition in 2005, when, for the first time, the judges decided not to award a second-place prize.

JULY

I'm not alone in my return to the piano. The manufacture of pianos has declined since the early 1960s, when music lessons for children were a common part of growing up, but many people who left the piano behind after their teenage years have come back to it as adults. This makes sense because the piano, though a percussion instrument, is the most complete instrument in itself—it seems to encompass everything that music can be—and has the richest solo repertoire. I continue with Chopin's B minor waltz and the Mazurka I've mentioned, add his beautiful E-flat major Nocturne (Op. 9, No. 2), the first piece of Chopin I played, and so familiar it's almost a cliché, and revisit my favourite sections of Schumann's *Kinderszenen.* Then I leaf through Schubert's Impromptus and my favourite Brahms Intermezzi. More choices than hours.

Away from the piano there are magazines like *International Piano* and *Pianist,* filled with profiles of great musicians past and present, interviews and reviews that lead me to CDs and books seldom discussed elsewhere—a specialized world, with its own rewards. Here the past isn't forgotten. *International Piano* appears six times a year, and after reading an issue I'm already impatient for the next. Where else would I find new profiles of Walter Gieseking, Wilhelm Kempff and Géza Anda, alongside those of young artists like Piotr Anderszewski? Or samples of new editions of piano music, like the second movement of Mozart's sonata No. 14 in C minor, K 457, from the Wiener Urtext Edition? *Pianist* (No. 54) even offered a helpful in-depth 'lesson' on the B minor Chopin waltz that brought me back to the piano.

Along with these magazines, books about the piano are also a part of summer reading and rereading. Old favourites like Charles Rosen's *Piano Notes: The World of the Pianist,* Harold C. Schonberg's classic *The Great Pianists: From Mozart to Present,* Arthur Loesser's *Men, Women & Pianos: A Social History,* even Thad Carhart's charming *The Piano Shop on the Left Bank,* make good companions, along with Mildred Portney Chase's always helpful *Just Being at the Piano* and Russell Sherman's thoughtful meditation, *Piano Pieces.* And I especially like collections of interviews. Elyse Mach's *Great Pianists Speak for Themselves,* a volume of personal essays, offers insights worth keeping in mind before settling down to practise. This month I'm reading David Dubal's *Reflections from the Keyboard: The World of the Concert Pianist.* One point is made over and over: the necessity of long hours of practice. Dinu Lipatti is credited with the remark that if he was away from the keyboard for two days, his hands felt like spaghetti, and Gary Graffman even called his memoir *I Really Should Be Practicing.* The names of a few titans come up again and again—Edwin Fischer, Dinu Lipatti and Alfred Cortot. Viennese pianist Paul Badura-Skoda praises Edwin Fischer for his 'wonderful non-percussive sound', a reminder that the piano's challenge is to achieve a singing tone, a legato the instrument seemingly withholds. I especially like Hungarian pianist Tamás Vásáry's idea that Chopin has to be played with the transparency of Mozart because 'the textures are almost Mozartian'. This is the crux of Chopin, and only a few—like the Portuguese pianist Maria João Pires, in her recording of the nocturnes—achieve it.

The other day I stopped at the music shop in Severance Hall, home of the Cleveland Orchestra, to pick up a recent recording of Mitsuko Uchida with the orchestra, one in a series of Mozart piano concertos that she played and conducted from the keyboard. There's nothing quite like a new CD that seems perfect from the first bar. I attended the performance for this live recording of Mozart's only concerto in a minor key—No. 20 in D minor, K 466—and No. 27 in B-flat major, K 595. Not just a souvenir of a memorable evening, this CD belongs on a shelf beside Géza Anda's Mozart concertos and Clara Haskil's wonderful Piano Sonata in C, K 330. How to get such transparency into my Chopin playing? Maybe I should take out the music for K 330, studied twenty-five years ago.

In the 1990s Philips had a wonderful series called 'Great Pianists of the 20th Century'—each volume included two CDs of remastered recordings. Though the series has been discontinued, a set occasionally crops up in a local music shop. Last week I bought one of Clifford Curzon, the British pianist known for his elegant musicianship, and this morning listened, transfixed, to his performance of Schubert's Impromptu No. 2 in A-flat. Recorded in 1952, when Curzon was at the height of his powers, the Impromptu stopped time. A great interpreter of the Classical school, Curzon was drawn to a quality he called *innerlich*—inwardness—a lyrical directness. It's similar, perhaps, to what the pianist Arthur Schnabel called 'the second simplicity'. Curzon's wonderful legato suited a piece of music marked *sempre legato*, and let me imagine the moment when Schubert put pen to paper. I knew in a flash that the A-flat Impromptu would be a piece to learn this summer. Fortunately I had an old Edition Peters of the Impromptus. The deceptively simple opening lines of the A-flat Impromptu mustn't be hurried, or the yearning in its stately theme can turn into something perfunctory. I listen to Curzon's version over and over until I feel the pianist is at my side, cautioning me: take your time. Simplicity demands patience.

AUGUST

Like film festivals, international piano competitions have proliferated in the last few decades, but the best of them do bring attention to gifted young musicians. This month is the nineteenth biennial Cleveland International Piano Competition, which was founded as the Robert Casadesus International Piano Competition at the Cleveland Institute of Music in 1975, in memory of the French pianist, who often performed with the Cleveland Orchestra (it was renamed in 1994). The competition offers a $50,000 first prize, one of the largest anywhere. In the last twenty years the audience has grown from 1,000 to over 10,000, and the number of applicants from under 50 to more than 250—impressive figures suggesting that the piano world is a healthy one.

I attend several sessions and listen to others on the radio, aware of the courage it takes to perform under such intense conditions. (The last time I joined in a student recital was after the tenth grade, when I played—too ambitiously—Chopin's Polonaise in A-flat, known as 'Heroic'. Somehow I got through it without a wrong note and promised myself 'never again'.) The competition's initial sessions began with twenty-seven pianists. It's moving to watch young performers, many in their early twenties, offer versions of some of the greatest music ever written. Half of them showed more than promise, and this made me wonder what they would achieve in the years ahead. A glance at past competition winners shows that only a few go on to international prominence. In the 1979 competition, for example, the second prize went to Jean-Yves Thibaudet, of France, and third prize to Canada's Angela Hewitt. I'm glad to predict three of the four finalists (that fourth I'd ruled out early on), with a slight preference for this year's winner, Alexander Schimpf, a twenty-nine-year-old from Germany who, unlike many of the other contestants, had *not* studied at either Curtis or Juilliard.

There's another side to playing the piano, and it happens during a late summer thunderstorm, rain beating on the windows. The storm fills me with memories of my teenage years, of similar nights when my mother would ask me to play the show tunes she loved, 'Smoke Gets in Your Eyes' or 'On the Street Where You Live'—music that used to be called 'pop standards' and is now known as 'the American Song Book'. I've kept those worn collections of Irving Berlin and Rodgers and Hart and Jerome Kern, and take out 'Smoke Gets in your Eyes'. Nostalgia music, it suits an end-of-summer mood.

SEPTEMBER

The new concert season begins. Marking it for the *New York Times*, in an article called 'Pride at the Piano', Vivien Schweitzer summed up every concertgoer's dilemma: 'Pianophiles in New York are privileged to hear many first-rate concerts each season by rising stars and established pianists. But only a few of them—including Mitsuko Uchida, Martha Argerich and András Schiff—can be counted on for revelatory and transcendent interpretations.' How, then, to value the concerts that aren't 'revelatory' or 'transcendent', which make up the bulk of concertgoing?

My first concert is with the German pianist Markus Groh. Scheduled at the St. Lawrence Centre, the recital was moved to Walter Hall at the University of Toronto, which meant drier acoustics. Groh is a favourite of the series' general manager, who in 2007 brought him together with the Tokyo String Quartet. A tall, lean, fortyish man, with hair pulled back in a ponytail that appeared to be held together by a rubber band, and dressed in tight black clothes, he affects the style of a bohemian romantic, perhaps to suit the first half of his program: Schumann's 'Papillons' and a selection of Chopin's waltzes and polonaises. After a stolid Schumann, several hurried waltzes and one okay polonaise, I debated about returning after the intermission to hear Brahms's 'Variations and Fugue on a Theme by Handel'. But I'm glad that I did. From the opening bars, this music suited his temperament. If the performance wasn't 'revelatory' it was 'first-rate', and I left the hall wondering what Groh would make of Haydn or Bach. As usual the audience was almost geriatric, though that didn't stop people from immediately jumping to their feet, as if a standing ovation was de rigeur. Schweitzer's remarks remained in my mind. With the start of classes, I miss my own time at the piano. Concerts aren't substitutes.

OCTOBER

This month, several surprises. The fall-term Reading Week allows for a visit to Cleveland, and I anticipated time at the piano with Franz Liszt's Consolation No. 3 in D-flat, my way of marking the bicentennial of his birth. A recent RCA compilation of Arthur Rubinstein's Liszt recordings included Consolation No. 3, and it inspired me. (The elegiac piece was used in the French film *Rue Montagne*, where a disillusioned concert pianist cancels his recital schedule to visit the cancer ward of a local hospital and play for terminal patients.) Liszt is a composer I want to like—perhaps because of my Hungarian forebears—more than I do.

October 6th brought the announcement of this year's Nobel Prize winner in literature: Tomas Tranströmer. The eighty-year-old Swedish poet has been partially paralyzed on his right side for the past twenty years, and he is also largely unable to talk. Yet his condition has not stopped him from creating a rich body of work, nor has it prevented him from playing the piano, but only with his left hand. In the poem 'Allegro' he has this to say (in Robert Bly's translation):

> After a black day, I play Haydn,
> and feel a little warmth in my hands.
>
> The keys are ready. Kind hammers fall.
> The sound is spirited, green, and full of silence.
>
> The sound says that freedom exists
> and someone pays no tax to Caesar.

I'm struck by the 'sound' that is 'full of silence'; the image—following 'spirited' and 'green'—for a moment seems like a contradiction. While the poet's discomfort with speech may shape the idea here, with a piano replacing his own voice, aesthetic decisions are often made in silence while playing or practising, and Tranströmer has the order right in his sound sequence.

Several days later I received a birthday package from Teresa Stratas. It contained an old German Schott score, *Das neue Operetten Buch*, that she had used and knew I would enjoy. I headed straight to the piano, wishing to be a better sight-reader. Playing through some favourite arias—'Einer wird kommen' from Franz Lehár's *Der Zarewitsch*, and the beautiful waltz 'Liebe, du Himmel auf Erden ...' from *Paganini*—I was delighted to hear familiar melodies come from my own piano and not from voices on a CD. I hummed along and felt the music a perfect match to a birthday's reflections. More than any other instrument, the piano can express every mood, every emotion. While it also reinforces one's limitations and inadequacies, like my poor sight-reading, it can, as Tranströmer wrote, give silence sound—a kind of freedom.

NOVEMBER

Ravel has been on my mind. It started with Roger Nichols's new biography called, simply, *Ravel.* Nichols is a great musicologist and his discussion of individual works led me to my favourite Ravel recordings by the French pianist Jean-Philippe Collard. The CDs soon took me back to an old, marked-up score for *Pavane pour une Infante défunte*, loved perhaps because my hands used to fit into it comfortably. Since I haven't played the *Pavane* for more than twenty years, it no longer slips on easily. And I'm self-conscious about practising in my Toronto apartment and disturbing neighbours; I won't learn new music here because every mistake seems louder.

Nichols doesn't bring me much closer to Ravel than Benjamin Ivry did in his fine book *Maurice Ravel, A Life*, so I read a short novel by Jean Echenoz, translated from the French and called *Ravel, A Novel.* Echenoz suggests that Ravel was influenced less by the sounds of nature than by the sounds of machines—for instance, the turbines in the engine room of a transatlantic steamship—and this notion helps explain the surface of Ravel's music, which often evokes the slick Art Deco style. Nichols has reservations about the *Pavane* ('But even if it is not great music, the melody is instantly memorable and far from obvious in its construction'), while Ivry calls the melody 'graceful' and notes that the piece was played at Marcel Proust's funeral in November 1922, possibly at his request. It's an easy composition to like but not that easy to play without turning it into a lugubrious moonlit cliché. Ravel famously objected to pianists who played the work too slowly, and quipped that it was the princess who was defunct, not the pavane. Maybe next summer, with more practise, I'll be happier with my efforts.

A concert by Lise de la Salle suited my reading and rusty efforts. With much advance press about the young French pianist, who is just twenty-four, I wondered if her reputation came from hype. She marched awkwardly onto the stage at the St. Lawrence Centre, head hunched forward with long blondish hair hanging down her back, like a Tenniel illustration for *Alice in Wonderland.* But I enjoyed de la Salle's diffidence, and from the first note of Ravel's *Miroirs* it was clear that she deserves her reputation, with technique and sensibility in ideal combination. What will she do in ten years? In twenty? I'd like to hear.

DECEMBER

With the end of the fall semester, marking essays takes over. There are few concerts other than the usual holiday music, along with Handel's ubiquitous *Messiah.* This time of year I always remember accompanying my fifth-grade class in the elementary school's Christmas concert. I'd practised the carols—'The First Noel', 'O Little Town of Bethlehem'—over and over, and Mrs Krausz had coached me. The afternoon concert took place in the school's gymnasium, with several hundred PTA mothers in attendance, and though I was nervous, once I sat down at the piano, and the choir director Miss Anton gave me a nod to begin, I was home free. Miss Anton—Helen Anton—was the school's art and music teacher, and with luck my homeroom teacher, so she knew of my piano lessons and wanted to encourage me. A classic spinster of the 1950s, wearing dark dresses with matching jackets and sometimes a cluster of artificial cherries pinned to her lapel, she had three white plaster busts on the upright piano in our classroom: Bach, Beethoven and Brahms, naturally. But she wasn't a musical snob, and I learned 'The Surrey with the Fringe on Top' from *Oklahoma!* to accompany class singing sessions. This month I anticipate the winter-term sabbatical that will leave me free to spend more time practising.

JANUARY

To start the new year I want something fresh, so out comes an old Wiener Urtext of Bach's Inventionen und Sinfonien (BWM 772–801), the two- and three-part inventions. I haven't looked at this music for decades, and am overcome with nostalgia because this edition was given to me as a Christmas gift almost forty years ago, by a friend, now deceased, who loved Bach and wanted me to play the inventions for her. Scattered throughout are pencilled notes and fingerings, which I'm glad to find (I can't recall who wrote them, but the handwriting isn't mine). One of my favourites, Sinfonia 5, in E-flat major, has this note: 'Pick up whole hand for each 16th.' Okay. The theme and inverted theme has a slightly improvisational quality, and, as usual, I begin slowly, counting aloud. These pieces were written for Bach's pupils but they're more than exercises. While Sinfonia 5 is only two pages long, it's not going to come back easily. If Dinu Lipatti's hands felt like spaghetti after two days away from the piano, mine are a bowl of cold oatmeal. According to the edition's foreword by Karl Heinz Füssl, the ornamentation in these works is sparing because Bach did not aim to teach his students 'mechanical manual dexterity'. More helpful is Bach's own foreword, from 1727, where he states his goal: 'most of all to achieve a cantabile manner of playing'.

This singing sound came to mind when I read in the morning paper that Alexis Weissenberg had died, at the age of eighty-two. A Bulgarian Jew who, as a child of twelve, managed to escape from Europe and the Holocaust with his mother, Weissenberg must have had much in common with Susan Krausz. After the war he ended up in New York, where he studied at Juilliard. A master of fiery technique, Weissenberg's Bach is fast and loud, and often overwhelming, but its thunder pulls one along, though it's hardly cantabile. I prefer his CD of Rachmaninoff's preludes, where music and musician are a more harmonious match. I've never heard Weissenberg play Liszt but they seem made for each other. In the current issue of *Piano* there's a fascinating interview with András Schiff where he explains that he doesn't like Liszt because of 'the direction that music took from Liszt, Wagner, Schoenberg and the others.' Preferring a Bachian line with counterpoint and polyphony, Schiff regards his dislike of Liszt as a matter of temperament, and admits, 'I must be the only Hungarian-born pianist who has trouble with his music!' I'm relieved to read Schiff's remarks.

FEBRUARY

More Bach—that's the sound I want to hear—along with last summer's Schubert Impromptu. It would be helpful to have a sympathetic piano teacher again, someone to consult for suggestions and corrections. I pick up another edition of Bach's Inventions, one of the Alfred Masterworks, edited by Willard A. Palmer, because it has detailed notes, unlike the Wiener Urtext. Palmer has studied the various autographs and other editions, and makes useful notes about Baroque ornaments (which were added by followers of Bach). While no edition can replace a good teacher, it's what I have for now.

A new book about the piano is rare, and I eagerly read Stuart Isacoff's *A Natural History of the Piano: The Instrument, the Music, the Musicians—from Mozart to Modern Jazz, and Everything in Between.* But Isacoff is often just frustrating. He divides pianists and composers into four arbitrary categories: alchemists (Debussy), melodists (Chopin, Schubert), combustibles (Beethoven, Liszt) and rhythmitizers (George Gershwin). Yet Beethoven wrote wonderful melodies (in the *Moonlight* Sonata, for one), and Debussy had a gift for rhythm (listen to 'Rain in a Garden'). Still, I enjoyed Isacoff's characterizations of some individual pianists (he calls Glenn Gould 'a master of personal theatrics'). But for my taste there's far too much about jazz, yet no mention of Keith Jarrett's rhapsodic 'Köln Concert' or Brad Mehldau, and not a word about cabaret pianists like Eddy or Peter Duchin. Isacoff favours the word *experimental* but every serious composer is experimental when you consider the previous generation.

MARCH

A frustrating month, it seems unable to decide what to wear, spring or winter. And my hands are frustrating too. I'm still working on several of Bach's three-part inventions but often my hands won't do what I want them to. My left wrist is sore from a strain last week, and after practising a short while I need to rest it. This reminds me that we play with our bodies, not just our hands. As compensation (sort of), I've listened half a dozen times to a CD by András Schiff—his recording of Bach's Inventions—from the Great Pianists series. The shaping of Schiff's performance has an appealing urgency, even lushness, but the base notes are occasionally muffled, not muddy yet not clear, like Glenn Gould's. The strength in Gould's left hand was amazing, and when he chose to, he could use that strength for nuances that other pianists seldom suggest.

APRIL

As brochures for the upcoming fall concert season arrive in the mail, I have to admit that this chronicle is coming to an end. The final concert of the season was the high point: Mitsuko Uchida playing two Mozart piano concertos: No. 9, K 271, written when Mozart was twenty-one, and the popular 21st, K 467, known for the beautiful andante movement that was used as the soundtrack for the Swedish film *Elvira Madigan* (1967), with Géza Anda's unsurpassed recording of it.

Uchida helped make a decision for me. Over thirty years ago I learned Mozart's sonata in F major, KV 332, and finally I looked for my Henle score. It's comforting to see old pencil markings for pedalling, fingering, and even corrections to spots which must have caused me trouble. I've decided to jump into the Adagio, which I loved. This past year I've left Mozart alone because the music can appear deceptively simple and I wasn't ready to face its demands. Several days before her Cleveland concert, Uchida spoke about Mozart to the local press: 'This music has so much in it. There are so many unbelievably deep, hidden things to be unearthed. I'm still scratching the surface.' Remarks like those almost make me want to close the lid on the keys. Somewhere I have a CD of her playing the F major Sonata but I won't look for it yet. It's odd but I'm less intimidated by a tremendous CD from a pianist I haven't seen in person—Lipatti, say, or Curzon—because I can't picture them at the keyboard, while Uchida's image remains in my mind.

After this year, I'm left with several questions: Will I find another piano teacher? Do I have the energy to embark on the hard work of lessons, and find time for practice? Can I accommodate my aging hands to the effort a piano demands? Of course there will be exciting concerts and new CDs and unexpected books ahead. I've learned to lower my standards for my own playing, or else I wouldn't be able to face any piano, which both saddens me and gives me hope. There's little perfection in life, and perfection can't last anyway, except on a few CD reissues of great recordings. I can set two 'perfect' performances side by side—say the Chopin nocturnes from João Pires and Rubenstein—and I'm unable to make a choice. Music practice teaches that there's always room for something more, something else, another perspective or inspired touch. My own small efforts, at least, are part of the admirable desire to make this big clumsy instrument called the piano sing. I'll have to live with that.

'Entering the Silence': Voice, Ethnicity and the Pedagogy of Creative Writing

The paradoxical nature of silence and its relation to ethnicity is starkly portrayed in a disturbing scene late in Maxine Hong Kingston's memoir *The Woman Warrior* (1975), a mixed-genre work that blends myth, folklore, family history, ghost story, *Bildungsroman* and immigrant saga into a postmodern portrait of the artist as a young woman. Taking up five percent of the book's length, the scene presents two Chinese-American girls in the basement washroom of their elementary school. The narrator, Maxine, is the twelve-year-old, partly Americanized daughter of Chinese immigrants living in Oakland, California, in the 1950s. The second girl, also the daughter of Chinese immigrants, is a year older, but smaller and more fragile. She reads aloud in class, yet seldom speaks. Maxine taunts and brutalizes the girl, pinching her cheeks, pulling her hair, and demanding repeatedly that she speak. 'Talk,' she commands. 'You have a tongue', 'Why don't you scream "Help"?', 'I'll let you go if you say just one word', and 'You'd better say something.' But the second child refuses to utter a sound. And Maxine soon pleads, 'Why won't you talk?', 'I'm doing this for your own good.... Please talk.' She stops only when her own sister enters the washroom. The reader is, inevitably, left to ask why Maxine tries to bully her classmate out of silence, and why the girl keeps silent.

This is a paradigmatic scene in literature of the immigrant experience because it deals with the relation of language to identity and voice. Beyond the particularities of Hong Kingston's cultural and historical situation, common issues are at stake. The scene will be discussed later, but first it's important to look at its cultural and literary contexts, in order to appreciate the pattern of transformation that silence signals.

The title of this essay, 'Entering the Silence', comes from the title of the second volume of journals by the American poet and Trappist monk Thomas Merton. However, the word *silence* is not used here exactly as Merton uses it, nor am I concerned with the theological import of silence for monastic life. But a cue is taken from this volume's subtitle, *Becoming a Monk & Writer*, because Merton links the growth of his religious and writerly vocations to silence. The verb *entering* not only suggests motion but marks the noun *silence* as a place or site. Merton, of course, is not alone in recognizing the importance of silence to writing. In 1934, when the Russian writer Isaac Babel spoke at the first Congress of the Soviet Writers' Union, he claimed, cryptically, that he was becoming a 'master of the genre of silence'. Exactly what he meant by the phrase has teased generations of critics, although it may represent a response to Stalin's accelerating purges. In any case, Babel's 'genre of silence' has echoes in the words of the American poet Muriel Rukeyser, who wrote in 'The Speed of Darkness': 'I am working out the vocabulary of my silence.' Rukeyser, who acknowledged her lesbianism only late in a long, distinguished career, perhaps had her sexual identity in mind in this poem. Certainly the idea of silence has been a crucial part of feminist literary criticism by creative writers, such as Tillie Olsen's classic *Silences* (1965) and Adrienne Rich's *On Lies, Secrets and Silence* (1960). And silence continues to be emphasized in writing about women writers, for example, in Kennedy Fraser's book *Ornament and Silence: Essays on Women's Lives.*

Recently, however, a number of women writers with immigrant backgrounds have applied the idea of silence not only to gender issues but also to concerns about race and ethnicity. The fiction writers Makeda Silvera and the poet Marlene Nourbese Philip, who share a Caribbean background and live and write in Canada, have made this connection in, respectively, *Silenced* and *She Tries Her Tongue, Her Silence Softly Breaks.* Yet the idea is not unique to them. Canadian-American novelist and poet Robert Kroetsch, in his essay 'The Grammar of Silence' (1984), linked silence to what he called 'the characteristic narrative of the ethnic experience', a narrative preoccupied with language. Of interest here is the way Merton, Babel, Rukeyser and Kroetsch have isolated silence as a crucial aspect of writing, even seeing it as a place, genre, vocabulary or grammar of its own.

Writers live poised between the power of silence and the power of language. Silence is essential not only to the writing process itself but to the process of building an identity as a writer. In a quite literal sense, claiming and transforming silence is a crucial aspect of finding a voice. While many writers have a resistance to silence, they also need it, which may explain the fear that some have of talking about current projects: they do not want to talk out their work rather than write it. The claiming of silence, then, is part of a transformative act that over time yields the writer's identity as well as the writer's work.

There are, of course, many kinds of silence. In its more positive associations, silence is linked to ecstasy, communion, rest, sympathy, identification, reflection, meditation—in both Eastern and Western religions—as well as secrets. The more negative associations include denial, concealment, evasion, punishment, rejection, depression, burden, threat, doubt, conspiracy and, again, secrets. In most of these senses, silence assumes the idea of some kind of community, or its absence. Inevitably, it is the companion of isolation, seclusion and obscurity. It may be imposed, as when someone or something defines another's identity and speaks for or about it. The idea that silence is the ground of language, that all speech comes from silence and returns to it, has a long history in Western culture. Augustine, in his *Confessions*, ca. 397–400, links silence and speech to time, arguing that language is an experience of temporal process.

Most people can think of favourite moments of silence in music, drama and film—even of works devoted to representing silence, such as Ingmar Bergman's film *Persona* (1966), in which a popular actress is hospitalized after she refuses to speak. When silence appears in literary texts it may be dramatized by characters who are either aware or unaware of its significance, it may be discussed as subject by characters or by a narrator and, finally, it may appear in metaphor, as seen in Babel and Rukeyser. The metaphorical use of silence may overlap with both of the first categories. In poetry, silence may be suggested by spatial arrangements and line and stanza breaks, while in prose it may be contained in section breaks and breaks between scenes and chapters. Such silences give meaning to the events of a text, just as silence takes meaning from the nature of these events, and from its context in a text. In her essay 'Line-breaks, Stanza-spaces, and the Inner Voice', American poet Denise Levertov wrote about line breaks and 'where the silence is', emphasizing how silence can be used to structure a poem. This concern is not only a technical matter of interest mainly to poets. Silence here is related to nuances of meaning and shifts in a writer's focus. Words—and meaning—depend on silence. (In Western music, when silence occurs, it is heard in the context of musical tonality, or key. A musical silence, however, usually does not signal a change in key.)

The transformative relation of silence to language and identity has a long history in North American literature. From the earliest twentieth-century fiction in English written about the immigrant experience by observers from the dominant English-speaking culture, child protagonists and narrators have been used to dramatize issues surrounding language that face all immigrants. In Willa Cather's *My Antonia* (1918), for instance, young Antonia's father asks Jim Burden, the novel's narrator, to teach his daughter English, and Antonia rewards Jim with a gift of a silver ring. Such child figures come to dominate representations of the immigrant experience, especially in books by writers who were part of that experience themselves, like Henry Roth's *Call It Sleep* (1934) and Anzia Yezierska's *Bread Givers* (1925); the examples seem endless. This association of language and child figures and/or narrators also occurs in the first important novels in the Canadian immigrant tradition in English by Adele Wiseman, John Marlyn and Mordecai Richer, novelists who took their immigrant and ethnic backgrounds as subject matter in the 1950s, a generation after their earlier American counterparts had. Three questions come to mind: Why are there so many child figures and narrators in the literature of the immigrant experience? Why are they so commonly associated with language? And why do so many of these child narrators become writers?

All of the writers already mentioned may be open to the charge that as writers they are naturally, even inevitably, interested in language and, consequently, have given it a privileged place in their books. But something more complex is happening. With their sensitivity to the demands and rewards of language, these writers are directing attention to cultural anxieties that most native speakers of English cannot understand since they tend to see language as a common activity, almost like breathing. It is worth remembering that language is made up of more than its words and grammatical system. A language brings its own culture and social history with it, and contains narratives—stories—which can help establish identity and, for a writer, voice.

North American writers who chose immigrants as their subject live and write in the larger context of Western literature. The figure of the immigrant child is a variation of the child figure in Western writing after the Romantic era and the Industrial Revolution, when the child began to replace the shepherd or shepherdess in nineteenth-century versions of the pastoral. Such child figures, whose lives embody a movement from innocence to experience, are well suited to reveal the contradictions that immigrants face in making lives in a new country. Learning a new language, and giving up the comforts of what is often thought of as the mother tongue, the language that nourishes, is the first step out of the silence that can torment immigrants. Perhaps language is so crucial to books about the immigrant experience because their authors found their own battles with language to be the crucial act of self-discovery.

Once immigrant children have finally mastered the new language, they may rarely hear or speak their native tongue. What happens then? Children seem to be natural language learners, yet immigrant children still feel conflict between their mother tongues and the language of their new lives, which silences the mother tongue and gives them a double consciousness about language. Will the immigrant child live in a world of self-imposed silences about the world of the old country, which is seldom known, or will the conflicts around language be resolved into new selves? John Marlyn dramatizes this subject in *Under the Ribs of Death* (1957), set in Winnipeg's North End during the 1920s. His novel tells the story of Sandor Hunyadi, a Hungarian immigrant who settles in Winnipeg with his parents, as Marlyn did himself. In the first chapter, Marlyn sketches the plight of a sensitive immigrant child who already knows that words have power. For example, Sandor is ashamed of the Hungarian boarders in his family's house: 'They were all foreigners, every one of them, and as though that were not bad enough they were actually proud of their foreign, outlandish ways. Not one of them had yet made a serious effort to learn English.' Sandor himself has no interest in anything but being accepted as a Canadian. Although he isn't sure what that entails, he knows that it means rejecting any ethnicity other than the culture associated with the British Isles. He is being educated in an English-language school that espouses the narrative of the English-speaking peoples, and there is no place for his ethnicity. Even his parents rarely speak their native language, which he has forgotten, except on rare occasions 'or when they had something to keep from him'. For Sandor, speaking a foreign language is a shameful thing. Since he lacks his mother tongue, he also lacks its stories—its narrative. Only English validates his experiences.

Of course Sandor also longs to change his name, a transformation that will finally, he hopes, make him belong. Describing an after-school fight to his father, he cries that everywhere he goes people laugh at his name, including the neighbourhood librarian and the school nurse. He says, 'If we changed our name I wouldn't hafta fight no more, Pa. We'd be like other people, like everybody else.' Sandor learns to feel ashamed of his background in schools and libraries, places of books and learning, and eventually he does change his name to Alex Hunter. 'Hunter' is not a translation of the Hungarian name 'Hunyadi' (*vadasz* is the Hungarian word for 'hunter'), but it shares its first syllable with 'Hunyadi', 'Hungarian' and 'Hun'. Symbolically, the new name conveys Sandor/Alex's situation: he is always on the prowl. It is a false transformation that keeps him locked in shameful silence. While Marlyn transformed the silences of his own background in his writing, he offered no such hope for his novel's protagonist. Sandor/Alex remains an example of the immigrant child who matures into an unsettled adult, nearly defeated by his conflicts with the values of a powerful majority culture.

In order to envision a way out of this isolating predicament for themselves and their characters, many writers with immigrant backgrounds have sought representations of themselves in the literature of their new homeland. American novelist Mary Gordon, in her essay 'Getting Here from There: A Writer's Reflections on a Religious Past', discusses the effect her family's Irish roots had on the development of her sense of herself as a writer, the 'artistic ego', as she calls it. For Gordon, Irish-Catholic Americans are part of a tradition 'committed to the idea of keeping silence', and this made it difficult for them to embrace language and storytelling. She laments the lack of 'Irishness' in American letters, in spite of such figures as Eugene O'Neill, Mary McCarthy and William Kennedy. The situation that Gordon delineates is not unlike the one Gay Talese describes in his essay 'Where Are the Italian-American Novelists?' As a young man in the 1950s, unable to find novels by Italian Americans, Talese felt drawn to Jewish and Irish-American writers, especially John O'Hara, 'in whose outsider's voice I heard echoes of my own'. Both Gordon and Talese were looking not only for reflections of themselves but for books that would serve as literary models. Each seemed to understand intuitively that silence cannot be transformed until a writer enters it.

Gordon and Talese are not unique in their observations about the contributions their ethnic groups have (and have not) made to the literature of North America. Many contemporary writers would argue that the situation has not changed radically, in spite of a publishing industry that seems occasionally drawn to exoticizing those ethnic writers it deems marketable. One example of this situation, in Canada, will illustrate the point. In an interview in 1990, the Canadian novelist Frank Paci, of Italian descent, emphasized that writers with ethnic backgrounds do not want to be marginalized as ethnic writers by readers 'who aren't ready to concede their mainstream ethnic biases—i.e. British—to "marginal" ethnic cultures'. Although Canada has several important writers of Italian background, including Mary di Michele, Nino Ricci and Pier Giorgio Di Cicco, they are too often lumped into the category of multicultural writers. Paci would have none of this. He went on to say that 'the language problems of Italian-Canadian writing are not the creation of writers but the real condition of miscommunication and silence among immigrants. The revolutionary aspect of writing here is that the author is giving these people a voice for the first time, and creating a language for them, and with them.' This is not an easy task. While growing up, Paci admits, 'What I remember most distinctly, however, was this tremendous pressure to transform myself by repudiating my Italian background. It didn't occur to me that the two cultures and languages could co-exist within one.' Note that he says 'within one' and not 'within me': the problem he faced was oddly impersonal. Paci had to learn that he could give a voice to silence and, in the process, avoid the false transformation of assimilation, instead transforming himself into a writer.

Conflicts between silence and ethnic identity may be part of the experience of most immigrants, but they may also be rooted in specific historical moments. Over time, the memory of even a traumatic event can be lost to silence. This process dominates Joy Kogawa's novel *Obasan* (1976), the story of a Canadian daughter of Japanese immigrants who reconstructs her childhood and her family's experience of internment during World War II. Like Paci, Kogawa's narrator, Naomi, feels the pressure to repudiate her family's suffering through several kinds of silence: of denial, and also of apparent acceptance. Naomi wants words for their story, but meaningful words. She sees the silence of her grandmother Obasan as a majestic but inadequate alternative to the almost compulsive talk of her aunt Emily. Namoi recognizes that any speech that transforms silence must understand the inherent pain in the act.

In the surreal psychic landscape that opens her novel, Kogawa presents the conflict between 'a silence that cannot speak' and 'a silence that will not speak' with language reminiscent of the beginning of many creation myths. 'Beneath the grass the speaking dreams and beneath the dreams is a sensate sea,' the narrator observes, longing to escape from silence: 'If I could follow the stream down and down to the hidden voice, would I come at least to the freeing word? I ask the night sky but the silence is steadfast. There is no reply.' By the end of the novel, which echoes this poetic language, Naomi finds her 'freeing word' in a vision of grief as a wailing scarecrow that shows her 'the song of mourning is not a lifelong song'. Yet the silence that has become a mourning song is only part of Naomi's knowledge, and in her imagination, silence can now honour private memories and be a genuine kind of acceptance because it is part of a larger narrative.

Kogawa, however, does not leave the last words of her novel to Naomi. The family's story, after all, is part of history, and Kogawa closes the book with an excerpt from an actual document, a letter sent in April 1946 from the Committee on Japanese-Canadians to the House and Senate of Canada. The excerpt condemns the policy of deportation and internment, describing it as 'an adoption of methods of Naziism'. This shift from a specific family's story to the general policy behind it suggests that writing is a collective act, an act that builds on the efforts of other writers. Kogawa can allow the words of other writers, quoted in the letter, to speak for her and to end her book because she has found her own 'hidden voice' in the act of writing *Obasan*, thus giving the book a kind of double ending. The individual writer here merges with her ethnic group and yet remains apart from it too.

With these thoughts about the power of silence, I'll return to the torture scene from *The Woman Warrior*, the relation of the two girls and how Hong Kingston reconciles some of the issues she has raised. Without understanding what she is doing, Maxine, the tormentor, tries to enter the silence of her victim because it reminds her of her own. As she hectors her classmate, she even begins to sound like her own mother, insisting that what she wants is only for the best. She becomes a parody of the stereotype of the intrusive immigrant mother. The child Maxine's conflict is one of finding a voice: What can she legitimately say? The claims of Chinese and American cultures have made her life a contest, and like the girl she torments, Maxine cannot say who she is, or choose either culture. She seeks a way out of the confusion of her silence by trying to make someone else—a kind of double, or shadow—resolve the dilemma for her. In this scene Maxine begins to value language as a way out of her isolation; language, in time, will transform it. Like Frank Paci, Maxine suffers the double perspective of two languages: the values of her family's culture that make her reject Americanness, and her own sense of self-hatred, which makes her see her Chineseness, her ethnicity, as something monstrous, something to expunge. And, like Paci, she needs to learn that both languages can coexist in her as she tries to find a language of her own—a voice.

After Maxine abandons the tormented other, she collapses physically. 'The world is sometimes just,' she reflects, 'and I spend the next eighteen months sick in bed with a mysterious illness.' Yet there is redemption for her after she abandons her double and her misguided attempt to make it speak. Only then can Maxine properly enter her own silence in a slow act of transformation. Rather than persisting as oppressor, and defining another, she sees that monster figures can be reflections of our own fears of ourselves. She is ready now to seek out her own voice, acknowledging the stories within her that need a place in the world. Hong Kingston's own solution to the conflicts of a dual ethnic perspective and cultural allegiance is to become a writer. Her choice is language as a way out of silence. Finding a voice moves her toward consciousness, and involves moral choices. It is a movement toward valuing her own experience that ends the confusion of silence with self-discovery.

The relation of silence and language to a writer's cultural identity is important for young writers from different ethnic groups. For example, the long tradition of African-American writing in English may affect the ways in which young African-American writers see themselves, their heritage, and their possibilities; the tradition of black gospel music further enriches the subject. Certainly issues around language and identity have been important to Zora Neale Hurston, Richard Wright and James Baldwin. As well, similar concerns have occupied Latina/o American writers such as Sandra Cisneros and Richard Rodriguez, whose Spanish, as Rodriguez noted in *Days of Obligation*, was a powerful kind of secret code language, usually unknown outside the home.

What can teachers of creative writing learn from the writers quoted here and the situations they describe? In light of the growth and profusion of creative writing courses and programs in North American universities over the last three decades, the question takes on added significance. Most people would assume that it is possible to teach the basic skills of writing, but 'creative' writing? At the very least it is possible to teach students some of the strategies used by both literary and commercial writers—even to look at their writing as models—as well as to encourage students whose work shows potential. But teachers of creative writing need to do much more than this. Their task is to help students connect to silence as a place for thought and for the tensions that can produce art.

From my experience, many students who enrol in creative writing courses have a limited sense of subject matter. They do not have a voice yet and do not know what they want to say, so they are liable to write in clichés. Frequently they can't explain why they think they're writers, or, more to the point, why they want to be. From the television shows and movies they watch to the books they read and the music they listen to, North America's popular culture industry shapes the way many of them see their world. Often they are drawn to stories about unhappy relationships, drugs, vampires and rock musicians—some of the preferred subjects of popular culture. The young writers today are most likely to have read and loved V.C. Andrews's series, including *Flowers in the Attic* (1979), the novels of R.L. Stine, horror fiction by Clive Barker, Stephen King and Anne Rice, the *Twilight* series and the Harry Potter books. It is, then, necessary to begin here and urge writing students to recognize the power these books have had over their imaginations. In her essay 'The Untaught Teacher', Denise Levertov wrote about teaching poetry workshops in the late 1960s at C.C.N.Y, and lamented the fact that her students had no common knowledge: 'But it seemed as if each individual had a specialty and none had a common frame of reference, so that each allusion I made—and such a course as I was attempting, with its personal core and its wide range of citations, must of necessity depend largely on comprehensible, suggestive allusion—was picked up by only one or two students.' As the saying goes, *plus ça change.*

In order to teach creative writing it's important to ask an almost unanswerable question: What shapes a writer? Most professional writers will admit that extensive reading has helped teach them how to write; naturally they have favourite books, many remembered from childhood or teenage years. Whether these books were important at the time they were read, or matter mostly as memory, is difficult to assess. Just as Mary Gordon and Gay Talese once sought representations of their ethnicities to help them develop as writers, so do all young writers, whether consciously or not, need books that will engage them in the process that can produce a distinctive voice. In this sense, young writers are all ethnic writers, without language and stories. But young writers from ethnic backgrounds have a special dilemma. They are doubly silenced by the majority culture and its manufactured popular culture, and yet they have an often pressing subject matter in their backgrounds that, once recognized as potential subject, can give them an immediate advantage in an alternative set of narratives.

In addition to directing writing students to significant books, another way of helping them expand their sense of subject matter is to ask them to write about something from their own childhoods. The autobiographical impulse, after all, has been crucial to twentieth-century fiction. In fact it is almost impossible to think of modern writing without D.H. Lawrence's *Sons and Lovers* (1913), Virginia Woolf's *The Voyage Out* (1915), James Joyce's *A Portrait of the Artist as a Young Man* (1916), and Ernest Hemingway's collection of Nick Adams stories *In Our Time* (1925). Childhood has been such a potent subject because it can contain something for everyone. But childhoods differ. Issues relating to ethnicity are particularly relevant to many large urban universities, where student populations may include many first- and second-generation immigrants, some with strong connections to their ethnic communities. As well, the recent emphasis on multicultural values in many secondary schools has encouraged students from a wide range of backgrounds to look to the traditions of their countries of origin for entertainment, solace and wisdom. These students often know prejudice first-hand, and speak of it willingly, if asked. Why not, then, take it too as a subject?

In 1996 the literary magazine *Granta* devoted an issue to 'The Best of Young American Novelists'. Of the twenty writers included, only five—Sherman Alexie, Edwidge Danticat, Jeffrey Eugenides, David Haynes and Fae Myenne Ng—show an interest in ethnicity and come from backgrounds that aren't immediately associated with the majority culture. When British novelist David Lodge reviewed this issue, he lamented the 'sameness' in the work and speculated that 'it is certainly tempting to look for an explanation of the influence of creative writing programmes in colleges and universities.' He's correct in noting that two-thirds of the writers selected were graduates of master's or doctoral programs in creative writing or teachers of the subject. With their emphasis on technique and style, too many creative writing programs may encourage students to perfect their poems and stories, their lines and sentences, before these students find the subjects that most fully engage their imaginations. This could account for the bland smoothness that does characterize much low-risk contemporary writing.

Among the exercises that can be assigned in writing workshops are narrative retellings of incidents remembered from childhood. Inevitably these will have a beginning, middle and end, or some sense of closure (even if unresolved), and some kind of conflict. Once this conflict is identified, various narrative strategies can be explored. Young writers who experiment with childhood as a subject usually find that they want to write about generational conflict. The child narrators they develop often see from a double perspective, assessing their own world as well as the apparent contradictions and hypocrisies of the ever-present world of adults. This double perspective is characteristic of child narrators and makes them a useful tool for young writers: characters with two perspectives are usually not one-dimensional. Writing students from immigrant backgrounds often find that a child figure or narrator can reveal the tensions and contradictions that most immigrants feel, at the same time inscribing their own ethnic backgrounds in a new literature of North America.

To suggest that students explore the autobiographical impulse is not to advocate treating fiction as artfully disguised autobiography, nor is it to urge them to write in search of an identity, or confine themselves to an ethnic literary ghetto. But fiction has to begin somewhere, in order for a writer to create a world. This is what Salman Rushdie had in mind when he discussed the origins of his novel *Midnight's Children* (1981): 'When I began the book it was more autobiographical and it only started to work when I started to make it more fictional. The characters came alive when they stopped being like people in my own family.... One of the discoveries of the book was the importance of escaping from autobiography.' This escape starts by admitting the claim that the autobiographical impulse makes on the imagination. Ironically the value of the autobiographical mode for young writers is that it can take them into the communities of their lives and away from the solipsism of the self, and the notion that all art is merely personal expression and, as such, equally good—a notion that naturally appeals to them.

James Joyce expressed this matter succinctly in Stephen Dedalus's discussion of narration in the final pages of *A Portrait of the Artist as a Young Man*. He observes: 'The narrative is no longer purely personal. The personality of the artist passes into the narrative itself, flowing round and round the persons and the action like a vital sea.' Once Stephen understands this relation, he can move toward artistic life without fearing isolation: 'I will try to express myself in some mode of life or art as freely as I can and as wholly as I can, using for my defense the only arms I allow myself to use—silence, exile, and cunning.' Of course Stephen's trinity of arms is not the only model—different writers will have their own—but what matters here is Joyce's recognition that silence can be the first line of defense for a young artist. It is worth remembering that Stephen admits he was raised to be a monk; in many ways we aren't far from Thomas Merton's link between silence and the monastic and writerly lives.

Whether as arms, grammar, vocabulary, genre or space, silence allows writers to transform their own battles with language in crucial acts of self-discovery that shape their voices. Representations of silence signal this process, which ends in language when, as Muriel Rukeyser wrote, 'silence is become speech'. It may be a truism that writers are particularly aware of the power of language. In acknowledging its importance, writers are, in a sense, claiming themselves as their subjects, and at the same time, paradoxically, in Rushdie's terms, 'escaping from autobiography'. Like Hong Kingston's narrator, they learn to admonish themselves—rather than the people around them—to speak.

A Matter of Descent: David Plante's Fiction

What makes a writer Canadian? In an era that places a considerable value on multicultural fiction, the question can be approached in many ways. If David Plante's paternal grandparents hadn't decided to emigrate from St. Bartholomew, Quebec (near Trois Rivières), to the United States, he might today be one of Quebec's leading novelists. This notion isn't as fanciful as it may seem, for Plante has written passionately—and frequently—about his French-Canadian background, in hypnotic short novels that recall the work of Marie-Claire Blais. I can't help but want to introduce the two of them, and then sit back and listen. 'Yes, let's do it,' Plante said with enthusiasm, in a telephone interview from his home in London more than twenty years ago. 'I liked *Une saison dans la vie d'Emmanuel* very much.'

Born in Providence, Rhode Island, in 1940, the sixth of seven brothers, Plante went to French-Catholic parish schools before studying at the Jesuits' Boston College. Like the narrator of his novel *The Accident* (1991), he spent an academic year abroad at the University of Louvain in Belgium. After graduating with a B.A. in French—English is his first language—he taught school in Italy and then in the U.S., until 1966, when he moved to London, England, where he still lives. Plante returns frequently to North America, and has been writer-in-residence at the University of Tulsa in Oklahoma, King's College, the University of Cambridge, the University of East Anglia, as well as at the Université de Québec, in Montreal, working with French-language writers, and a professor of creative writing at Columbia University; he was also the first writer from the West to teach at the Gorky Institute in Moscow. The author of sixteen novels and four non-fiction books, he has received a Guggenheim Fellowship and awards from the American Academy and Institute of Arts and Letters and the Arts Council of Great Britain.

During that long-ago conversation, Plante discussed his thoughts about writing, and also—with great good humour—answered my questions about his atheism. His fiction never shies away from ideas, yet Plante explained that he doesn't set out to write books about ideas. 'A vision,' he said, 'is more a sense than a clear idea that can be articulated—the vision comes very, very early on in life and every novel is an attempt to find the images that express the vision.' Plante had been asking himself, 'What is the central image of my culture?' Living abroad naturally made him contemplate his national background in ways that might not have occurred to him if he'd stayed at home. The image he conjured is powerful: 'I remember very early in my childhood the image of Mass being said in the woods, of the priest holding the host, and the Indians peering out from behind the trees, watching. The colonials, the forest, and the Indians—it's all there.' Asked if he feared appropriating the culture of the native people, Plante reminded me that he is part Blackfoot—one eighth, through his paternal grandmother. 'To the extent that my Indian culture means something to me, I feel I have as much right to say I'm an Indian as anyone else.'

He once said his obsessions and preoccupations were American, but Plante's early experimental fiction reveals a number of influences—especially the French *nouveau roman* of the 1950s, along with Henry James and Gertrude Stein. Five novels later, he developed the distinctive voice of his Francoeur-family trilogy: *The Family* (1978), *The Country* (1981) and *The Woods* (1982). These spare and brooding books are admittedly autobiographical. (Because of a change in publishers, they appeared out of the order in which they were written—*The Woods*, Plante cautioned, is 'an interlude', and should be read as a bridge book.) The name 'Francoeur' contains the French word *coeur*, or heart, and its combination with *Fran* gives a symbolic dimension to the 'French heart' family's saga. Not heavily plotted, the novels rely on an accumulation of incidents, almost like a musical theme and variations. Plante has reinvented the *nouveau roman* for his own purposes, at the same time echoing the French tradition of the *conte*, an intense short novel generally about troubling love.

Although *The Family* is narrated from the point of view of twelve-year-old Daniel, it dissects the hermetic world of a working-class French-Catholic family in Providence, who love each other with an inarticulate care that supports and drains at the same time. Reena, the mother, suffers an emotional breakdown while Jim, the father, is in conflict with his toolshop's union, eventually losing his job. This devout couple are not easy on each other or on themselves. Yet when *The Family* concludes with Daniel's prayer for his troubled home—a prayer for grace and understanding—forgiving love seems almost possible. Patriarchal and superstitious, the Francoeurs recall several of James Joyce's characters; novelist Mary Gordon—the other great contemporary American-Catholic novelist, and a friend of Plante's—has written that 'the ghost of Stephen Dedalus, that professional writer-son' haunts Plante's trilogy. But his intensity and gravity make Plante very much his own writer.

The Woods finds Daniel in his first year of university. Fearing the draft and eager to explore his sexuality, he has a brief affair with an older woman. The oppressive world of his childhood has been broadened, but Daniel remains confused by his body and curiously asexual in his attempts to understand his sexuality. This is not untypical of the young characters in Plante's novels, for their struggles with the body are monumental efforts to understand themselves and the nature of their heritage. In *The Country* Daniel, now a writer living in London, makes several visits home to his ailing parents, ultimately attending his father's funeral. As he watches the elderly Francoeurs flounder in senility, he wants desperately to make sense of his inheritance. It's no surprise that his first questions are about language. He asks why the family no longer speaks French, what old French expressions they remember, what language his grandmother learned from her Blackfoot mother. Daniel's questions are urgent, for his parents have taken on the stature of powerful ruins. As he cuts his father's thick toenails, or helps his mother bathe, careful of her modesty, he wants them to express their understanding of themselves in an articulate way—surely they can still teach him something. Being who they are, of course they can't find the right words. But when the exhausted Jim Francoeur says goodbye to his son, suddenly asking if it's difficult to write a book and adding, 'Be a good boy', the moment is one of the most poignant exchanges between a father and son in contemporary fiction. That Daniel's quest for language should also lead to God is almost inevitable in Plante's world. As Daniel thinks of his father, with his 'old parochial French', he prays to 'my Canuck God. *Seigneur, Seigneur, ayez pitié pour nous.* It was religion, not of recourse, but stark truth: death is what we live for, and as terrible as it is, to die is better than to live.'

Perhaps Plante needed a break from the almost claustrophobic Francoeurs, for his next book, *Difficult Women* (1983), is a non-fiction account of his friendships with Jean Rhys, Sonia Orwell and Germaine Greer.

Plante had been helping Rhys with her memoirs, *Smile Please*, when he decided to write about their encounters. Lively, frank and witty, this extended piece of gossip transcends itself as Plante examines the affection and esteem he feels for these women, and the way they returned his regard. Especially strong is the profile of feminist writer Germaine Greer, a fellow teacher at the University of Tulsa in the late '70s. When she and Plante drive at breakneck speed through the wintry hills of New Mexico, swigging champagne on their way to Santa Fe while watching for police cars, the reader is glad to be along for the ride. *Difficult Women* probes Plante's attachment to women who give and withhold simultaneously; the patterns described there aren't far from the way Reena Francoeur treats her son.

Plante returned to the Francoeur family with *The Foreigner* (1984). Although its hero is unnamed, anyone familiar with his previous novels will immediately spot Daniel. Plante once acknowledged the influence of Henry James, even paying tribute to it in the title of his first novel, *The Ghost of Henry James* (1970), about five young Americans in Europe; in *The Foreigner* he takes up one of James's quintessential subjects: American 'innocents' abroad. Befriended by a knowing young black woman, the narrator begins to ask himself what it means to be an American, particularly one of French-Canadian descent. European condescension makes him impatient and fills him with self-doubt, yet he gradually sees that identity is something earned, not given. Asked about his life at home, he remarks, ironically, 'Oh, in America I live among Red Indians.... My aunts and uncles smoke pipes made from ears of corn, and they smear their bodies with bear grease in the winter to keep warm.' Somehow he will make a world for himself outside of the family, though relationships there seem just as strange and unknowable.

Plante's next book *The Catholic* (1985) focuses on the conflicts between sexuality and religion. At college in Boston, Daniel tries to understand and accept his homosexuality—a monumental task in light of his background—as well as the nature of sexuality itself. The erotic descriptions reveal Daniel's dilemma: if he rejects his body and his desires, he will have to reject himself. Refusing, he sees that sexuality can be a trap, but substituting spiritual lust for physical desire would be a betrayal of his Church. Like Christ, a beloved body remains a mystery: 'You knew you were missing what gave the real shape. You never saw what counted, but what distracted you.' Claiming his self in the act of sex,

Daniel turns from his heritage: 'I was born and brought up in the Mystical Body ... The Church I was part of lay on the earth, its arms and legs wide, its head thrown back, and Christ loved this body. Every time people made love, they re-enacted in their love act the mystical love of Christ for his Church.' The book is a profound *cri de coeur*, for no one will ever love Daniel as much as the Christ of his childhood. That such a book could be written with generosity of spirit and elegance is simply amazing.

Plante told me, 'Yes, I am an atheist, I don't believe in God, but my belief or not has absolutely no bearing on God.' The *but* is important because it allows him to confront his Catholicism without bitterness. He has never written denying the existence of God because 'I don't believe that God is a subjective thing, but an objective one.' Philip Roth once told Plante to 'write about the most extreme feelings you've ever had', and he has honoured the advice. 'I was brought up a devout Catholic, and I can't deny those feelings.' The memory of them is still palpable. On the day we first spoke, Plante had just been talking with Mary Gordon. 'Do you think our losing our faith was the worst thing that ever happened to us?' she asked. Plante's reply—'Yes, yes, but you can't say to yourself "Now I want to believe again"'—reveals a great deal about his fictional method. He may not rediscover his faith by writing about it, but he has transformed that loss into something affirmative.

Since *The Catholic*, Plante has depicted spiritual crises with a depth of feeling rare in modern fiction. In *The Native* (1988), one of Daniel's older brothers and his tormented daughter are locked in a battle of wills as the father tries to help his unhappy child deal with her suicidal impulses. Three years later, in *The Accident* (1991), an unnamed narrator struggles with the after-effects of a loss of faith. This book, which many have called Plante's finest, includes a dramatic episode similar to one that happened to Plante during his year in Belgium, when the camaraderie of several American students turned to conflict, petty jealousy and death. The incident—a deadly car accident in Spain—has haunted Plante ever since, and he knew it would eventually appear in his fiction. Plante admits to developing his subjects slowly, often over years, and he has returned to the event twice. In 1982 the *New Yorker* published his short story 'The Accident'. Comparing it with the novel is a study in the evolution of fiction. The short story has many of the details about Louvain that appear in the novel, along with its key episodes, but here the similarity ends. The story's protagonist, a young woman, is replaced in the novel by an unnamed narrator, clearly Daniel Francoeur, who has left his Boston college with a numbing sensation that follows a crisis of faith. The addition of this element heightens the stakes, permitting Plante to pose a difficult question: Is faith an act of choice or a matter of grace?

Told with his spare, elegant style, Plante's portrait of Catholicism in *The Accident* will be familiar to his readers, but with a European twist. One summer in the late 1950s, the narrator begins his junior year at the University of Louvain, where the seventeenth-century theologian Cornelius Jansen taught and developed a dark strain of Catholicism that was imported to North America by early French settlers. Like most students abroad, the narrator quickly befriends contemporaries he might have ignored back home: Karen, the rebellious daughter of a wealthy businessman; Vincent, her sarcastic and sinister shadow; and, most important, the plump, devout Tom. As this quartet tries to enjoy their year of freedom, while debating heady new ecumenical reforms, they begin to question themselves about the nature (or lack) of their faith. True to his Jansenist background, the narrator wants a religious experience that will shake him to his foundation. 'For religion to be a religion,' he insists, 'it has to descend on you, and knock you to the ground and make you totally helpless and possess you and make you believe whether you want to or not, so it's not you who decides if you believe, never, never you, but something that insists you're going to believe, or die, or believe and die.' Plagued by his envy of Tom, which he feels unable to escape, he suffers unexplainable nightly seizures that leave him in despair. Although Tom insists that it is more important to choose God than to be chosen by grace, he remains uncertain how to live his own religious convictions—a fact that only makes the narrator's obsession with him more intense. The two men, who at first seem to be opposite sides of a coin, can neither resist nor help each other.

The religious thoughts of these characters are driven by a youthful egotism that Plante catches beautifully (he is often at his best with characters verging on adulthood). When the narrator remembers an island off the coast of Providence, which he yearns to purify of all traces of human corruption, his longing embodies every dream of an unfallen world; Karen's cleverness and Vincent's cynical poses seem all the more poignant because they are untested. The centre of the novel, however, is Tom, whose struggle with his apparently innate goodness balances the other characters' attempts at sophistication. As Tom captures everyone's attention, even grudging admiration, he becomes a key to the mystery of faith. These 'innocents' drift through comic moments without even recognizing them; self-delusion mounts. The bleak atmosphere of wintry Louvain, sketched in precise and almost loving detail, provides their metaphysical reflections with an essential reality.

Increasingly troubled by his friend's depression, Tom arranges an automobile trip to Spain, with the hope of distracting him. But during a terrible rainstorm their car crashes into an oncoming truck. Victor, Karen and the narrator survive while Tom is killed at once, leaving the narrator overwhelmed by a sensation that Tom survived the accident while he died; the curious pair seem to exchange fates, and merge. When Tom's body is returned for the funeral, his parents do not recognize their son's face. Plante wisely leaves the transformation a mystery. At the end of the novel, the narrator remains in Louvain, consoling Karen with an ominous calm. The Jansenist emphasis on predestination, though unstated in the novel's final pages, permeates every line. Tom may have died to save the narrator, or taken over his spirit. Or, random chance, which brought them together in the same car for a fatal accident, may be part of God's design. Rejecting final explanations, Plante lets his tale challenge materialist assumptions through an ending as disquieting as that of Henry James's *The Turn of the Screw.*

During our first telephone conversation, Plante told me that he would eventually like to write a book about England. Having lived there for most of his adult life, he knows the country and its people well. He referred to England as 'a peculiar country going through a very bad patch. Thatcher has done a great deal of damage, and right now culturally, morally, artistically, it's a very shallow country.' When I mentioned that Doris Lessing had some positive things to say about John Major before giving a reading at Toronto's Harbourfront, Plante agreed at once: 'He's trying to introduce elements of humanity and morality. One feels a kind of softening up of Thatcher's hard, absolutist stance.' Other projects included a novel about a middle-aged American writer in Moscow. Plante noticed that there was little serious fiction in English set in Russia and decided to take up the challenge. His Russian novel was definitely 'not a thriller, and has nothing to do with the KGB or the CIA.' Then titled *The Centre*, it would deal with a man looking at his heritage—a David Plante subject if ever one existed.

It took several years but Russia finally appeared in his next two novels,

Annunciation (1994) and *The Age of Terror* (1999). Plante may have left the Francoeur family behind but not the mysteries that animated their lives. Family conflict appears in *Annunciation* after a teenage girl, Rachel, is raped, and decides to keep the resulting baby; her mother, Claire, wants to find a way to help her recover. Interested in art, Claire befriends Claude, a weary New York art editor who has moved to London, and together they pursue an unknown Renaissance painting of the Annunciation. From England to Italy to Russia, Plante takes them on a quest for a way of life worth living without the consolations of faith. *The Age of Terror* opens like a mystery novel, with a photograph of the frozen corpse of a Russian woman, Zoya Kosmodemyanskaya, who was murdered by Nazis in 1941. Jumping ahead to 1989, before the collapse of the Soviet Union, Plante brings several foreigners to Leningrad—a disillusioned young American college dropout named Joe (reminiscent of Daniel Francoeur), and a sinister older alcoholic, Gerald, who is involved in supplying the international sex trade with young girls and boys through a mysterious Russian woman, Zoya, named after the murdered martyr. But this is not a Cold War espionage thriller. As the characters attempt to save each other, economic hardship comes to symbolize spiritual disintegration. Grimmer than the foreigners abroad in Plante's earlier fiction, these characters have lost their innocence, though Joe, haunted by gangster-ish Stalinesque dreams, has a sense of déjà-vu that posits an alternate to the fallen world.

Unlike his Francoeur books, Plante's recent novels have a wider social and cultural range. Without the narrower focus that suited his myth-making imagination as well as his struggles with family and Catholicism, Plante's writing has taken on a more cerebral quality. His next novel, *ABC* (2007), presents a father who, after the accidental death of his young son, follows mysterious letters scrawled on a piece of paper to seek out the origins of the alphabet, the letters mirroring mysteries of the human heart. During his search, Gerard (a professor of French-Canadian descent at a small New England college) travels from Boston to Manchester to Athens and, eventually, to the Syrian desert, along the way meeting people with similar tragic losses. Gradually he comes to understand that love and grief are a common alphabet. The central character's concluding epiphany ('His grief did finally what grief does: grief expands into phenomenal love') may not convince every reader—many people are only embittered by grief—but one might wish it so.

Two memoirs give a candid picture of Plante's life. *American Ghosts*

(2005) covers some of the ground of his autobiographical novels. However, Plante's travels through Quebec in search of the roots of his abandoned Catholicism, recorded with tender appreciation for his family's history, add a new dimension to the confessional aspect of his writing. (He traced his lineage back to a distant relative, Jean Plante, who married Françoise Boucher on September 1, 1650, at Notre-Dame de Québec.) The memoir's meditative tone suits a writer who wants to avoid any nostalgia in his backward glance. Plante also wrote of his struggle to accept his sexuality, and about the life he made with Nikos Stangos, a London-based publisher and Greek poet. ('With Nikos,' he claimed, 'I felt that *I* had no history, but that *he* had a history.') While suggesting that with Nikos he was 'free of my Canuck God', Plante never explored their life together in his fiction, as if it were too private to serve as subject matter. But after Nikos died of cancer in 2004, Plante used the second person to address him directly in *The Pure Lover: A Memoir of Grief* (2009), an elegiac account of the nearly four decades they spent together. A Graecophile like many young gay men of his generation, Plante was drawn to Nikos as well as to his cultural tradition, which held tremendous imaginative appeal in a pre-liberation era. Consequently, Greek poetry and history play an important role in *The Pure Lover*, giving the book the added dimension of a love story about ideas. Broken into poignant short fragments of memory, Plante's grief memoir evokes the powerful elegiac strain running through classical Greek literature.

Plante's memoirs allowed him to mythologize the people of his life. It's not a big leap from reclaiming his Blackfoot heritage, which his family largely ignored, to regarding Nikos as the 'pure lover'. The gratitude Plante felt that such a paragon would love his imperfect self may be an understandable part of mourning, but it let Plante make a curious statement about his life as a writer that seems at odds with the psychologically probing nature of his fiction: 'He [Nikos] understood that I wrote not to understand but to negate understanding; that I wrote not for discursive thinking but, by describing a wet pebble, to stop thinking, to be purely aware. He understood that not only did I have no opinions of my own but I wanted no opinions of my own.' This self-portrait of a writer without opinions culminates in the claim that 'The sexual, familial, social, political, and civic duties I abided by became, in my detachment from them, as spontaneous to me as they had always been to Nikos....' The pure lover in death has turned into a kind of spirit guide, almost a secular saint. Plante followed this memoir with an engaging selection from his long-kept diary, *Becoming a Londoner* (2013). In this account of his love affair with a city and its literary life, past and present, Nikos again plays a central role, while the Francoeurs' Rhode Island and Quebec remain in the background. But any reader familiar with Plante's novels will sense the heavy shadow his background has cast. For *Worlds Apart: A Memoir* (2015), Plante returns to his years with Nikos, along with accounts of some of the famous cultural figures he'd known in London and New York: Claire Bloom, David Hockney, R. B. Kitaj, Philip Roth and Stephen Spender, to name only a few. Aptly reviewing the memoir, Allen Ellenzweig remarked, 'Plante's "Canuck" identity, more than his being gay, seems to have been central to his sense of self, and the marginality of Americans descended from Québécois ancestry remains an especially painful wound.' Ellenzweig saw this 'wound' as the 'hidden scar beneath his [Plante's] external worldliness,' a psychologically astute character reading.

In 1992 Plante came to Toronto for a reading at Harbourfront, and I was pleased to show him the city. That weekend's lively talk—ranging from expatriate life to favourite painters—remains a fond memory. David was interested in the English-language editions of Russian classics published by Progress Press in Moscow, also an interest of mine, so we spent part of a rainy Saturday looking for books, later enjoying the mystical film *The Double Life of Veronique* from Polish director Krzysztof Kieslowski, with a subject that suited one of David's novels. The next day I invited several friends to join us for brunch—the biographer Rosemary Sullivan and playwright Larry Fineberg. David asked for a vegetarian soup, so I made a lentil-spinach concoction, and we happily talked the afternoon away, of course about religion and childhood. A year later he kindly gave me a blurb for my first book, a collection of short stories, and we corresponded occasionally, losing touch in the late 1990s. But I continued to anticipate his new books. The world, however, is sometimes a small place. While revising this essay I mentioned my interest in Plante's work to Teresa Stratas, who exclaimed, 'David Plante! He's a good friend of Fabrizio's.' Fabrizio Melano, an opera director and one of Teresa's oldest friends, has known David since the 1960s. An hour later Fabrizio and I were on the telephone, and he offered to make a reintroduction, since David had a new London address. I hadn't planned to interview him again but the connection felt serendipitous.

During our first phone conversation so many years ago, my last question for David, now admittedly tactless, concerned a remark several critics have made, that he was a humourless writer—an odd notion, for it's difficult to imagine someone without a sense of humour writing his books. Plante laughed heartily. 'Never mind my critics,' he said. 'Sometimes even my friends say, "Why do you write such gloomy books? You're so much fun at dinner parties." Yes, one day I'd like to write something very very funny.' And what a funny-sad book it will be. I'm still looking forward to it.

On *Deaf to the City*

When I came to Canada in 1968 as part of the Vietnam-era American exodus, Marie-Claire Blais and Mavis Gallant were among the few Canadian fiction writers I'd read, courtesy of Edmund Wilson's *O Canada: An American's Notes on Canadian Culture.* The wise cosmopolitanism of Gallant and the fierce, visionary romanticism of Blais have remained for me the quintessential Canadian voices. Blais is, arguably, Canada's finest novelist, and her greatest books—*Deaf to the City*, along with *A Season in the Life of Emmanuel*—are achievements of rare stature in contemporary fiction. Since her literary debut with *Le Belle Bête* (translated as *Mad Shadows*) when she was nineteen years old, Blais has produced a compelling body of work that has won international acclaim and brought her France's Prix Médicis, several Governor General's Awards and a Guggenheim Fellowship. She is a fearless writer.

At first glance, *Deaf to the City* may seem a challenging, even formidable book. It is made up of a single long paragraph of over 200 pages with continually shifting points of view, often in mid-sentence. Yet after several pages, readers will find that the novel is propelled forward by Blais's unusual approach to narration, and its use of alternating voices becomes a kind of stream-of-consciousness of the suffering human spirit. As these voices move back and forth, *Deaf to the City* builds in a crescendo of accrued meaning: a more traditional narrative technique would seem inadequate to suggest the connections, and disconnections, at the heart of Blais's vision. The novel has rhythmic energy, which gives Blais's story a crucial breathless quality. The story itself, rooted in observed details of daily life, unfolds hypnotically through the charged narrative. There is no polemical thrust to Blais's work, just the urgent sense that all life is fragile and besieged: pay attention. Look and see.

One day in late spring, Florence Gray, wife of a prominent Montreal physicist, arrives at the Hôtel des Voyageurs in a rundown section of the old city, where she seeks temporary refuge from her life. Unlike a Ritz or

Plaza, this hotel has known better days. It is, in fact, closer to the Hotel Savoy of Joseph Roth's eponymous novella (and one of the greatest short novels of the twentieth century) than to Vicki Baum's glamorous Grand Hotel. The Hôtel des Voyageurs, like all hotel/train/ship settings in pilgrimage stories, as far back as Chaucer's *Canterbury Tales*, is also a psychic space, an in-between world where people from all walks of life can gather in a microcosm of humanity. It echoes the medieval motif of the ship of fools (popularized in modern fiction by Katherine Anne Porter's bestselling novel of that name), yet Blais, never a simple moralist, writes without the satire commonly associated with the motif. Life is too short and serious a matter for easy outrage or humour, while all-embracing irony, the characteristic tone of much fiction of our time—and frequently a defence against seeing—doesn't tempt Blais.

The central characters at Blais's hotel include, as well as Florence—one of the novel's two principals—a young boy, Michel/Mike, who suffers from a terminal brain tumor and, like Florence, faces imminent death; Gloria, his mother, a tough, part-time stripper who runs the hotel; her daughters Berthe (hiding from her family at an Anglo university), thirteen-year-old Lucia, well on her way to a life of prostitution, and baby Jojo; old Tim, an alcoholic Irishman, nearly homeless, and his dog Tim, now dead; and Judith Lange, a young philosophy teacher at a local college, and sometime confidante of Florence. Other notable characters, from various backgrounds, are Gloria's gangster husband; Florence's son, who is doing graduate studies in Europe; and Judith's mother, Madame Langenais. Repeated claims are also made on the reader by a stray cat who follows Berthe; a white lilac bush blooming outside Judith's classroom window; the concentration camps that haunt her teaching; and famed works of art, such as Munch's painting *The Scream*, Kafka's stories and music by Mozart and Bach. Blais is a writer whose love of art, ideas and culture contributes to the emotional depth of her own books—her intelligence never decorates her fiction. In this sense she embraces the Latin heritage of our word *education*—*educio*, meaning to 'lead out'—because art and ideas (the imagination, in fact), can draw people from isolation and solipsism.

Blais's characters all share in some way a deafness to each other, and to themselves, even as they struggle to move forward in the face of suffering and death. Death, of course, is deaf to all of them. The French word *sourd* in the original title (*Le sourd dans la ville*—literally *The Deaf*

One in the City) suggests not only physical deafness but a lack of comprehension, a failure to understand or grasp meaning. At the end of the novel, when Florence commits suicide, a sense of inevitability and loss brings the book to an elegiac close that leaves the reader wanting another sentence, another clause, another shift in focus and page of print to stop *Deaf to the City* from ending, as all life does. No reassuring plot conventions tie up the situations of Blais's characters, yet they are not open-ended either, since death hovers over the city. Alongside sorrow, fleeting impressions remain—the abandoned furniture in Florence's home, old Tim's missing dog, the branches of a white lilac bush.

It would be unfair to conclude these remarks without acknowledging Carol Dunlop's exemplary translation, in part because it introduces English-speaking readers to Blais's novel. A fiction writer in her own right, the Boston-born Dunlop died of cancer in 1982, at the age of thirty-six, only a few years after completing her work on *Deaf to the City*. Dunlop found an English-language equivalent for Blais's sinuous, lapidary prose, and her translation remains a testament to her own talents. Speaking to Montreal's *Le Devoir* shortly after Dunlop's death, Blais said: 'Sa traduction du *Sourd dans la vie*, a été pour moi une joie de partager la compréhension d'un univers littéraire et sa connaissance intime de la mort m'a beaucoup touchée dans ce travail de collaboration. Nous perdons un être cher et précieux.'

On a personal note, in the early 1980s I had the privilege of working with Blais when I edited *The Oxford Book of French Canadian Short Stories* and asked her to contribute an introduction to it. More than two decades later, we had a happy reunion when she agreed to write a short story for another anthology I was editing, *The Exile Book of Canadian Dog Stories*. I decided to translate the story myself—one long, intricately winding paragraph that ran several pages—which only increased my respect for Dunlop's achievement. Soon after, Blais spoke to my university classes, attended a conference I'd organized and, over dinner at Toronto's Turf Club, we even enjoyed making a few bets on the televised horse races, with the advice of Barry Callaghan. An extraordinary presence, Blais is as wise and compassionate as her books, which deserve to be read again and again. Welcome, then, to the Hôtel des Voyageurs—and to one of the finest novels in any language.

The Biographer As Snoop: Exposing E.M. Forster

One spring day in 1922 Virginia Woolf saw her friend E.M. Forster—then forty-three—on a London street, and later wrote in her diary: 'The middle age of buggers is not to be contemplated without horror.' What, I wonder, would she think of Wendy Moffat's much-praised biography of Forster, *A Great Unrecorded History* (2010), with its focus on her friend's sexuality? Unlike P.N. Furbank's official study, simply titled *E.M. Forster: A Life* (1978), which discusses Forster's sexuality as only one facet of his works and days, and Nicola Beauman's *E.M. Forster: A Biography* (1994), which expands somewhat on Furbank's account of Forster's sex life, Moffat treats his search for homosexual expression and identity as the essential explanation of his creativity. She is, on the whole, convincing.

A richly detailed biography can turn you back onto your own life, and this happened to me while reading Moffat's book. Following Forster's sexual fumbles as an undergraduate at Cambridge University, I recalled a classroom at Western Reserve University in Cleveland, Ohio. The year was 1967, the course a senior seminar in American Romanticism, with a professor who had a book on Mark Twain to his credit. Darkly handsome in a Gregory Peck-ish way—like his Atticus Finch in *To Kill a Mockingbird*—he kept long office hours when he talked about literature to any undergraduate who was a true reader. I often climbed the steps to his attic office to test my ideas on this thoughtful man. That term we were reading Walt Whitman, and all the passages about young male bodies in the Calamus poems obviously, to me, had something to do with homoeroticism (I'd been reading Plato's *Symposium* and other Greeks in translation). Although this was the late sixties, with talk of free love a commonplace, the Stonewall riots were several years off and homophobia was the norm. Listening to my classmates discuss Whitman's imagery as if we were in a political science seminar, I ventured the comment that perhaps those hunky bodies had something to do with the poet's reputed homosexuality, not American democracy. The room went dead, the professor looked as if I'd violated an unspoken law and then dismissed both my suggestion and any notion that Whitman would write about such a topic.

Jump ahead to the spring of 1970 and a graduate seminar on the Bloomsbury Group in the English Department at the University of Toronto. Now the professor was a scholar who went on to write several fine books about this subject. Stonewall had received scant attention in the Canadian newspapers. We were reading E.M. Forster, a writer I found curiously flat, as if he wasn't writing about whatever he really wanted to write about; I couldn't put my finger on my objection. There was rumour of a long-unpublished novel by Forster, the story of a homosexual romance set during the years before the First World War. Someone asked about it (not me, I'd learned my lesson) and our professor explained, dismissively, that he'd seen the book and it wouldn't do much good for Forster's reputation. When *Maurice* was posthumously published in 1971, I hooted at an early Cambridge scene where several undergraduates are translating a Greek classic aloud: 'They attended the Dean's translation class, and when one of the men was forging ahead Mr Cornwallis observed in a flat toneless voice: "Omit a reference to the unspeakable vice of the Greeks."' More than half a century had passed since that fictional classroom, hadn't it? I should add that the academics I've mentioned here were men of goodwill and not bigots—truly—yet somehow they expressed the values of their times.

Moffat offers a wealth of detail about Forster's sexuality—history and preferences, foibles and successes. We never learn his favourite season or colour, his preferred breakfast or what he cooked for dinner ('simply', we're told), which composers he loved, if he wore scent, or where he bought his books. This isn't an objection, but it means that his sexuality is the foreground of Moffat's research, which includes previously unpublished diaries and letters as source material. After his mother's death, in 1945, Forster destroyed most of his family's papers (later regretting it) but he preserved the records he'd kept of his sexual affairs—with an eye to their future historical value—so it's fair for Moffat to go digging through his past. What's fair, however, can lead to a kind of distortion. Halfway through the book, I wondered if Moffat would like her own sexual history to receive the meticulous attention and recreation she gave to Forster's.

I don't think I'm being prudish, and my remark about Moffat's own sex life is not meant to be flip. It's rare for people to share the complete details of their sexual life, and the focus of *A Great Unrecorded History* raises questions of what is worth recording, what we mean when we speak of a 'private life', and even why Moffat adds the word *Great* to her title. We learn from one of Forster's young conquests (I hesitate to write the word *lover*, which Moffat over-uses) that he often had holes in his socks; we read of his frequent masturbation in childhood and in old age; we follow as he picks up a ship's stoker, a French sailor, a cabdriver, a policeman; and we hear from the writer himself that his penis had a great deal of foreskin—but I'm not certain what to make of these facts. Do they humanize Forster? Or explain his art? Socks wear out, children and adults masturbate, people meet people, the male half of the human race has a penis, some circumcised, some not. All these details come with a steady, almost hagiographic, assurance that Forster was a great writer, a great friend, a great man, a great human being. Moffat's an apologist mounting a defence.

Yet Moffat's portrait of Forster's sexuality makes me think of a canvas by Francis Bacon covered over with Norman Rockwell images. Forster's sad sexual conquests while travelling in India and Egypt read like adventures in sexual tourism, his persistent pursuit of much younger working-class men, who were often married (or soon to be), seems downright self-defeating, and the way he used his fame, money and class position to charm and, later, manipulate his partners, almost makes mincemeat out of his talk of friendship, ethics and the examined life. That some of these young men responded, and even involved Forster in their marriages as a friend of the family (Forster bought one couple, the Buckinghams, a house nearby, which gave him easy access to the husband) only suggests that all sorts of people do all sorts of things.

Forster's claim that 'I want to love a strong young man of the lower classes and be loved by him and even hurt by him', has an Edwardian ring that also brings to mind Lady Chatterley and her gardener—a fantasy still alive in our culture. Moffat may prefer to focus on the word *love* in such a passage, but the word that stays in my mind after completing her book is *lower*, because Forster never seemed to forget *who he was* even while loving. Unintentionally, Moffat recounts his yearnings in the language of a romance novel. At the age of fifty-two, when Forster (whom she calls Morgan) met Bob Buckingham, a policeman who was twenty-five years his junior, Moffat writes: 'Morgan began to fall deeply in love.' This is on page 223, and Forster has been 'in love' so many times by then I almost sighed. What does the word *deeply* add to her description? The two men remained involved until Forster's death, at the age of ninety, though afterward Bob denied their sexual relationship (his wife admitted it). Forster wanted commitment from his partners—he felt frustrated that he couldn't share the life of the mind with Bob (he felt this about all of his lovers), and was annoyed when Bob's passion cooled after he bought him a house—yet he always chose people who were essentially unavailable.

Moffat's record of Forster's affairs rarely allows for the fact that he may have been taking advantage of his lovers, although she does quote one friend of Forster's who claimed that he liked feeling superior to people. Only once does Moffat show some impatience with her subject. She writes: 'But it is disquieting to hear Morgan record with such heartlessness Bess's complaint to her husband as he leaves once more for a day to roll in the hay with his new friend.' Moffat may be sensitive to the feelings another woman might have had in such a situation, but she might have also shown sympathy for Forster's male partners. While this isn't exactly a reverse sexism, it suggests that Moffat is not entirely comfortable with all of the messy male couplings she has to chronicle, and she doesn't want to appear to be passing judgment on them. When the object of Forster's affection isn't a young Englishman (Syed Ross Masood, then Mohammad el Adl) Moffat does suggest that he may have been influenced by colonial attitudes, though his lovers welcomed his attention. Her subject, after all, is a hero.

Forster knew he was living a double life, and spoke of his divided self or conflicted identity, which makes his counsel 'only connect' gratuitous. This double life was accompanied by lying, distortion, betrayal and even blackmail. We should remember, however, that he lived during a dangerous time of official homophobia almost unimaginable today. Forster came to his maturity under the shadow of Oscar Wilde's imprisonment, and saw the persecution of gay men continue throughout the course of his adult life. Five years before his death he wrote: 'When I am 85 how *annoyed* I am with Society for wasting my time by making homosexuality criminal. The subterfuges, the self-consciousness that might have been avoided.' This seems as honest a declaration as Forster ever made about his life, yet the word '*annoyed*'—italics his—somehow trivializes his condemnation. Given Forster's emphasis on human relations, *annoyed* is a pretty lame word. Too often he sounds like a spoiled only child (which in fact he was) who wants his way and nothing else. This is, of course, a common emotion that most people learn to hide or disguise, but I want something more, or better, from Forster.

My own life has seen a change from the Stonewall challenge through the plague of AIDS to a time of gay soldiers and gay marriage, where claiming civil rights for same-sex relations has turned some committed couples into the ordinary folks next door, with little of the old power to challenge bourgeois norms and values. It's here that I balk, and wonder what Forster would have thought now. He died in 1970 and could never have envisioned a homogenizing future. Maurice and his working-class lover Scudder may have ended their novel in each other's arms, but that's the happily-forever-after ending of a fairy tale.

Forster may have put such an emphasis on his loves—and loving—because he needed a constant reflection of himself in another person; he felt incomplete. In his private papers he was frank about his sexuality, but he had no use for Freud, and for the kind of probing that went with his theories—he wanted to find a place for living his sexuality rather than understanding it. This is admirable in a time of oppression, as it affirms the importance of each individual life, but it doesn't help us understand the significance that sexual expression can have over anyone's lifetime. Nor does it shed light on the way a moment in time can shape an individual's sexual preferences and practices, and if these are idiosyncratic or generalized. As he aged Forster came to praise 'Half-understanding the truest wisdom, at least in private matters....' There may have been much about his life he preferred to overlook. But I can't imagine how he would have lived if he'd been born several generations later—would he have wanted to be one of the folks next door? He may have hinted at an answer when he wrote, at age seventy: 'For I cannot speak to others of my worst trouble, which is that I have got tired of people and personal relationships....' He came close to admitting, finally, that love doesn't conquer all. We are more than our loves, our friends, our families. Surely he knew that his novels proved this.

Are gay men and women better off today than Forster's generation? A young undergraduate like Forster would now be able to enrol in gay literature or gender-studies courses at many large universities, but I've noticed that these courses often have larger enrolments of straight women, and many of the gay men who take them seem hell-bent on acting out old-fashioned stereotypes. A few young or middle-aged or even senior gay couples may now have their wedding announcement in the Style section of the Sunday *New York Times*, but gay bookstores are closing for want of customers and readers. Despite the increased global legalization of homosexuality, and in some places even gay marriage, the growing threat from orthodox religions—and not only in our own backyard—makes me pause. At the university where I teach, which has a large multicultural student body, I'm frequently taken aback by the casual yet intense homophobia of students from what we refer to, carefully, as traditional backgrounds. I hear, then, echoes of Forster in the 'Terminal Note' he wrote for *Maurice* in the late 1950s, describing the shift in public attitude towards homosexuality during his lifetime: 'the change from ignorance and terror to familiarity and contempt'. Contempt, of course, can easily flare into something much crueller, especially when people need to feel superior to others. Over time this situation may change, but you can't always count on your own times to be benevolent, as Moffat's biography of Forster reminds us. Perhaps we have more in common with that nervous young man than we may like to admit.

Getting to Know Her: Fact and Fiction

Most people have some special friend, relative or acquaintance who passed through their lives but got lost along the way. We may wonder about their stories, but we seldom try to search them out. I wrote about such a person in my novel *Pack Up the Moon* (2001), and after the book was published had many opportunities to learn more about her. While my novel isn't a *roman à clef* (which is what writers usually say), there are correspondences between my character Charlotte Fleury and a young woman named Madeleine Darte, who was once an important part of my life.

When I settled in Canada in 1968, I met Madeleine in a graduate class at the University of Toronto. We became instant friends in the way that can happen with young people adrift on ideas and idealism. But that friendship came to an abrupt end. The reasons aren't important but like my novel's narrator, Karl Marton, for many years I wondered what had happened to Madeleine. Then, at a dinner party in 1993, I learned that she had been murdered in Florida in the mid-seventies. And that night, while I was working on my first novel, a new one started to write itself.

Several years later I decided to research some of the details of Madeleine's death. Like Karl, I even contacted Florida's Department of Records, and for $19.95 ordered a copy of her death certificate. But then I stopped. I didn't want to know any more facts—true crime has never interested me. And at that point Madeleine had merged into my character Charlotte Fleury, so I wasn't always sure where one left off and the other began. I was, after all, writing Charlotte's story, and like all strong characters—and memories—she had her own way of directing me.

What interests me now is the effect *Pack Up the Moon* had on people who also knew Madeleine, many of whom I'd never spoken with before the novel appeared during the weekend after 9/11, as inauspicious a debut date as possible. Of course I'd wondered if anyone would spot echoes of another person in its heroine. I didn't have long to wait. The critic Philip Marchand, who had known Madeleine as an undergraduate at the University of Toronto's St. Michael's College, soon wrote an article about my book's Madeleine connection. He also told me that Marshall McLuhan had written about her death in his unpublished journals (Philip had written a well-received biography of McLuhan), now in the National Library. I was pleased and not surprised. Madeleine was hard to forget.

One morning, a week or so later, I was stopped on the campus where I teach by the wife of a colleague. She'd just finished the book and remembered an English class she'd taken more than twenty-five years ago at Memorial University, in Newfoundland, where Madeleine had been teaching. She described her as an intense, nervous lecturer who'd held the lectern tightly as she spoke, a woman who'd worn either long flowing skirts or the shortest of minis. Charlotte could have been like that, I told myself, if she'd had the opportunity to teach. Or maybe not.

Another day, outside a grocery store near the Yonge and St. Clair intersection, a woman recognized me from a television interview and asked if I knew Madeleine's mother. No, I said, I'd never met her. 'Are you sure?' she persisted. I was positive. This woman had another story to tell, about how a mother had faced her daughter's violent death. Soon I received the first of several e-mails from a man who, with his ex-wife, had known Madeleine and her family. He told me what had happened to Madeleine's ex-husband. I won't discuss that here because it's nothing I know first-hand, so it belongs to the realm of gossip. It's true, however, that gossip and fiction are closely related, as the American novelist Mary McCarthy once acknowledged.

Such encounters began to pile up, with coincidences that would seem contrived in a novel (one colleague, for instance, got his first teaching job because of Madeleine's death). I found that Charlotte was leading me to Madeleine, to details of her life that I couldn't have imagined, although they made perfect sense. Life, like fiction, thrives on plausibility.

The tone of the gossip—'Let me tell you about ...'—is never far from the pages of most fiction. If the gossip concerns someone we've known, it may even have a special resonance. But do fiction's roots really matter? Does anyone north of Toronto's Bloor Street really care about the true-life origins, say, of Margaret Atwood's characters? For some readers it's easy to spot resemblances to writers like George Jonas or Rick Salutin, but for most, the stories have to stand without such counterparts; we tend to think about actual stories as sources, not gossip. Of course celebrities who influence fictional creations belong to a special category—the portrait of

Gertrude Stein and Alice B. Toklas in Monique Truong's novel *The Book of Salt* immediately comes to mind.

Gay writers have long been in the forefront of turning fact into fiction. Marcel Proust, who recorded the *belle époque* in volume after volume, may be the most famous, but closer to our time Truman Capote and Edmund White saw how fictionalized portraits of real people can backfire. Capote, who revealed the steamy secrets of several prominent socialites in a notorious chapter of his novel *Answered Prayers* found himself ostracized by former lunch pals. Edmund White—a writer noted for his generosity to other writers—lost the friendship of Susan Sontag, the critic and novelist, after she saw herself and her son in his novel *Caracole.* According to Sontag's biographers, gossip had it that Sontag even threatened a lawsuit. They go on to quote gay novelist David Leavitt (who himself had been sued by British poet Stephen Spender over Leavitt's own novel *While England Sleeps*): 'Writers who are famous advocates of freedom of expression are the first ones to pounce, the first ones to sue, the first ones to scream when something is written about them.' Well, yes—no one should be surprised. Writers like having things their way.

With Madeleine/Charlotte, I'm talking of course about a more private world. I was glad to find myself sharing it with strangers, and was struck again and again by the goodwill of the people who wrote to me. They all seemed pleased that someone else had remembered Madeleine, and cared enough for a spark in her story to occasion a novel. They were not too shy to ask about individual episodes in the book, but like me they may have had memories of Madeleine's roast chicken, with tarragon butter stuffed under the skin (a dish Charlotte cooks), or her intense, Bette Davis eyes (also Charlotte's). Apparently one or two true details stood in for the rest of Madeleine's story, true or not.

Although Charlotte is buried in Toronto's old Mount Pleasant Cemetery, Karl never visits her grave. I don't know where Madeleine is buried, but recall someone saying that her grave might be in Port Colborne, Ontario. I'd like to visit it now. Not to take flowers, nothing so simple. But I would be tempted to leave a copy of my book. I can't help thinking that the young woman who once sat cross-legged on her bedroom floor, passionately waving a paperback novel by Margaret Drabble with one hand while clutching a glass of red wine in the other, would somehow be pleased that she is still remembered, and that a part of her story has shadowed a book.

Not long after this essay was published, to coincide with the release of the paperback edition of *Pack Up the Moon*, I received an e-mail from a man named Richard Tallman. He identified himself as Madeleine's last partner and suggested we meet, perhaps to visit her grave together.

Nothing came of his overture, so I put it out of my mind. Occasionally I still meet someone who had also known Madeleine—the Canadian novelist Greg Hollingshead, for instance—and the mention of her becomes a kind of bond. Around this time Barry Callaghan gave me a copy of the bound doctoral thesis Madeleine had written about his father's work, 'Moral Vision and Naturalistic Technique: The Conflict in the Novels of Morley Callaghan', and I was reminded of the tragedy of her early death, the lost promise of her life, the talks we'd had about her love of Callaghan's novels and even the copy she'd once given me of his *Such Is My Beloved* (1934), a favourite of hers. Then, several years later, Tallman wrote again, this time asking permission to use a quotation from my novel in a self-published *roman à clef* he'd written about Madeleine. Of course I agreed if he would send me a copy of the book.

He did, and it's called *The Turning Year: a memorate* (2012). I read it eagerly, looking for the young woman I remembered, and for any hints of my Charlotte too (here she's called Marie—and sometimes Martie—Bertrand). The book turned out to concentrate on the story of a woman who helped Tallman through his grief over the loss of my old friend (who was murdered by his first wife), with an emphasis on religious healing; eventually he married this woman. But there were flashes of the Madeleine I had once known, and the ensuing years vanished with Tallman's description of her as 'a dark heroine' who 'made the eating of escargots a delight to behold if not something to partake in, who ate her steak so very rare that her eating of it became an animal act; Martie of the running slow motion on the wind, reaching out for someone or some thing just beyond her reach.' Fact and fiction blended together, and for a few minutes I was once more in my early twenties, eager for a telephone call from a voice that I would never hear again.

Which Paris?

When I made my first trip to Paris more than forty years ago, like many tourists I arrived at a place that belonged to other people, though it seemed *almost* mine through books. Along with French verb conjugations memorized in high school, my head was stuffed with images of historical figures, characters from novels, famous paintings, a few buildings (like Notre Dame), lines from poetry, familiar melodies from opera and Edith Piaf. The first French record I'd purchased as an undergraduate—an LP of Juliette Gréco's best-known hits—had the Latin Quarter chanteuse singing 'Sous le ciel de Paris', and I knew the words by heart. Central to the geography of the Western imagination, this near mythical city had become a museum, even an interactive one, if you were lucky enough to afford a plane ticket there. In his touchstone essay 'Paris, Capital of the Nineteenth Century', written in 1935, the German-Jewish critic Walter Benjamin (1892–1940) extolled the city's arcades and boulevards, and I was ready for all of them. I wasn't, of course, interested only in the *belle époque*, but in every nook and cranny where Abélard might have walked about in the twelfth century, where Madame de Sévigné wrote her engaging letters in the 1600s, and where, much closer in time, Albert Camus had his Saint-Germain-des-Prés office.

Once I finally got to Paris, I wondered if I could find the city of those fabled years of the early twentieth-century modernists, the era of Proust and Gertrude Stein, Stravinsky and Picasso. Of course I dutifully marched off to Stein's apartment at 27, rue de Fleurus, climbed the hillside steps in Montmartre to locate the Bateau-Lavoir, where Picasso painted his proto-Cubist masterpiece *Les Demoiselles d'Avignon* in 1907, and lingered over an *omlette roulée* in a patio restaurant in the Palais-Royal, Cardinal Richelieu's old mansion, so that I could look up at the second-floor window of Colette's last apartment and imagine her there, peering down on the quadrangle's elegant garden. One night there was a mediocre meal of *pintade*, or guinea fowl, at Café Procope, a tourist trap where the Encyclopédistes had gathered in the eighteenth century, another night brought a performance of Debussy's *Pelléas et Mélisande* at the ornate Opéra Garnier, with Pelléas wearing tight-fitting leather gear and Mélisande flapping about in something flimsy. I felt that I was in the set of a movie by François Truffaut or Eric Rohmer. Wonderful as the feeling was, I wanted something more.

My second trip to Paris let me think of myself as a flâneur—that uniquely Parisian figure, thanks to Baudelaire, who found meaning in wandering the city's streets for 'refuge in the crowd', in Benjamin's words. With a map of the Metro lines now memorized, I planned to take on the city. I no longer hoped to spot Juliette Gréco around every corner (I did, however, see Catherine Deneuve walking near Place des Vosges, in the Marais, as exquisite in life as onscreen), but I soon fell back on old cultural associations, making my way through Père Lachaise to the graves of some of my heroes: Chopin, Maria Callas, Gertrude Stein, Oscar Wilde (not a native Parisian on the list). No matter where I looked in Paris, there was something beautiful for the eye, from the Art Nouveau Metro stops to the city's silvery light, though such beauty can be unnerving after a while. What was I seeking? The government of France spends a king's ransom to keep Paris spruced up as the world's leading tourist destination, and this meticulous buffing has managed to remove most vestiges of its sometimes violent and painful history.

By my third trip, I had a pastry shop to return to for perfect *financiers*, favourite bistros and concerts to attend at the Baroque Church of Saint-Roch, where the premiere of Berlioz's *Messe solennelle* was held in 1825. Finally the nostalgia I felt for Paris had something to do with my own experience of the city, not simply borrowed nostalgia, literary nostalgia or the romance of another person's life. Yet my experience merely touched the surface of things. Yes, I enjoyed seeing Proust's narrow, metal-framed bed in the Carnavalet museum, but I'd begun to feel restless after such encounters. To my surprise the city's past can start to weigh heavily, and if you're not always in good spirits (and who is?) all that beauty can be oppressive. I now admitted that one has to live in a city in order to appreciate its opportunities and accept its drawbacks. Gertrude Stein had the right to quip 'America is my country and Paris is my hometown' because she'd made the city her own, remaining in France during two world wars, although as a privileged writer/celebrity. Unless you live in a place for a serious stretch of time—and I don't mean a long holiday or academic sabbatical—you can't truly claim to know it. You don't really belong, you're just passing through, enjoying the treats.

I wasn't, however, going to turn my life upside down and move to Paris, though others had done that, and I've always enjoyed accounts of their adventures. I would remain a traveller, a tourist, what have you—forever. Increasingly I found myself drawn to books about Paris by writers who had settled there but kept some distance. Two women especially showed me the way out of my dilemma, and both did it through language: the Russian fiction writer Nina Berberova (1901–93), who came to Paris from St. Petersburg in 1925, and recorded, in Russian, the life of the White Russian community in exile, and the Canadian short-story writer Mavis Gallant (1922–2014), who settled in Paris in the 1950s and took French life (not only émigrés and ex-pats) for her subject, in English. Eventually I knew what I had to do.

During my undergraduate years I'd become friends with a fellow student in a French class, and we'd kept in touch since then with letters, occasional long-distance phone calls and even biannual visits. An American-Jewish woman escaping a difficult family, she had moved to Paris after graduation and the death of her mother, a Holocaust survivor, taken a job teaching English at Berlitz and remained put. During my visits to Paris I often stayed at Anita's apartment, in an unfashionable neighbourhood, where I met her ex-pat friends as well as several of the loves of her life, including two young Algerian men and a middle-aged Frenchman. By this time I'd published a collection of short stories and was ready for the challenge of a first novel. I didn't have to look far for my subject. I would write myself into Paris.

With my friend's encouragement I set out to explore a corner of Paris that didn't tempt travellers: the nineteenth arrondissement and its environs. In the early 1990s this was still a working-class neighbourhood with few distinctions, not exactly seedy but rough, unpolished, and often quite poor. The newer immigrant populations—Vietnamese, North African, Chinese—lived side by side with native Parisians, people who had left their homes in the provinces for work in the city, and older refugees from across Europe whose lives had been shaped by hardship, struggle and loss. While 'the nineteenth' wasn't the North American ideal of multiculturalism, it had its own kind of tolerance. In my best flâneur fashion, I wandered the streets, ate in dingy restaurants, shopped in unglamourous shops, entered apartment buildings that still had communal Turkish toilets, and even visited the Tenon hospital, where I determined that one of the scenes of my novel would be set. I was often shadowed by a fiction writer's sense of distance and guilt—there's a thin line between being a flâneur and a voyeur. But I told myself this was Paris too, and I wanted to get it right, or make the best effort.

It pleases me now to think back on that novel, *The Paris Years of Rosie Kamin*. It was published in 1998 and won several awards. I write this with a sense of awe, because the novel had the aspect of a gift to it. One of its American awards, the Ribalow Prize, is given to the best Jewish novel of the year, and I was the first and only non-Jewish writer to receive it; Elie Wiesel was among the judges. At the ceremony in Manhattan an elderly guest came up to me and said, 'This book is your *beshert*.' She asked me if I knew what the Yiddish word meant, and I told her I did—it's your intended, your predestined soulmate—and that's what the novel was, something I'd been heading toward without quite knowing it.

Writers should always surprise themselves, and that book surprised me. Half a year later I gave a reading from it in Paris. I hadn't been nervous before similar events in New York or San Francisco, but this was Paris after all! And sitting in the middle of the audience was Mavis Gallant, one of the greatest short-story writers in any language. She had told a mutual friend that she would be present that night, but I didn't believe it. Nor did I expect to sit next to her for the dinner after the reading, and talk about her cataract surgery and writing about Paris. I almost had to pinch myself. Sometime later Mavis wrote to me about my book, and that letter is a treasure of my writing life. Speaking of my novel's heroine, she wrote:

> She is one of those characters of fiction who seems to have written the book—something like Joseph Roth's Trotta, not the one in *Radetsy March*, but the cousin who comes back from the Russian prison camp in *Grotte des Capucins*. (I don't know what it was called in English.) It is that particular Trotta who has haunted Vienna for me rather than Roth. Or (another example) I see Odette walking along the Champs-élysées with a swarm of admiring men but not Proust. I'm sure this makes no sense, so I shall stop it at once.

But it made sense to me: Rosie and I had almost been flâneurs together.

No one can know all of Paris, write about all of Paris, or see or love or claim to understand all of Paris. We can only glimpse a vast, ever-changing subject, at the angle one's life has allowed. I'm reminded of a remark in that classic movie *Casablanca* (1942), when the nightclub owner Rick, played by Humphrey Bogart, turns to his lost love, Ilsa, the luminous Ingrid Bergman, and says, 'We'll always have Paris.' I'm fortunate to have had my moment in Paris—my own Paris—and I'm grateful. I wish the same for everyone.

On Books and Baby Boomers

Suddenly, it seems, everyone is turning sixty. The baby boomer generation—born after World War II, between 1946 and 1960—has had a profound impact on North American cultural, economic and political life, and they're about to be at it again. Over dinners, at parties, in busy business corridors, they're reassuring each other that 'Sixty is the new forty'. Well, good luck. But how will the publishing world face the onslaught of spending that the boomers are going to enact? What will happen to serious and popular fiction, and books in general? What, in the end, will matter to the boomers, and what might they change?

I ask these questions because I'm part of the boomer generation too, and I've completed a novel, *Winter in Hollywood*, that looks directly at some of the issues about aging that the boomers—and all of us, eventually—have to face. It's a truism that our culture likes to emphasize youth, from the stories of young love that dominate TV, the movies and popular culture in general, to ads and articles hawking Viagra, Botox and plastic surgery. Age itself has come to be seen as something unnatural, to be avoided at almost any cost. Or, as the seventy-five-year-old heroine of my novel remarks, while walking down a street of fancy shops in Los Angeles: 'age hid itself—bad news, bad luck'. The reasons for our fear of aging are complex and perhaps ancient. And it's ironic that the boomers, who were always youth obsessed, now have to put their own stamp on aging. Can book publishers and booksellers help humanize this process, and offer an alternative to fear and loathing? There has to be more than Andrew Weil's bestseller *Healthy Aging*, sensible as it may be.

One of the most popular non-fiction books of 2005 was Joan Didion's *The Year of Magical Thinking*, a memoir about the death of her husband, the novelist John Gregory Dunne, and the fatal illness of their daughter. Apparently everyone in the book business was surprised by Didion's runaway success, as if no one had noticed the boomers at the gates. One newspaper critic, commenting on the phenomenon, concluded rather too cleverly, 'Translation: Aging boomers are becoming interested in their own mortality.' The snide tone here is common when aging and mortality rear their twin heads. Yet when Annie Leibovitz photographed Didion for *Vanity Fair*, she avoided the soft focus often reserved for elderly celebrities (Didion was seventy-one) and instead recorded the novelist in her wrinkled glory, with claw-like hands, in an image that evokes famous portraits of Karen Blixen (Isak Dinesen) made by Richard Avedon and Cecil Beaton several years before her death, at age seventy-seven. The fierce expression on Didion's face will fool no one who has read her memoir. This is a woman shocked by mortality hitting so close to home. Despite years of bearing witness to late twentieth-century injustice and angst, Didion, it seems, never quite expected to be part of the passing scene of suffering.

I claim no special knowledge about aging. In recent years the circumstances of my own life have let me spend a big part of it with my aging parents, and other relatives and friends, in hospitals and nursing homes. I've found myself at different times troubled, frightened and saddened by what I've seen, and on a few occasions amazed at the kindness of some of the caregivers. Life happens in such places too, with its own rules and logic, in a kind of alternate universe to youth and middle age. *Winter in Hollywood* began in one of these nursing homes as I watched an elderly woman—a stranger to me—rocking a naked rubber doll back and forth in her lap, lost in dementia. Where was she, I wondered. She must have been someplace. How could I follow her there? Rarely recognizing anyone, she sometimes smiled to herself, knowing perfectly well where, in her mind, she happened to be. People walked past her as if she was invisible. We should have been ashamed.

Where, in our literature, are the best examples of aging? Read *King Lear* or *The Stone Angel* and there's little consolation for the thought of what's ahead, if you live long enough to get old. In my day job of teaching, I've had the opportunity to regularly reread many of the classics, and I'm often struck by the fact that older characters—characters over fifty deemed too old for love stories—fall into minor roles; they're priestly advisers, spunky spinsters and walk-on figures who have a few helpful, or not helpful, words to offer to young characters with issues other than aging on mind. Occasionally we find an interesting septuagenarian, but such figures are far removed from the cheery mouthpieces in TV ads for luxury retirement communities and adult diapers.

The explosion of books by women writers in the last forty years has fortunately offered some corrective to this situation. From the popular journals of the poet and novelist May Sarton, beginning with *Journal of a Solitude* and ending with *At Eighty Two: A Journal*, to such novels as Barbara Pym's *Quartet in Autumn* and Muriel Spark's *Memento Mori*, real aging—and the hard work of it—has started to find a place in serious writing. And in Canada, Mavis Gallant was never afraid of the subject. Multiculturalism has also broadened the picture as writers drawn to the generational novel—with characters living in extended families (in versions of 'the old country')—inevitably include older characters. Often, however, these oldsters exist to provide plot opportunities for cultural conflict, and belong to that category of 'minor' characters who in themselves have few stories, or opportunities, of significance.

Too many middle-aged male fiction writers worry mainly about their diminishing sexual selves, and portray aging as a bleak time when characters dream only of young bodies. One recent example will suffice. Our book-chat culture, like many elderly people, has a poor memory. Most reviews of Gabriel García Márquez's novel *Memories of My Melancholy Whores* were struck by the originality of its premise (an elderly man dreams of young girls) as if the reviewers had never heard of a once famous precursor, Yasunari Kawabata's *House of the Sleeping Beauties*, published in the early sixties. Men need to find more life in aging than sexual longing, although that is an important part of the experience of time passing. And the task is a daunting one. Unlike fiction writers, poets have done a richer job of recording age. They seem less afraid of the subject, perhaps because they think in images as well as in narratives. Of course poetry welcomes reflection while narrative favours action. And most poets realize that their work is unlikely to find a large readership—knowledge that can free them to write about painful subjects with a heartfelt directness most fiction writers, aware of market pressures, may feel they can't afford. I personally know of several published young writers who have been persuaded by their editors not to develop older characters in drafts of new novels.

A central problem starts to emerge. Most people want to put off aging, which appears as the end of life rather than a part of it. While various religious traditions hold out the image of wise detachment as something to strive for, and folk tales offer icons of aging, contemporary fiction, with its emphasis on story and desire, is in many ways incompatible with aging, unless we start to rethink fiction. As people live longer lives (lifespan figures have, after all, changed considerably since Virginia Woolf wrote, not to mention Tolstoy), writers need to look at those extended years and claim them as subject matter. When my heroine thinks to herself, 'There had to be a way of growing old without going crazy from the grief of it', she is uttering one of the most unspoken universal thoughts, and not trying to convince herself that seventy-five is the new sixty.

Our culture likes to see itself as one that embraces diversity, but the uniformity of much popular entertainment belies this notion. In a *New York Times* article about the popular TV sitcom *The Golden Girls*, one of the show's original producers said that he would never propose such a program today because the characters were 'too old'. Book publishers share this prejudice too, and have their own versions of 'hip' youth culture. Harry Potter is only part of the problem. Today's university students often claim to prefer the children's books they've loved to books written for adults about adults. In a sense their attitude reflects our culture's ambivalence about maturity. It also seems the opposite stance of readers of my generation, who can recall the adult books they yearned to read as children. I was particularly fascinated by my mother's collection of John O'Hara's novels, and at the age of ten read them when she wasn't around. I didn't know what an affair was, I'd never tasted a martini and I'd yet to see New York City, but I knew that all of these were mysteries connected with being grown-up. I longed for them, not for magical paraphernalia in a pseudo-English countryside, and many writers I speak with today also recall their first literary encounters with adulthood in books we weren't supposed to read. Romanticized adulthood, yes, and sometimes even sensationalized, but seldom infantilized. O'Hara, come to think of it, never shied away from aging as a subject, even if his characters fell into adultery and alcohol and isolation as they struggled with the problems of being fully human.

But we have to return to our world, and to the possibilities it offers. Marketing specialists argue that product loyalty is gained by aiming advertising (and the products encasing it) at the young. This notion, sometimes challenged but still powerful, seems to determine too many publishing lists, which overlook the fact that readers over forty, people with discretionary money for entertainment and reflection, aren't always fascinated by the exploits and travails of characters in their twenties, including the recent spate of memoirs by writers who have yet to live much of a life. I'm not saying that young people shouldn't write books, or that their lives aren't an important subject. Not at all. Young characters are a significant part of my own novels; several young women—one is eighteen, the other twenty-three—are crucial to *Winter in Hollywood*; and the memory of youth shadows almost every story of aging. I am, however, suggesting that the many possibilities of aging still await serious fiction writers, and that literary representations of aging that challenge the pervasive anti-aging assumptions of our culture may strike a chord with boomers looking for something good to read, and also appeal to younger readers who want to see beyond the definitions our culture embraces. There are new truths to be found, old boundaries to be broken and even money to be made. Sixty is *not* the new forty, just as forty is *not* the new twenty, but each age is something to discover. I hope that *Winter in Hollywood* will contribute to a discussion not only about aging and mortality, but about living itself, and what it is that all people might do with the unknown time that remains to them.

The Taste for Fiction: Rereading Novels, Reading the Self

The headline caught my eye: 'Philip Roth Gives Up Reading Fiction'. As I read on, the *New York Times* article cited an interview where Roth said, 'I've stopped reading fiction. I don't read it at all. I read other things: History, biography. I don't have the same interest in fiction that I once did.' When asked for an explanation, the novelist replied, 'I don't know. I wised up ...' and changed the subject. Regretfully, I knew what he meant.

For as long as I can remember I've been a devoted reader of fiction. One of my first loves was Anna Sewell's novel *Black Beauty* (1877), and as a boy I insisted on sleeping with a copy of it under my pillow. I didn't long for a horse, I wanted the book nearby. Ever since, I've been puzzled by people who didn't care for fiction, or who claimed they lacked the time for it. Even stranger were the people, always a few decades older than I, who said they had stopped reading novels: from my twenties, a Russian-born engineer who refused to read any novel longer than 200 pages, and in time not even those; from my thirties, a university librarian who gave away all her novels, except for *Don Quixote* and *The Hobbit*; and from my forties, an editor who lent me out-of-print novels by Henry Green—the last novels he had truly loved. What had gone wrong? This lack of interest in fiction, almost a distaste for it, would never happen to me.

Then decades passed. Gradually I picked up new fiction without much enthusiasm, more from duty than interest. And for the first time in my reading life I found myself setting aside novels halfway through them. I continued to value fiction, and had even written three novels and a collection of short stories. Was I becoming detached from our culture, increasingly out of sympathy with it? Most of the pirouetting contemporary fiction by male writers—Martin Amis, Michael Chabon and Jeffrey Eugenides, for example—tried my patience, while novels by much-praised women writers such as Ann Patchett and Alice Sebold struck me as contrived or trite. I no longer wanted to read about alienated adolescents, impossible love affairs and messy marriages; supernatural or postmodern effects were too clever by half; and the social commentary seemed like easy satire. Of course this wasn't true of every new novel I purchased—I loved Cynthia Ozick's *Heir to a Glimmering World*, Philip Roth's *Indignation*, Jill Clement's *Heroic Measures* and Ward Just's *Forgetfulness*—but these were exceptions. Like Roth, I turned with greater pleasure to historical studies, biographies, memoirs and journals. What had gone wrong? Could I recover a taste for fiction? I needed a plan. I needed to understand what was happening.

Fiction has many functions, which inevitably change over one's lifetime. We read novels and short stories to satisfy our curiosity about how others live in the world as well as for entertainment, for comfort and consolation. Very few people, I suspect, read fiction mainly for the pleasures of language, though that shouldn't be discounted. Yet readers' interests evolve, and reading preferences may change along with them. Why, for instance, would anyone over sixty still *need* book after book about the love problems of fictional twenty-somethings, a popular subject with writers and publishers? It's not that I want only novels about aging—though I've long admired Barbara Pym's *Quartet in Autumn*, which concentrates on it—but subject matter counts. As well, my work as a teacher determines some of my reading, and teaching classic novels has kept me close to books that have been favourites since I first discovered them. The pleasure of introducing *Anna Karenina* or *To the Lighthouse*, for example, hasn't flagged. Rereading such books (which stand up well to rereading) has also shaped my dissatisfaction with the thinness of most contemporary fiction.

The publishing, reviewing and academic worlds distinguish between literary and popular fiction, a distinction both unavoidable and arbitrary. The popular nineteenth-century writer Charles Dickens would now be considered a classic or literary writer by most people. Other distinctions—such as 'middlebrow', 'bestseller' and 'trash'—only suggest the trouble with categories. Grace Metalius's *Peyton Place* (1956), for example, once belonged to the categories of 'bestseller' and 'trash', but the novel is now available in paperback from the University Presses of New England, with a 24-page introduction that explains why it was considered shocking. Many books once thought to be literary (from 1957, James Gould Cozzens's turgid *By Love Possessed*) are now dismissed as middlebrow, and even pretentious, while other literary bestsellers—J.M. Marquand's clever *B.F.'s Daughter* (1946)—are long forgotten. And it's amazing to recall that copies of a bestseller like Betty Smith's poignant *A Tree Grows in Brooklyn* (1943) were sent to American soldiers during the Second World War, perhaps to remind them of the folks back home, because that novel has been relegated to the ghetto of books for teenage girls, who, as my students have told me, much prefer Stephenie Meyer's *Twilight* series about high school vampires. Much of today's 'literary' fiction—often reviewed glowingly by young writers with an eye to their own careers, or by more senior writers who have figured out how to play the game of literary reputation—is of no more value than once-praised novels that current writers, critics and academics would dismiss. Reputations see-saw, but we like to overlook this fact and admire our own taste.

My plan to reinvigorate an appetite for fiction would begin with rereading, and I've now followed this plan for several years. Rereading includes not only the act of reading a book once again, either an old copy or a new edition, but it also involves the memories evoked, and the reflections that follow—a bit like looking through an old family album, and rediscovering parts of one's self. In his essay 'On Reading Old Books', published in 1821, William Hazlitt began his defence of rereading bluntly: 'I hate to read new books. There are twenty or thirty volumes that I have read over and over again, and these are the only ones that I have any desire ever to read at all.' It would be wrong to regard Hazlitt simply as an eccentric. A political radical with an interest in the English Romantic poets, he valued the satisfaction to be gained from books well known to him, and was glad to avoid having his 'palate nauseated with the most insipid or vilest trash.' Strong language, but some of the books he liked to reread—such as Henry Fielding's *Tom Jones*—reveal him as a reader of sound judgment. Hazlitt was forty when he wrote his essay (not an old man for his era, but not a young one, either), which may help explain his remark: 'Books have in a great measure lost their power over me; nor can I revive the same interest in them as formerly. I perceive when a thing is good, rather than feel it.' Age and experience can produce a sense of repetition—that one has seen 'it' all before—and Hazlitt could have been suffering from this state.

Closer to our own time, among the novelists who have written about rereading, both Larry McMurtry and Susan Sontag emphasized the importance of rereading as an act of understanding, with Sontag quipping, 'Most of my reading is rereading.' And John Irving has remarked frankly, 'When I love a novel I've read, I want to re-read it—in part to see how it was constructed.' The literary critic Patricia Meyer Spacks has even written an academic book about the subject, *On Rereading* (2011). All of them would likely agree with the critic Harold Bloom, who has argued that rereading is the only way to truly know a book. But rereaders aren't always teachers or novelists. In the summer of 2009 a cluster of articles about rereading appeared. Verlyn Klinkenborg in the *New York Times* ('Some Thoughts on the Pleasures of Being a Re-Reader'), Roger Angell in the *New Yorker* ('Two Emmas'), and David Gates in *Newsweek* ('Now, Read It Again') all wrote about it, and David Bowman returned to it for the Book Review of the Sunday *New York Times* ('Read It Again, Sam'). One recurring idea was best expressed by Klinkenborg: 'The characters remain the same, and the words never change, but the reader always does.' It's this notion of change that intrigues me. Whether from curiosity or for escape or nostalgia, we reread in the shadow of memory, which may be part of the pleasure. Who were we? Who are we? What matters? What doesn't? Meyer Spacks suggests that rereading can seem like an indulgence because most people have limited time and there's always an unread book waiting. I'm not convinced by her argument. Reading can never be exhaustive as long as people keeping writing. As we reread, we have to look at ourselves more closely. Tastes may change, or evolve, but do individuals change as much as we sometimes tell ourselves?

The books of one's teenage years vary from one generation to another and shape reading habits for years to come. From the seventh grade on, when I read my mother's copies of *From the Terrace* and *A Rage to Live*, I longed to be an adult, with the freedom to go to the theatre, enjoy martinis and have an adulterous affair—though I wasn't quite sure why. I may have belonged to the last generation of young North Americans to carry around thick copies of Russian novels. Somehow we knew that these were the books we *should* be reading, books that belonged to the Western canon before it came to be regarded as oppressive rather than liberating. Where did our idea—a kind of aspiration—come from? As a teenager I had part-time jobs as a library page, first in my high school and then in the local library, and as books passed through my hands, one after another tempted me. I recall this instance vividly—after watching a Hollywood version of *The Brothers Karamazov* in the ninth grade, I borrowed the library's copy and convinced myself that my family resembled the Karamazovs because my maternal grandfather reminded me of Lee J. Cobb as the movie's difficult Papa K. This was unfair to both

Dostoevsky and to my grandfather, but that didn't matter then because I wanted to measure my own experience against the books I read.

Fiction's capacity to take readers back in time to moments in history may explain the teenage taste I had for novels by Thomas B. Costain (*The Black Rose*, 1945), Anya Seton (*The Winthrop Woman*, 1958), Margaret Mitchell (*Gone with the Wind*, 1936), and Irving Stone (*Lust for Life*, 1934), all once bestsellers. Though the dull, flat prose of these books now surprises me, I do recognize the research that went into producing them. The years that followed led me to prefer Marco Polo's *Travels* to Costain, John Winthrop's *Journals* to Seton's bodice-ripper, Mary Chesnut's Civil War *Diary* to Mitchell's romantic saga and Van Gogh's letters to Stone's bio-novel. Growing up explains a lot—growing up and growing away from the taste of the dominant culture's bestsellers. Still, I remember the sense of discovery these novels once gave me; the fact that they were library books gave them a kind of stature. But why should I now care for Kathryn Harrison's novel *Enchantments*, about Rasputin's daughter, or Geraldine Brooks's Civil War fantasia *March*, about the father of the March family in *Little Women*? One day Harrison and Brooks will take their places beside Costain and Seton. Such historical romances are substitutes for the real thing. Of course great writers have set novels in the past—Tolstoy's *War and Peace* (1868) and Lampedusa's *The Leopard* (1958) come to mind—but they weren't using the past to justify colourful adventure or to piggyback on a historical figure. And they were both great writers.

From my plan of rereading I also saw that movies led me, at twelve or thirteen, to many book choices, as if Hollywood validated the library's collection: *The Vikings* introduced Edison Marshall's historical romp and Alfred Hitchcock's *Rebecca* brought up Daphne du Maurier's modern Gothic. And I still have affection for some of these once-popular titles. It's fascinating to thumb through *Books of the Century: A Hundred Years of Authors, Ideas and Literature* (1998), edited by Charles McGrath, which contains reviews culled from the *New York Times*. While there's an emphasis on books that have lasted, reviews of some now-forgotten novels did make it into the 600-page tome—for instance, Herman Wouk's 1955 bestseller, *Marjorie Morningstar*, which *almost* survives a reread. (In his 1956 review of it, Maxwell Geismar concluded with a sniff: '*Marjorie Morningstar* is very good reading indeed. But to this reviewer at least, the values of true culture are as remote from its polished orbit as are, at base, the impulses of real life.') *True culture?* Today I can guess at his meaning, but not at fifteen. Even better than McGrath, the critic Jonathan Yardley has examined his reading life in *Second Readings: Notable and Neglected Books Revisited* (2011). His book strikes me as serious and apt, which means that we probably share some common values and tastes. Yardley finds much to admire in John P. Marquand and praises du Maurier's *Rebecca*, whose 'sales would be envied by many a Flavor of the Month author of ostensibly "serious" fiction'. Wisely, he admits that 'one of the built-in liabilities of doing a series of literary reconsiderations is that it exposes one's treasured youthful tastes to the cold light of a more mature reading.' Rereading can be humbling.

Many of the books I once enjoyed were probably no better than the contemporary novels I easily set aside. My taste and standards, however, have been shaped by half a century of reading. And Sontag, McMurtry, Roth and Meyer Spacks also had decades of reading—and living—under their belts. Age probably accounts for some of the impatience I share with Roth, because a growing sense of mortality does make a difference in what a reader wants from a book, and the consciousness of less time ahead contributes to a shift in taste. One wonders how real people, rather than fictional characters, face the end of their lives: biographies and memoirs, after all, are just obituaries writ large. It's no surprise that much contemporary fiction echoes a novelistic tradition that for centuries has thrived on the twists and turns of a love story. But the search for love—its richness and disappointments,—tells me, with each passing year, less and less that I still *need* to know.

In the spring of 2012, when the Pulitzer Prize committee declined to offer an award for the best novel of the past year, Ann Patchett, who had published a book that some reviewers considered a contender, wrote an op-ed piece for the *New York Times*. In it she took the high road: 'Let me underscore the obvious here: Reading fiction is important. It is a vital means of imagining a life other than our own, which in turn makes us more empathetic beings.' If only it were true. I've known many fiction readers—and writers—who are *un*empathetic to say the least, and my experience surely isn't unique. There's a self-serving edge to Patchett's remarks ('Buy my book,' she implies, 'and you'll be a better person') that troubles me. According to Patchett's logic, fiction suits mainly the very young. If a person hasn't learned empathy by the age of forty, it's probably too late for hope. Think of Cervantes, Balzac, Dickens and Tolstoy: if their novels haven't made better people of us, there's little reason to expect much from new fiction writers. Patchett's touching notion is reduced to a sweet platitude by any daily newspaper.

Although my plan to spark a new taste for fiction wasn't a complete success, perhaps I'm an optimist, at least when it comes to books. I just purchased a copy of the English translation of Herta Müller's novel *The Hunger Angel.* Born in 1953, Müller won the Nobel Prize for literature in 2009. Why not give her a chance? The book sits on my bedside table and I eye it with some trepidation. I *want* to like it. Müller's own story—her girlhood in Romania herding cows, her life in a German-speaking minority under Nicolae Ceaușescu's dictatorship, and the fact that she wrote herself into another life, as well as her mother's years in the Gulag—makes me wish *The Hunger Angel* was a memoir. But it's not, it's a novel. Okay. I reach for it. Maybe this time.

Marginalia

Anyone who keeps a personal library knows the sometimes strange sensation of opening an old book to find marginal comments you've previously made staring you in the face. How long ago did you add that aside? Who were you then? And if you've ever bought an out-of-print book from one of the many online sites, you'll have seen descriptions of available titles that include references to damaged jackets, watermarks and even marginalia. Other people's marginal notes usually seem more objectionable than one's own, but not always.

During a trip to England in 1974, I visited Sissinghurst Castle, an Elizabethan tower beside the famous garden of novelist Vita Sackville-West and her husband, Harold Nicolson (1886–1968), a diplomat and prolific non-fiction writer. I had read his three-volume diary as well as several of her novels, and as a student of the Bloomsbury Group knew something of their unusual marriage. After a morning in Vita's lush white garden, I stopped at the castle's gift shop and purchased a copy of Nicolson's memoir *Some People* (1927), about his early diplomatic career, in a hardback reprint from 1958. The pages had started to yellow but I didn't mind. On returning to Canada I took up the book, found it dull and set it aside for another time.

Forty years later, while pruning books from my overstocked shelves, I came across *Some People*, flipped through a few pages and was now captivated by Nicolson's account of his early years and diplomatic training. What also caught my attention were the faded pencil checks in the margins. I knew they weren't mine, and saw that I must have purchased a used copy of the memoir. This didn't matter, of course, but I was charmed by the fact that the book's previous owner had ticked off clever passages, witty rejoinders and unusual turns-of-phrase that I might have noted myself. I began to look forward to these checkmarks (only 20 in a book of 247 pages), and wondered about this like-minded reader. Who was he or she? Our kinship grew—at least in my imagination—as I read on. Was that reader a member of the Nicolson family, or a guest at Sissinghurst? Might the marks have been made by Harold himself? Unlikely, yes, though they could have been, since he didn't die until 1968. Had my copy of *Some People* been remaindered from a publisher's overstock? All unanswerable questions, but I did enjoy a brief bond with a congenial reader who remains anonymous.

A decade or so after purchasing *Some People*, I borrowed another memoir from the Robarts Library of the University of Toronto: Nina Berberova's *The Italics Are Mine* (1969), in Philippe Radley's translation from the Russian. (The Russian edition, *Kursiv Moi*, appeared much later, in 1983.) Berberova's wonderfully wry, tragic short novels about the White Russian community in Paris after the revolution of 1917 were mostly written in the thirties, becoming popular in translation in the 1990s. After admiring several of them I wanted to know more about Berberova (1901–93). She left St. Petersburg in 1922, settled in Paris three years later, wrote for émigré publications and in 1950 arrived in the United States, where she taught Russian, first at Yale University and then at Princeton.

The library copy of her memoir contained a dozen or so handwritten comments in an elegant bold script that struck me as old-fashioned, perhaps European. They corrected some of Berberova's remarks, with a cumulative tone of distrust. The passages challenged facts, noting, for example that someone had died earlier than Berberova said, or been divorced later. Often the comments began with a phrase like 'but she knew ...' or 'they weren't friends then' or 'she wasn't there ...'. They appeared to come from someone who read and spoke Russian, had been part of the community Berberova discussed, and had once known her. Of course every memoir depends on a writer's personal agenda and memory, yet I wondered why someone had taken the trouble to object in the margins of a library book, feeling compelled to set the record straight, to have their say. When I returned that copy of *The Italics Are Mine*, I urged a librarian to preserve it in a special collection—the marginalia might someday be of interest to a scholar of Slavic literature and didn't belong in the ordinary stacks. Since my suggestion was ignored—the librarian had referred to the book as 'defaced'—those anonymous annotations, and any value they might have had, are lost to us. (Still, it's interesting to think of a book as having a 'face'.) While I now own a paperback of the memoir, yellowing badly since its purchase in 1993, I long to see again that 'defaced' volume from Robarts.

Marginalia is usually anonymous, but not always. In the summer of 1987, Betty Jane Wylie, a Canadian playwright and non-fiction writer, attended a writers' retreat at the Banff Centre. While there she became friends with Tillie Olsen (1912–2007), the American author of a much-loved feminist classic, *Silences* (1978), about the way creative women had been silenced for centuries. Olsen was especially supportive of Wylie's work, and at the end of their time in Banff, Wylie asked Olsen to sign her copy of *Silences*. Olsen agreed, but said she wanted to think about her dedication: she would take the book home with her to San Francisco and mail it back later. Wylie didn't expect to see the book again, since good intentions are easily lost to the claims of daily life.

But after several months Olsen did return the book, and she had annotated many passages that Wylie had ticked, along with many others. (Olsen's handwriting is so minuscule it has to be read with a magnifying glass.) A few examples give the flavor of her remarks. Beside a passage about the poet Rilke, who did not attend his daughter's wedding or even allow a two-hour honeymoon visit to interrupt the solitude he wanted for his writing, Olsen added an asterisk, and another asterisk at the bottom of the page, writing: 'years later I learn he managed time for a love affair though'. Near a passage about writers who have struggled with silence, Olsen addressed Wylie, 'You [underlined twice] already a quality writer These years to be—you will no longer be a silence, an absence—but a presence.' She then quickly returned to the pleasures of literary gossip. Under the italicized heading *Exclusions; Isolations; Patriarchal Atmospheres*, Olsen had quoted the editor/poet A. Alvarez about an encounter with the young poet Ted Hughes and his wife, the writer Sylvia Plath. After this meeting, Alvarez wrote, 'I was embarrassed not to have known who she was.' Alert to marital slights, Olsen added in the margin, 'And Ted Hughes had said, done nothing to tell him about—or include S.—as poet—in any way.' Later, near the end of her book, she scribbled a few words, almost summing up her own philosophy:

> Most of our ills not sexual
>
> ....
>
> Not sexuality over the centuries
> the lifetime language of our bodies but
> tasks, tasks, tasks

Perhaps Olsen felt that she hadn't made her point emphatically enough. (Incidentally, Wylie's copy of *Silences* is now with her literary papers in the Archives and Special Collections of the University of Manitoba.)

The presence of marginalia in any book can raise serious issues. Our own notes are informal, off-the-cuff records of what we once thought, along with the spontaneity of it, and it can be good to pause over them and gauge the way our opinions may have changed, or not. (I don't lend books in which I've made notes—they're for my eyes alone.) The marginal comments of another person, however, take us out of ourselves and our own reading histories. I can't help but think of the anonymous medieval scribes who, in copying ancient manuscripts they couldn't read or decipher, occasionally made marginal jottings. Who were they writing for? That check-maker of *Some People* may have been making tick marks without another reader in mind, but the scribbling reader of Berberova's memoir meant those notes for public consumption, in a kind of dialogue with the book, while Olsen's remarks were a correspondence with both Wylie and with Olsen's own text, adding thoughts from a decade after its publication.

It has become a contemporary practice—or journalistic shtick—to end literary interviews by asking a writer to name historical figures or writers they might like to invite to a dinner party. I would certainly want to meet Nicolson and Berberova, and be joined by the anonymous readers who'd marked up their books. Yet my interest in marginal notes doesn't mean that the next time I order a used book online, I'll look for one with marginalia. I still prefer a pristine copy—ready for my own pen or pencil—but at least I know I might be missing something worthwhile.

Anatomy of *Anatomy of a Murder*

Everything rests on the bones. A screenplay functions like a skeleton, with the joints making movement—a plot or story—possible. In the opening credits of Otto Preminger's film *Anatomy of a Murder* (1959), 'Screenplay by Wendell Mayes' precedes 'Based on the novel by Robert Traver'. Of course there's nothing wrong with this, and Mayes's screenplay was nominated for an Academy Award for best screenplay based on material from another medium (it lost to Neil Paterson's *Room at the Top*). Today Robert Traver's novel *Anatomy of a Murder* (1958) is long out of print and largely forgotten, though his bestseller was once a Book-of-the-Month Club selection. If remembered at all, it's for Preminger's film version, which regularly crops up on the Turner Classic Movies channel, and has been available in various VHS and DVD offerings. The high-definition edition from the Criterion Collection (2012), a stamp of approval in itself, was praised by Dave Kehr in the *New York Times* because it 'returns substance and shading to this black-and-white classic'. In his essay for Criterion's brochure, Nick Pinkerton notes that the film is 'widely considered among the finest trial films ever made', though he adds, rather sniffily, 'maybe more universally loved by law students than cinéastes'. And Foster Hirsch, in his biography *Otto Preminger: The Man Who Would Be King* (2007), concludes: 'It's unlikely that there has ever been a more lucid, more unexpected, and more entertaining movie about the law.'

Yet Hirsch has little to say about Traver's novel, or the bones of the bones; and the seven 'additional features' that make up the second disk that accompanies Criterion's release of the film largely ignore Traver. The features include interviews with Hirsch, with Gary Giddins on Duke Ellington's score, with Pat Kirkham on Saul Bass's credit designs; newsreel footage from 1959 about the making of the film in Ishpeming, Michigan, and Marquette County; location photographs by Gjon Mili; selections from a 1967 episode of the television program *Frontline*, where Preminger debates a stuffy William F. Buckley Jr. about censorship; and scenes from a documentary film in progress about the making of Preminger's film, drawn from a memoir by Joan G. Hansen. Enjoyable and sometimes enlightening, none of these addenda discuss Traver or his novel, although he did spend time on the set and appears in various location photographs. If the contribution of screenplays is to be taken seriously, and adaptations regarded as valuable in themselves, it's important to look not only at the differences between a screenplay and a novel but also at the issues raised by them.

The historical and literary context of Traver's book matters to any discussion of the film. The 1950s are often considered puritanical and prudish, a sexual void. Whatever was happening in the bedrooms across North America—sketched by Alfred Kinsey in *Sexual Behavior of the Human Male* (1950) at the start of the decade, and followed by *Sexual Behavior of the Human Female* in 1953—it took years for novels and movies to catch up with the Kinsey Reports, although the moral status quo of Eisenhower's America sometimes seemed to be under siege by entertainers, from Marilyn Monroe to Elvis Presley. Three controversial bestselling novels from the late 1950s focus on a rape and a sensational trial: Grace Metalious's *Peyton Place* (1956), James Gould Cozzens's *By Love Possessed* (1957) and Traver's *Anatomy of a Murder* (1958); each book was transformed into a successful feature film: *Peyton Place* (1957), *Anatomy of a Murder* (1959), and *By Love Possessed* (1961). Of the three novels, none is read today, and the once-scandalous *Peyton Place*, banned in many American cities, and in Canada, is now available in a paperback edition from Northeastern University Press, with a 24-page introduction explaining what the fuss was about. Of the three films, only *Anatomy of a Murder* has retained its power, and has grown in stature over the last half century. (While the subject of sexual assault had been raised discreetly in several earlier 1950s films—for instance, Elia Kazan's *A Streetcar Named Desire* [1951] and John Ford's *The Searchers* [1956]—the word *rape* was not spoken, nor was the act discussed in any detail.) In his thoughtful study *Movie Love in the Fifties*, James Harvey refers, in passing, only to *Peyton Place*, which he calls a 'Gothic small-town melodrama'. Yet through their legalistic and clinical discussions of rape, these films offered a franker treatment of sexuality than viewers were accustomed to; in fact, the courtroom settings made possible a discussion of sexual relations that would otherwise have been avoided. These films, therefore, paved the way for subsequent representations of consensual sexual relations.

Robert Traver was the pen-name of a Michigan trial lawyer, John D. Voelker (1903–91), who had served as prosecutor of the Upper Peninsula's Marquette County before his appointment as a justice of the Michigan Supreme Court. Also a writer, he published eleven books, including novels, collections of short stories and essays, a memoir and a book about his great love, fishing. (Traver was the maiden name of Voelker's mother.) Although he retired from the bench in 1959, after the success of *Anatomy of a Murder*, none of his subsequent books achieved the popularity of that bestseller. Its power probably relates to its origin. Voelker based his novel on an actual case of his own. On July 31, 1952, an Army lieutenant, Coleman Peterson, shot and killed Maurice 'Mike' Chenoweth, owner of the Lumberjack Tavern in Big Bay, Michigan, and a former policeman, for allegedly beating and raping Peterson's wife, Charlotte Anne. The principals involved were middle-aged and not particularly glamorous. Because of Voelker's defence, Peterson was found not guilty, on the grounds of temporary insanity. Both the novel and the film take their narrative strength not only from Voelker's experience, and the trial itself, but also from his love of legal ambiguities (as well as trout fishing).

Compressing the characters and events of a popular 437-page novel into a screenplay for a film that runs 161 minutes had to be daunting. Before working with Preminger, Wendell Mayes (1919–92) had written and co-written several successfully produced screenplays, including *The Spirit of St. Louis* (1957) with Billy Wilder; *The Hunters* (1958); and *The Hanging Tree* (1959), with Halsted Welles. He worked with Preminger again, on *Advise and Consent* (1962), and penned more than a dozen other filmed screenplays before his death—*Hotel*, in 1967, and *The Poseidon Adventure*, with Stirling Silliphant, in 1972, were the most notable—but *Anatomy of a Murder* is his most significant project. Like Preminger, who had a doctorate in law from the University of Vienna (his father had been the attorney general of the Austro-Hungarian Empire), Mayes brought a parental legal connection to his work—his father was a California lawyer. Yet any sympathy for the legal profession had to serve the requirements of a commercial film, where a courtroom drama, Hollywood style, replaced the mundane realities of an actual trial.

The filmed screenplay resembles a two-act theatrical piece, with Act 1 setting out the case and its complications and Act 2 focusing on the trial itself. Mayes, naturally, cut back on Voelker's long descriptions of legal precedents and conflicting psychiatric theories regarding the insanity defence. He also removed many minor figures (and their histories), who gave the novel its depth and moved it along, and deleted a sub-plot—the conflict between the defence lawyer and the prosecuting attorney, who are running for the same political office. Such changes almost inevitably foreground the rape. Traver's editor at St. Martin's Press, Sherman Baker, had already trimmed back much of the original manuscript's pre-trial exposition to emphasize the drama of trial. That Mayes adheres as closely as he does to the carefully plotted novel, often taking lines of dialogue directly from it, suggests not only his skill as a screenwriter but also his awareness of the book's popularity. Significant changes might have disappointed a public familiar with the story, and damaged the film's box office draw. Mayes was smart enough to recognize the good story at hand, tightening plot lines to make them more filmable.

As the fictional characters who replaced the real-life Petersons, Lieutenant Frederic Manion and his wife, Laura, needed their own unique qualities. Travers took his time setting up the novel's central dilemma, and the troubled marriage at its core. After his hero Paul 'Polly' Biegler receives a telephone call from Laura regarding her husband, who has been accused of the first-degree murder of Barney Quill, a local bar owner, Traver's first-person narrator (and stand-in) describes his initial meeting with Manion: 'My prospective client sat back and regarded me calmly, with eyes that were neither black nor brown, but bafflingly dark; an expression that was neither interested nor disinterested, but aloof, aloofly detached to the point of scorn.' Manion explains that he is thirty-six years old and his wife is forty-one, not thirty-five, as reported in the newspapers. Laura finally enters the novel on page 66, long after Biegler has committed himself to the case. At the courthouse she steps out of a black sedan, followed by her small dog, a terrier:

> The woman wore dark glasses and as she advanced across the lawn toward us I thought for a moment it was a certain Hollywood tigress: she had the same buoyant step, the same free-swinging stride and same generous blouseful; she had even the same mass of piled-up russet hair, the high color, the full cherry-red lips. But, no, it wasn't my lovely celluloid dream queen. Before she reached my car I knew this was the woman over whom my client had killed Barney Quill.

This 'tigress' evokes Rita Hayworth, a 1940s force of nature, and not an ingenue.

Mayes's screenplay, and the casting of two attractive young actors as the Manions—twenty-nine-year-old Ben Gazzara and twenty-four-year-old Lee Remick—heightens the sexual dynamic around the trial and sets the couple off from the frankly middle-aged legal team played by Jimmy Stewart, Arthur O'Connell and Eve Arden (who were all, coincidentally, fifty-one years old). Lana Turner, then thirty-nine, had agreed to play the role of Laura, but withdrew (or was fired), according to Hirsch, because of conflicts with Preminger about the character's down-market wardrobe. Turner's more mature sexuality would certainly have been truer to the novel and changed the dynamic of the film. (She did star in movie versions of *Peyton Place* and *By Love Possessed*, bringing to her roles the notoriety of her personal life—in 1958, her daughter Cheryl had stabbed to death Turner's underworld lover, Johnny Stompanato.)

When Lee Remick's Laura first meets Stewart's Biegler, the scene is underscored with an alto sax glissando, immediately establishing Laura as a B-movie tramp. Remick plays her that way, implausibly flirting with her husband's lawyer. While leaning against her car, outside the county jail, with her dog on a leash, she says, 'This is Muff,' nodding at the dog and then, looking Biegler over, adds, 'You're tall.' In Traver's novel, the dog's name was Rover, but in the film it's changed to Muff, a not-so-subtle shift since *muff* is a slang term for female genitalia. The screenplay reinforces this raunchy aspect of the character with several scenes that do not appear in the novel. When Laura visits Biegler at his house, where he keeps his office, she suggestively lies across the sofa, sipping a beer (and feeding some to her dog). 'What do you do alone in the house if you're not married?' she asks, and as she fondles her beer glass, Stewart asks, 'How about it, are you ready?' There's a pause as they look into each other's eyes. 'I mean,' he continues, 'are you ready to tell me the story?' 'I know what you mean,' she replies breathily. The subsequent interview about the alleged rape is much longer than Stewart's first meeting with the accused murderer, and viewers might be forgiven for thinking that the movie should have been called *Anatomy of a Rape*. When Biegler asks if a woman doesn't know when a man is interested in her, Laura smiles, saying: 'Oh, sure. But that's only usual with me. With men, I mean. Almost all men. Ever since I was a kid. You, for instance, you're interested.' Stewart denies it but his words say one thing and his eyes another. 'It's just the way you look at me,' Laura tells him, and he replies, 'Well, it would be very difficult not to look at you.' Persistent, she adds, 'Oh, the way I dress, you mean. You don't like it?' Her tight sweater and slacks have made their point, and Biegler mumbles, 'Oh, I love it. I just love it.' Oddly, Laura goes on to tell him that she doesn't wear a girdle, but the sexual tension in the scene begins to flatten as Remick, a patrician young woman from New England, exaggerates the character's rough sensuality like a slumming debutante.

By this point in the film, Laura is an ambiguous figure. But she also has to be made a sympathetic one, so the screenplay builds on the tensions in her marriage, emphasizing her husband's irrational, jealous nature. She has never been unfaithful, she assures Biegler: 'Not once. Not ever.' But is she telling the truth? Later, during the trial, when Biegler finds her gallivanting about in a roadhouse, he takes her away from her male friends, cautioning:

> Now until this trial is over you're gonna be a meek little housewife with horn-rimmed spectacles, and you're gonna stay away from men and juke joints and booze and pin-ball machines, and you're gonna wear a skirt and low-heeled shoes and you're gonna wear a girdle, and especially a girdle. Look, Laura, believe me, I don't usually complain of an attractive jiggle, but you save that jiggle for your husband to look at if and when I get him out of jail.

Back at her trailer, Mayes has Laura confess that she wonders what it would be like if Manion wasn't freed: 'It would be one way to end it. No. I didn't mean that. I may think it sometimes but I don't really want it.' Continuing to vamp Biegler, she asks, 'Do you want to come in, Paul? You can if you want to, you know.' Declining, he says softly, 'I'm sorry I had to spoil your fun at that place.' As he goes, she adds, 'I'm lonely, Paul. I'm awful lonely.' Stewart is such an asexual actor that it's difficult to tell if Biegler is even momentarily tempted, but the screenplay has given the audience reason to doubt Laura's veracity. The next scene takes place in the courtroom—the beginning of the trial—where she is as much on trial as her husband.

In an interview from 1989, Mayes told Val Robbins: 'The only thing Otto ever had to say as we went through the script was, "Wendell, I don't know how to shoot this scene," and then he would explain to me why he didn't know how to shoot it. And I would make the necessary changes. He was very considerate, and never changed a word, or even a comma, without my consent.' Whether it was Mayes's idea, or Preminger's, is unclear, but one crucial difference between the novel and the screenplay came with the decision to delete the budding romance between Biegler and Mary Pilant—the young woman who serves as the hostess and manager of Barney Quill's Thunder Bay Inn—and develop Mary's role, with unexpected melodrama. In the film Mary turns out to be Quill's daughter, not just an ex-teacher hired to improve the image of his roadhouse, although their blood relation is not known in the community. Late in the film we learn that Mary is not Quill's mistress, as many locals believe, but his illegitimate daughter, from an Ontario town suitably named Blind River (since Oedipus, blindness has been a trope commonly associated with sexual transgression). In our time of single-parent families, it's worth remembering that illegitimate offspring were once considered shocking; the subject of unwed mothers provided the first of many dark secrets, for example, in *Peyton Place.* Mayes's decision to shift Mary's role from employee to daughter tightens the plot and has a powerful impact on the outcome of the trial, but it also involves one of the film's more bizarre episodes—the matter of the 'panties'.

The film's reconstruction of events leading to Quill's murder, and the alleged rape of Laura Manion, required the direct treatment of an explosive sexual subject. Film audiences of the fifties, however, were accustomed to sparer representations of sexuality than book audiences; as well, the publishing industry faced nothing quite like the Motion Picture Production Code and the Catholic Legion of Decency. Traver's novel is fairly matter-of-fact in its courtroom discussion of the rape, although for legal reasons the prosecution lawyers try their best to keep the matter out of the trial. In the novel, it takes two pages for Biegler to convince the judge that he should be allowed to cross-examine a prosecution witness who has inadvertently brought up the rape by referring to it euphemistically as 'some trouble'. Pleased with the opportunity, he offers only legal reasons, adding, 'It would be a pity, Your Honor, to inject grave error into this case when we are so close to being done.' After Biegler notes that 'the prosecution wants to separate the motive [for murder] from the act', he offers a Biblical metaphor, comparing this approach to 'trying to take the core from an apple without breaking the skin. I beg the court—I beg the court—to let me cut into the apple.' Like Adam, he wants to consume Eve's sinful apple—sex and knowledge are combined.

Mayes must have known that his adaptation would face the censors: the words *rape*, *raped* and *raping* appear thirty-four times in the film, along with *sperm, spermatogenesis, sterile, intercourse, fertile, relations, contraception, completion, violation* and *sexual climax*, which are mentioned at least once. (It does not include such words from the novel as *gonorrhea, vaginal orifice, cervix, womb, dilator* and *seminal fluid.*) It's a commonplace in criticism about Preminger that he welcomed censorship battles, and that his struggles around the words *virgin* and *pregnant* in *The Moon Is Blue* (1953) taught him the publicity value of defying censors. His decision to film *Anatomy of a Murder* surely reflected his desire to have another go at them.

While neither Traver's novel nor Preminger's film show the much-debated encounter between Laura and Barney Quill, one detail is constant in both: after Laura accepts a late-night ride home from Quill, and he drives to a dark road where he may or may not have raped her, her underpants disappear; the police search for them to no avail. Traver is content to leave it at that, but not Mayes. In a scene that addresses the jury and the courtroom as well as the movie's audience, Judge Weaver (played by an actual judge, Joseph N. Welch), brings up the matter of the missing underwear. With the defence lawyer (Stewart) and two prosecuting lawyers (George C. Scott and Brooks West) all looking up at him in the frame, Weaver states: 'There's a certain light connotation attached to the word *panties*. Can we find another name for them?' 'I never heard my wife call them anything else,' replies West; 'I'm a bachelor,' Stewart says; and 'I was overseas during the war, your honor. I learned a French word. I'm afraid it might be slightly suggestive,' says Scott. 'Most French words are,' Weaver replies. None of these legal minds can come up with the simple word *underpants*, and the dialogue's true intent—titillating the audience with the word *panties*, which is repeated thirty times in the film—has taken place. The camera then closes in on Weaver, who adds:

> This pair of panties will be mentioned again in the course of this trial and when it happens there will not be one laugh, one snicker, one giggle, or even one smirk in my courtroom. There isn't anything comic about a pair of panties which figure in the violent death of one man and the possible incarceration of another.

Of course everyone in the courtroom snickers.

The screenplay builds on this fascination with Laura's missing underwear, and when she takes the stand and, finally, is allowed to discuss the rape, prosecution lawyer Dancer/Scott, moving closer and closer, until their faces almost touch, asks, 'Do you always wear panties, Mrs Manion?' She shakes her head negatively when he repeats the question. With Laura's underwear now taking a central role in the trial, the film deviates from the novel. In an unexpected turn of events—a kind of eleventh-hour rescue for the accused—Mary Pilant appears as a last-minute defence witness. Bringing with her the missing underpants, which she found at the hotel, she hands them over to Biegler. Offering the garment as proof of the rape, he describes them as 'badly torn, as if they'd been ripped apart by powerful hands'. Exactly why rapist Barney Quill tossed the dangerous lingerie into the hotel's laundry, rather than disposing of it, is bypassed—he was careful not to leave it at the crime scene, yet he wasn't saving it as a perverse souvenir. No matter. Stewart/Biegler has won his case. Meanwhile, Mayes's decision to delete any romance between Pilant and Biegler improves the story, leaving the middle-aged legal team alone with their habits—fishing, drinking, obsessive secretarial tidying up—in a more realistic portrait of aging than appears in the novel. Both film and novel conclude with the Manions skipping town, which was Voelker's actual experience with the Petersons. By setting aside the novel's happier, potentially fairy-tale ending (middle-aged lawyer finds attractive young love), Mayes closes on a darker portrait of sexual bondage—one that gives the film not only its integrity but also its currency. However, since Laura's 'panties' remained missing in the novel, the book finishes with a powerful ambiguity (had she accepted Quill's advances? had she been beaten by her jealous husband? did she and Manion conspire to cheat the justice system?); the recovered torn garment in the film confirms Laura's story, and undercuts Traver's ambiguity.

Sex is the driving force in Preminger's *Anatomy of a Murder*, not the law. This is one of the key differences between novel and film—a difference generally overlooked in commentary about it, which regards Preminger's *Anatomy* as his paean to the American system of justice. Although this may be superficially true, everything in the film that honours the legal system comes from the novel, while some of its more curious digressions are pure Hollywood. While Voelker happily became part of the film company, his presence also seems like a publicity gimmick. Preminger even included him in the film's clever trailer, where both men appear in a mock swearing-in of the cast, which Voelker finds 'highly irregular'. But, asks Preminger in a thick accent, 'Didn't you approve the screenplay by Wendell Mayes?' 'Yes.' Voelker nods. 'And didn't you, being not only a bestseller novelist but also a justice of the Supreme Court of Michigan, didn't you supervise every single legal detail in the film?' 'Yes, Otto,' he agrees.

Preminger had wanted Burl Ives to play the trial's presiding judge, but ultimately, at the suggestion of a press agent, he cast eminent Boston lawyer Joseph N. Welch in the role. Admired for his work as Army counsel in the Army-McCarthy hearings of 1954, Welch had famously addressed the demagogue with a question that punctured McCarthy's hold on power: 'Have you no sense of decency, sir, at long last?' Criterion's brochure includes Ernest Havermann's notable article, 'Joe Welch in Juicy New Role', from the May 11, 1959, issue of *Life* magazine. Welch agreed to participate in the film as long as it treated the legal system accurately, and his letters to Voelker criticize the romantic falsifications of most screenwriters (he claimed, for instance, that he never saw a judge use a gavel to quiet an unruly courtroom, and he wouldn't use one in the film). According to Havermann, Welch was particularly concerned about courtroom humour, and at his request one scene was rewritten to accommodate an objection. A memorandum, reputedly from Preminger, notes that the jury will laugh only at remarks from a witness, not from a lawyer, and that 'They will laugh at any damned thing in the world the judge says if the judge himself obviously thinks it is funny.' That said, there are courtroom antics aplenty in *Anatomy of a Murder*. If some of these sound suspiciously like the behaviour on an episode of *Perry Mason*, the popular television drama that began its decade-long run in the fall of 1957, well, Preminger had to be aware of the tremendous popularity of the series. When critics like Hirsch and Pinkerton suggest that Preminger's hero has nothing in common with the righteous Mason, they need to look again at a few episodes, available on DVD. Some of the more theatrical moments during the film's trial include: bringing Muff, the dog, into the courtroom, where the dog jumps into the lap of the fussy prosecuting attorney, Dancer; during the prosecution's cross examination of the coroner, Biegler's ostentatious fiddling with a fishing lure (which he later gives the judge); the predictable moment of revelation when Laura/Remick, who wears glasses and a large hat to cover her pinned-up hair, removes the hat and tosses her mane about, to illustrate her desirability, evoking loud outbursts of anger and sarcasm from various lawyers. The trial scene with the dog is itself instructive. In the novel, Biegler asks the judge for permission to bring in the dog for demonstration. When the judge queries the demonstration, Biegler explains his reasons for it:

> 'First, that the dog is both small and friendly and was unlikely either to dissuade the deceased or protect the witness and, second, that the animal and its flashlight could indeed have lit the witness through the stile near the park gate, as she testified.' I paused. 'And there is a third reason, Your Honor,' I said. 'To prevent Mr Dancer from thereby making a slavering mastiff out of this little dog if we are not allowed to produce him.'

In the film no reasons are given, and the dog simply occasions laughter in the courtroom and probably the movie theatre. Perry Mason never had it so good. Erle Stanley Gardner, his creator and also a lawyer, knew the value of melodrama, and like him, Voelker did include some courtroom antics in his novel, but the film emphasizes them, sometimes as a kind of comic relief but also to keep the audience—if not the jury—on the edge of their seats.

Many of the other differences between novel and film may at first seem slight, especially when compared to the compression of two strands of plot into one, and the emphasis on sexuality, but in their own way the film's changes influence its impact. In life, Peterson shot Chenoweth on a night at the end of July, and Traver kept the same seasonal background in his novel; an aura of end-of-summer ripeness overlay the subsequent September trial. Once Preminger decided to film on location in Michigan's Upper Peninsula, to give the film its unique atmosphere, the shooting schedule—which began at the end of March 1959, and ran through much of April—could not capture the heat of summer. The screenplay includes no seasonal references. While the characters sometimes drive about in convertibles with the tops down, the wintry beginning of spring provides the film's dour setting. The trees are barren and leafless, and even the bushes around the courthouse appear, skeleton-like, only as bare branches. Preminger decided to use Voelker's actual Michigan house for Biegler's home, while in the novel he lives in an apartment over the town's five-and-ten, in an inherited family building (the family money came from brewing beer). However, Mayes's hero, like Traver's Biegler, smokes 'stinky' Italian cigars and devotes considerable time and thought to fishing, though exactly why the trout season appears to be in full swing so early in the year is unclear (Maida, Biegler's secretary—played by Eve Arden—quips at one point, 'If this refrigerator gets any more fish in it, it'll swim upstream and spawn all by itself'). Traver's hero had once played some drums at the Thunder Bay Tavern, but the film's Biegler appears to be a gifted jazz pianist, who naturally joins Duke Ellington when he appears, with his combo, as a character called Pie-Eye—out of place in his flashy sports coat in a backwater roadhouse, which comes across as definitely more urban than what one would find in an Upper Peninsula resort town. The film's jazzy score by Ellington reinforces the *noir* quality that makes *Anatomy of a Murder* echo Preminger's most memorable success, *Laura* (1944), a film also thick with conflicting sexual tensions. Details, yes, but all significant.

Preminger's *Anatomy of a Murder* has earned its place among admirable mid-century American films, but what about Traver's novel? Is it worth reading today? The strengths of the film depend so much on the book itself that the question is inevitable. It is disingenuous to praise the contribution of the film's credit designs or the soundtrack or the location footage while bypassing the genesis of the film, or simply referring to the novel as a bestseller, as if that was Preminger's sole reason for acquiring the film rights. Traver's novel, in fact, has far more energy, wit and intelligence than any of John Grisham's currently popular legal thrillers. It's important to remember that yesterday's bestsellers aren't always dated, that the canon of worthy books does change over time and that forgotten, entertaining novels—like once popular but neglected movies—may still have a great deal to tell us about ourselves.

The Return of Two Writers: Eleanor Perényi, Grace Zaring Stone and Ethel Vance

Books rarely get a second or third chance, but the reprint of Grace Zaring Stone's novel *The Bitter Tea of General Yen* (1930), and an upcoming reprint of Eleanor Perényi's memoir *More Was Lost* (1946), will give them a well-deserved lease on life. And, oddly enough, it was Bette Davis who made their connection for me, even pointing the way to Stonington, Connecticut, although I don't know if the born-and-bred Yankee actress ever visited there herself. When I arrived, during a bicentennial that marked the three-day battle of August 1814 in the War of 1812, my visit focused on meeting Peter Perényi, the son of a writer I much admired.

In 1981 Eleanor Perényi published a garden book that seemed destined to become a classic. *Green Thoughts: A Writer in the Garden* took the form of an abecedarian, from 'Annuals' to 'Woman's Place', and was praised by Anatole Broyard, Brooke Astor, John Hollander and Mary McCarthy. Perényi told of making her garden outside an old house in Stonington, offering not only practical advice but a rich cultural perspective. The book is still in print, as part of the Modern Library Gardening Series. Soon after reading it, I found Perényi's memoir *More Was Lost*, which attracted me because of my own Hungarian-American background. In 1937, an adventurous young American visiting Budapest with her parents is courted by a dashing, liberal-minded baron twice her age, they marry and she settles on his family's estate in Ruthenia, once part of an old Hungary whose borders frequently changed during the twentieth century. It's a tale of romance (and gardens too) but also of terrible loss, and was reviewed in the *New Yorker* by Edmund Wilson as 'always lucid and crisp' and in *Harper's* as 'disarmingly frank ... a charming story in spite of its tragic overtones of war'. Reprinted in 2001, it is scheduled to become a New York Review Books Classic. One title can lead to another, and I next located a used copy of Perényi's *Liszt: The Artist as Romantic Hero* (1974), which Richard Howard called 'one of the most searching, sophisticated and sensible books' about the romantic hero/composer. As an amateur pianist I devoured every page. Here, apparently, was a writer who could do just about anything.

Now Bette Davis enters, via the Turner Classic Movies channel. One night I tuned into an unfamiliar 1948 film, *Winter Meeting*. During the Second World War, a New England spinster poet (Bette, of course) living in Manhattan befriends a heroic young soldier; they have a brief affair—frankly sexual for its day—and discover secrets about each other that transform but isolate them. I spotted the name Ethel Vance in the credits, located a copy of her out-of-print novel, from 1946, and was won over by an exceptional book that deserves rediscovery. Vance wrote several bestsellers that, along with *Winter Meeting*, were made into movies, including *Escape* (1939, filmed in 1940 with Robert Taylor and Norma Shearer). Advertising for *Escape* claimed that 'Ethel Vance' was a pen-name to conceal the author's identity because she had a daughter who lived in a country falling under Germany's influence. A Google search increased my curiosity: 'Ethel Vance' was the pseudonym of Grace Zaring Stone, author of *The Bitter Tea of General Yen* (also made into a movie, in 1933, starring Barbara Stanwyck and directed by Frank Capra), and—more important to me—Stone turned out to be Eleanor Perényi's mother.

Because I'm drawn to out-of-print books, neglected writers and reputations that have often faded unfairly with time, Ethel Vance's books soon formed a pile on my desk that even included a historical novel by her daughter Eleanor, *The Bright Sword* (1955). After a few telephone calls my visit to Stonington followed, almost inevitably.

Peter Perényi has a gift for storytelling—perhaps inherited?—and a striking resemblance to photographs of his father, Baron Zsigmond (or Zsiga), in *More Was Lost*. Peter's long foreign-service career provided wonderful stories of his own. First we talked in the garden his mother had made (adding to earlier plantings by her mother), and later in the kitchen, with its ambience of former days still maintained. The house, officially dated to 1787, sits on a third of an acre just a block from downtown Stonington—not far from the James Merrill House, where the poet lived for several decades (it is now a museum with a writer-in-residence program). Peter's grandmother Grace, as I've come to think of her, bought the house in 1941 with money from book sales to Hollywood, and it's filled with mementos of family travels from Europe to China and Japan, as well as books and more books. In the dining room an old oil portrait of Peter's great-great-great-great-grandfather, the influential social reformer and utopian writer Robert Owen (who founded the New Harmony community in Indiana) looks out over the mantel.

Our talks naturally began with *More Was Lost*, which closes on an open note—'So perhaps the story has not ended after all'—with Eleanor, pregnant, returning to the United States, and Zsiga remaining in Europe, where he eventually joined an underground group. Were his parents reunited after the war? The moving full story is Peter's to write, but a 1947 divorce ended the marriage, although Peter got to know his father years later (they never discussed *More Was Lost*, but Zsiga did own a copy of it, and the book was finally translated into Hungarian in 2003). Eleanor once said that she wrote her memoir because she 'didn't want to forget'. When Peter visited the ancestral estate in 2002 and brought back pictures of its Soviet transformation, she looked at them and said they reminded her of 'the photo of a friend's corpse propped up'.

It's a long way from Hungary to Connecticut. Stonington in the 1940s drew writers and artists from Manhattan who travelled there conveniently by train, and the town claimed a range of talented residents—some part-time, some full—including the Director of the Metropolitan Museum of Art, Francis Henry Taylor. The poet Stephen Vincent Benét had a house there, Merrill moved to Stonington in 1954, and numerous New Yorkers stopped by—Truman Capote came for the summer of 1956, complained that Medaglia d'Oro coffee was unavailable in the village and called it 'creepyville'; later literary residents included the novelist Peter Benchley of *Jaws* fame and the poet and librettist J.D. McClatchy. Grace settled in full-time after 1956 and the death of her husband, a naval captain, with Eleanor following around 1962. (*Winter Meeting* includes a visit to a small New England seaport clearly patterned on Stonington, which is located three miles from the more touristy Mystic.) Merrill became close to both women, dedicating *Water Street* (1962) to them, and he wrote several poems for Grace, including '1939' from *Nights and Days* (1966) and 'Grace', about the aging writer, from *The Inner Room* (1988).

In his memoir *A Different Person* (1993) Merrill noted that 'Grace was the most cosmopolitan of our Stonington neighbors', and recalled her 'exhaling smoke and taking on the aspect of the famous novelist she had once been'. (Peter said his grandmother and mother both 'smoked like chimneys', though Eleanor eventually had to stop because of emphysema.) Their circle came to include Merrill's longtime companion David Jackson and Robert Morse, a painter and poet who lived across the street from Grace (his oil portrait hangs in her old bedroom). At our second meeting, Peter and I visited the Stonington cemetery, where Grace and Eleanor are buried beside each other, a stone's throw from Merrill's grave. This part of the cemetery is known as 'the poet's corner' (the drama critic John Mason Brown's grave is also nearby) and Eleanor once remarked that 'the cemetery would make the most amusing cocktail party in Stonington'.

But what about two writers, mother and daughter, living in the same house? Each had a studio on the top floor, on opposite ends, but Peter has no recollection of their discussing works in progress, or sitting together and working on something. Eleanor, 'a perfectionist', likely kept her writing to herself. According to Peter, mother and daughter 'saw eye to eye on an awful lot. They were a social unit, accustomed to each other's company from living close by if not together'. And both enjoyed gardening; Grace was especially interested in the idea of the garden. Their Stonington land had been planned as a series of outdoor rooms, including Grace's rose beds and Eleanor's vegetable plot. Grace sometimes liked to write under the grape arbour.

As a child Eleanor had been told that the most important thing was to have an interesting life, and she took this to heart. Both women loved travel and its adventures, and found a way to be intensely independent. Yet as writers with a deep emotional and blood connection, they must have learned to accommodate each other. In an evocative short memoir of the writer and photographer Carl Van Vechten, a friend who took handsome photographs of mother and son, Eleanor recalled meeting him at a dinner party in the 1940s: 'I was much the youngest and least important person present—an appendage, really, of my mother ...' That status didn't last. It is, however, interesting that the possibilities of literary work were divided between the two women, with Grace devoting her time to fiction and Eleanor, with one exception, to non-fiction; they had split the prose world in half. As well, the subject of mother-daughter relations seems to have been off limits. The bond between mothers and sons has a significant role in Grace's fiction (*Escape, The Grotto*), but her books with young women as central figures focus on motherless women (*Reprisal, Winter Meeting, The Secret Thread*).Grace's own mother had died in childbirth, a psychic wound any writer might be expected to address, but she treats the subject only in passing. (In a 20-page poem called 'The Summer People', a rueful satire about Stonington from his 1969 collection, Merrill based two characters—a mother and daughter team named Nora and Margaret—on Eleanor and Grace, and his portrait of their affectionate but sometimes lively bickering nearly caused a permanent rift in the friendship.)

The relation between a writer's life and work is easily over-simplified, yet the connection here merits attention. Grace lived a peripatetic childhood, moving from relative to relative. She spent time in New Harmony and later lived with an actress-relation, even working as a child actor. For the jacket of *The Secret Thread* (1948) she wrote: 'In New York we lived in an actors' boarding house like the one described in my book. Also, because the family so disapproved of the whole thing, I was given a stage name. An old coloured woman in the boarding house picked it out from some book or play she enjoyed. It was Ethel Vance.' After studying at the Sacred Heart Convent in New York and Paris, Grace travelled in Europe, even acted in Australia (Peter also remembers stories of horseback riding in New Mexico). During her marriage to Ellis Spencer Stone they were stationed for a time in the Virgin Islands, where she began to write. Her second novel, *The Bitter Tea of General Yen*, brought the success many writers dream of, with praise in *The Nation* ('extraordinarily effective') and a film adaptation that opened the Radio City Music Hall. It was followed by a historical novel, *The Cold Journey* (1934), about an Indian massacre in Puritan New England, which Carl Van Doren called 'a novel of concentrated power and sensitive beauty'. Next came *Escape* (1939). In *What America Read: Taste, Class, and the Novel, 1920–1960* (2009), Gordon Hutner calls Grace's pseudonymous work 'the first best-selling book about Nazis and one of the most popular novels of 1939', adding that 'It was rumored to have been written by almost every woman writer but Stone.' Her identity was revealed by the *Saturday Evening Post* in May 1942.

A pattern had been set. Matters of captivity, escape and rescue—usually within a clash of cultures—are at the core of Stone's fiction. In her earliest books, extreme situations dominate: a New England missionary woman is held captive by a refined Chinese warlord in *Bitter Tea*, and, in a reversal that hints at miscegenation, he becomes captive to his feelings for her; French and Indian raiders forcibly take Massachusetts settlers into Canada in *Cold Journey*; a son rescues his actress/mother from a Nazi concentration camp in *Escape*; and an entire French village is threatened because of anti-Nazi activity in *Reprisal* (1942). Although the threat is external, in each novel the victim has to examine the self because of his or her plight. Later, after the Second World War, captivity takes on a deeper psychological dimension. In *The Secret Thread* a university president has a nervous breakdown after witnessing end-of-war horrors, and must confront his past; in *Winter Meeting*, two almost-lovers face debilitating personal confusions; and in *The Grotto* (1951, published in England as *My Son Is Mortal*), a mother tries to understand her son's homosexuality in one of the first novels to broach the subject.

Grace's long friendship with the Charleston novelist Josephine Pinckney, discussed by Barbara L. Bellows in her biography of Pinckney, *A Talent for Living* (2006), illustrates the obstacles women writers faced in the years before World War II. It's no surprise they sometimes used feminine charm to survive in a publishing environment where successful writers such as Edna Ferber and Fanny Hurst mainly claimed the field of popular fiction. Yet Grace enjoyed the role of the 'femme fatale', according to Bellows, with quips like this: 'What the American businessman can't stand, his wife can!' Her books, however, bear no relation to the romantic novels of the era. Her male characters are not erotic projections but rather believable beings often preoccupied with internal conflicts, and her female characters have strong, subtle minds. Grace's interest in ideas and philosophy enlarges her fiction, and her books often explore ethical matters and religious belief. Peter aptly described his grandmother's vision to me as 'a dark one', yet his portrait of her suggested a warm-hearted woman of deep understanding, which the rich characterizations in her fiction confirm. That she also had a mischievous side made sense. 'She liked to say she was a witch', he remarked, acknowledging the mystical aspect of her Celtic heritage. She must have been a powerful role model.

Eleanor, born in 1918, travelled widely with her parents as a child, and later remembered being taken to China at the age of nine, where, during the civil war, she had counted human corpses on the Yangtze River (the details of her mother's novel about China came from first-hand experience). After doing time in an English boarding school, which she hated, Eleanor attended the National Cathedral School for Girls in Washington, which she was asked to leave, without graduating, for smoking on the roof. A passionate autodidact, she intended to become a painter and studied at the Phillips Gallery, but after returning from Hungary in 1940 (first to Washington, D.C., where her son was born), she settled in New York and worked for several years at the notable Julien Levy Gallery, bringing Arshile Gorky's paintings to the attention of Levy, as Hayden Herrera acknowledges in *Arshile Gorky: His Life and Work* (2003).

With *More Was Lost* Eleanor discovered her flair for writing. Dedicated to her son, the book was brought out by Grace's Boston publisher (Little, Brown and Company) in the same year as *Winter Meeting*. The memoir's title evokes an old Hungarian saying: 'More was lost at Mohács' (*Több veszett el Mohácsnál*); the phrase encourages a philosophical shrug at life's tragedies by referring to the Battle of Mohács of 1526, when the small Hungarian army was defeated by the Turks, leaving much of the country subject to a century and a half of Ottoman rule. The baronial way of life that Eleanor recorded has the historical detail of Patrick Leigh Fermor's much-praised account of his 1933 travels through Hungary and Romania, *Between the Woods and Water* (1986), yet there is none of the traveller's distance in her writing since she intended to put down roots. That her youth, beauty and intelligence charmed her husband's family and acquaintances almost goes without saying, and her hard work on the 700-acre estate surely impressed everyone. But history—in the guise of the Nazis—intervened. (Lauding the memoir's 2001 reprint in the *New York Review of Books*, Gore Vidal, who regarded Eleanor as a friend, compared her to Maggie Verver in *The Golden Bowl*, and then added, 'So an Ethel Vance story becomes Henry James.')

The publication of *More Was Lost* must have convinced Eleanor to devote her energies to writing, and she developed her craft with light essays on travel and fashion, as well as book reviews. Like many autodidacts, Eleanor appears to have had great self-confidence, writing about the things that interested her, some closer to her own life than others. A few examples: her time at the Julien Levy Gallery became a smart 1947 satire called 'Art's Sake' for *Town & Country*; she appeared in *Harper's* with 'Dear Louisa' (1955), an appreciation of Louisa May Alcott ('One is not surprised to learn that she did, indeed, die of overwork, at the age of fifty-six, and in the same year as her father, who did so much, in his simple-hearted way, to kill her off'); again in *Harper's*, in 1960, 'After Hours' was a witty account—based on personal experience—of the travails of a magazine editor flooded with proposals for fashion and cooking articles, and 'A Thoroughly Highbrow Cruise', a dry-eyed 1962 travelogue about

Mediterranean culture seekers, with a cameo appearance by the classicist Sir Maurice Bowra, that is wickedly funny. Versatile writers like Eleanor resist simple categorization. With the passing years she went on to write thoughtful essay-length reviews on a wide range of subjects for the *New York Review of Books* (from 1984, 'The Bloom Is Off' refreshingly punctures Bloombury's snobbism). A collection of Eleanor's occasional prose deserves publication: apart from the intrinsic merits of her essays, they belong to a moment of cultural/literary history and help illuminate it.

Introduced to the New York literary world by her mother, Eleanor had earned her own place there through her talent and sophistication. Among her friends she counted Mamaine Koestler, Arthur Koestler's second wife and one of the twin sisters who visited the Perényi estate in 1937, a visit noted in *More Was Lost.* Mamaine characterized Eleanor in a letter to her sister on January 18, 1951: 'It was awfully nice seeing her because she is really intelligent and owing to her European background easy to get on with ... it was so nice to be with an old friend and somebody who knows Europe and likes talking about it.' But New York couldn't hold Eleanor then. To work on her novel *The Bright Sword* (1955), she settled for a year in Mexico, and Peter accompanied her. Although in hindsight he didn't think much writing got done because of the lively artistic and ex-pat community, eventually she did produce a rich historical novel about General Sam Hood and the Civil War battle at Chickamauga, dedicating it 'To My Father and Mother'—to a military man and to a writer, both aspects of her psychic heritage. However, she was deeply sympathetic to the growing civil rights struggle, and chose not to list the novel—with a Southern general as its hero—on her subsequent book jackets.

Once her novel appeared, Eleanor settled back in New York City and for nearly a decade pursued editorial work for magazines, with jobs at *Harper's Bazaar, Charm* and *Mademoiselle*; her own essays appeared in *Atlantic Monthly, Esquire, Harper's, Town & Country* and *Saturday Review.* Now part of the Manhattan literary milieu, she wrote the first feature article about Edmund Wilson for *Esquire* in 1963 and, like her 1988 memoir of Carl Van Vechten for the *Yale Review*, it's worth reading today. In *The Tastemaker: Carl Van Vechten and the Birth of Modern America* (2014), Edward White pays short shrift to his subject's last decades, but Eleanor's essay (not mentioned) offers one corrective. She concluded with an anecdote about photographs that Van Vechten—affectionately known as Carlo—had taken of her son when he was six years old:

Prints were sent to the boy's Hungarian grandfather in Budapest, who because of the war had never seen him, and as it turned out never would. The old man died within a few months of receiving them, but we heard later that he had asked for them to be buried with him. Carlo wasn't strong on family feeling. He had no children and was, as he put it, 'wildly against childbirth. People will be starving in the streets'. But when I told him this story he had tears in his eyes—the only time I ever saw that happen.

Eleanor enjoyed having her say. When Jeffrey Meyers interviewed her in 1993 for his biography *Edmund Wilson*, she commented that Wilson, who claimed to be fluent in Hungarian, couldn't speak the language 'and was unfamiliar with nuances of usage', while of her friend Mary McCarthy—Wilson's second wife—she said, 'Nobody could make Mary do what she didn't want to do.' In his youthful travels with his mother, Peter encountered many of the famed writers of the era, and he remembered one weekend visit at Mary McCarthy's when Hannah Arendt dropped by and the three women debated the best way to load a dishwasher.

Eleanor's Liszt biography came next. While the Stonington house no longer has the baby grand that had taken up space in the living-room, classical music mattered to both mother and daughter (James Merrill recalled that 'a tattered score of *Manon*' was kept on the piano). *Liszt* is a group portrait, not simply a musical biography, and as such a contribution to studies on the Romantic sensibility. From the first page Eleanor's sympathy and reservations are clear:

The Romantic ego is insufferable and Liszt is of all Romantics the most insufferable. He had to be. He had somehow to keep afloat in the era that replaced the diligence with the steam engine, invented the telegraph and the universal press. He was a witness at the birth of the philistine. The pit-falls are familiar now that we know about mass taste and the maw of fame that devours all but the most resistant of culture heroes, the blowing up of a personality until it bursts. He had no such examples to go by.

Reviewing *Liszt* for *High Fidelity*, the editor Patrick J. Smith wrote that Perényi, though not a trained musicologist, 'has succeeded in stripping away all of the myths about Liszt and the figures around him and has evaluated each of them and the times in which they lived more thoroughly than ever before'. If there's a caveat, he handled it gracefully: 'While some may object to Mrs Perényi's frequent use of the first person in the expression of opinions, these opinions generally show so much insight that the objection quickly fades.' After all, the root word of *amateur* is *amour*. In 1979 she returned to the subject of classical music with a 23-page booklet called *Great Men of Music: Shostakovitch and his Music* that accompanied an RCA set of four records devoted to the composer. Peter remembered Grace asking, 'Who does Grandmother love?' and rather than giving the expected answer 'Peter', his impish reply was 'Beethoven and Mozart'. Eleanor might have added Liszt and Shostakovitch.

A gardener's work is never finished because the idea and reality of a garden are bound to daily life, and inhabit flux. Eleanor understood this conundrum and wrote accordingly. *Green Thoughts* is a masterwork that sits comfortably on any shelf beside the best of Gertrude Jekyll, Vita Sackville-West and Katharine S. White. The title—taken from Andrew Marvell's poem 'The Garden' (circa 1680)—suits the task Eleanor set for herself. And a daunting one it was, for she admitted that she was not a horticulturalist: 'All I can claim is some thirty years of amateur experience, which is to say that I know something about a lot of things and not enough to call myself a specialist in any.' But she was a writer, and, as her foreword concludes, 'a writer who gardens *is* sooner or later going to write a book about the subject—I take that as inevitable'. In meditations that range from the pleasures of a summer garden's night scents to reflections on the 17th-century tulip-mania in Holland to the challenges of managing an asparagus bed, she bridges the world of the enthusiast with that of the specialist (including local nurserymen and famed gardeners), as well as discussing matters of history and literature that touch on her subject—whatever strikes her fancy. Yet the seriousness of her study never overwhelms her wry sense of humour and enthusiasm for the quotidian. In one brief essay called 'Reward' she quotes a passage from Merrill's poem 'From the Cupola':

> Finally I reach a garden where I am to uproot
> the last parsnips for my sister's dinner
> Not parsnips mastodons …

and Eleanor exclaims, 'Those parsnips, you see, were mine. I planted them, then went away that winter, commending the vegetables to his care.... The parsnips have made it into literature.' The crisp, elegant style that grounds Eleanor's sharpest insights makes her book essential reading for anyone interested in what good prose can be. And her style—with its clarity, balance and harmony—shows a debt to Grace's.

While Eleanor's non-fiction has stood the test of decades, if not a larger span of time, what about Grace's novels? Popular fiction from the past has often been dismissed since Virginia Woolf offered her critique of 'middlebrow' writing in *The Death of the Moth* (1942), and Dwight Macdonald followed in 1960 with an influential essay 'Masscult and Midcult', later included in his collection of that name (and reprinted as a New York Review Books Classic). More recently, books such as Joan Shelley Rubin's *The Making of Middlebrow Culture* (1992) and Franco Moretti's *The Bourgeois: Between History and Literature* (2013), have taken the subject for academic study. I raise this issue because writers like Grace can too easily be lumped under the heading of 'past bestsellers' and set aside. That does justice to no one—not to the writers and their books, not to the past, nor to contemporary readers. Too often 'popular' and 'middlebrow' are seen as the opposites of 'modernist' or 'avant-garde', which may reveal a critical bias against realism. And we may still be too close to the 1930s and '40s to appreciate their ambiguities.

Grace's fiction is not experimental, and her prose is spare and fluid rather than self-consciously literary. In an interview for the *New York Times* in 1942, she said: 'I know that my stories don't resemble in the least the books of Virginia Woolf. I don't try to imitate genius—naturally. Why should I? I work terribly hard to tell a story effectively, and do a good tight construction job, because I can do that much. I can be a craftsman.' Her lapidary style suits her record of the dilemmas and contingencies of trying to live humanely. While she doesn't avoid situations that might tip a less skillful writer into melodrama, Grace's plot turns emerge from her characters' temperaments and are not imposed on them for the satisfactions of a page-turner. And she has a keen sense of irony that never falls into smugness. Anyone who has admired Alan Furst's engaging espionage novels would do well to pick up *Escape* for its wartime plot, strong characterization and palpable intrigue, and *The Bitter Tea of General Yen*—a more nuanced version of the East-West cultural clash than anything by Pearl Buck (and published two years before *The Good Earth*)—is as historically smart as recent fiction by Amy Tan and Lisa See. Arguably her most intense and original novel, *Winter Meeting* is a psychologically probing account of desire that rejects the conventions of its day. The struggle of its characters to reveal themselves through loving has few counterparts in American fiction by women writers of the forties. *Winter Meeting* evokes the best of Elizabeth Bowen, and prefigures subsequent work by novelists such as Mary McCarthy in the 1950s. Like Grace's other novels, it doesn't offer easy certainties or the 'middlebrow' reassurance that life is always worth living.

The two women aged together. Grace lived to see one hundred, and died in a Connecticut nursing home in 1991; her last novel was published when she was seventy-seven. Eleanor's final book appeared when she was a young sixty-three. Caring for her mother, and surviving various debilitating illnesses of her own (including legal blindness), kept her occupied until she died in 2009 at ninety-one, with Peter by her bedside. During our visit to the Stonington cemetery Peter wondered aloud if he should clean the lichen from Grace's gravestone. I said that I liked it, somehow the mossy growth seemed right. What matters now is that two writers left us some very fine books, and we owe them both a debt of gratitude. It can only be repaid by reading these books.

The Cyborgs Next Door: Thinking About Posthuman Studies

The lure of vampires made a kind of sense. While androids, avatars, mechanical dolls, cyborgs and their like never caught my imagination, zombies gave me pause. But when an imaginative student proposed a senior independent-reading course called 'Posthuman Studies', I finally had to ask what was going on? Have we now finished with being human? Or are we just tired of it?

In the last few decades, posthuman studies—a hybrid offshoot of science fiction, anthropology, technology studies, literary theory, philosophy and futurology—has become a hot academic field. It's an umbrella term that covers artificial intelligence, biotechnology, cybernetics, even neuroscience and psychology. Just a century old, the word *posthuman* made its first appearance, according to the *Oxford English Dictionary*, in 1916, in relation to speculation about human evolution, genetic or bionic. With the tradition of Victorian science fiction behind it, *posthuman* also incorporated nineteenth-century evolutionary thought. Subsequent usage both echoes and expands the sci-fi (or SF) tradition. In her influential essay 'The Cyborg Manifesto: Science, Technology, and Socialist-Feminism in the late Twentieth Century' (1985), anthropologist Donna Haraway used the cyborg figure to argue that there was no such thing as fixed human identity, thus erasing the boundaries between humans and machines, to advocate the idea of fluid identities. This challenges the Western humanist concept of the 'human' as well as ideas of free will and natural law, which regard human nature as constant, perhaps unalterable.

Who, then, is posthuman? The cyborg figure—a bio-organic, mechanical and electronic being, hence part human and part machine—is only one model. Alterations to the human, as we currently conceive it, could, for instance, be brought about by genetic engineering, computer implants, neural therapies, longevity extension and psychopharmacology. Humans and posthumans might exist side by side, rather like Neanderthals and early humans once did, even interbreeding, although the greater abilities of posthumans could suggest that they finally triumph, as humans superseded Neanderthals.

Naturally there have been additions to Haraway's work. In *The Post-Human Manifesto* (1988), Steve Nichols argued that humans were already posthuman, while in *How We Became Posthuman: Virtual Bodies in Cybernetics, Literature, and Informatics* (1999), N. Katherine Hayles—a research chemist turned literary critic—posited that 'information lost its body' and is now 'an entity separate from the material forms in which it is thought to be embedded'. If, as she argued, the essential function of both humans and machines is processing information, then, like machines, we're merely processors. Eventually the cultural critic Francis Fukuyama, of the-end-of-history fame, applied the term in *Our Posthuman Future: Consequences of the Biotechnological Revolution* (2002), which discussed the impact of biotechnology on democracy. All of these writers ponder human transformation in an advanced technological age.

But let's begin at the beginning, with the prefix *post*, which exudes an elegiac air. In the term *posthuman* it almost suggests that humanity has been left behind in some extraneous era. One problem with *post*—derived from Latin, and meaning 'after'—is that we've become addicted to it. Think of just the following terms: post-Romantic, post-Impressionist, postmodern. (In some instances *post* is followed by a hyphen, but not always.) As an adjective, hyphenated terms with *post* often refer to art-historical styles, such as post-Impressionist painting and post-Romantic music. The term *postmodernism*, without a hyphen, has been commonly embraced by theorists since Jean-François Lyotard's now-classic study *The Postmodern Condition: A Report on Knowledge* (1979), although many of the vaunted features of literary postmodernism—the fragment, irony, collage, pastiche and parody, and an emphasis on relativism—are also features of modernism and appeared, as well, in some Romantic texts. Our fascination with categories almost seems to have exhausted itself in *posthuman*. Just as difficult are the terms *post-history* and *post-historical*, associated with posthuman studies but popping up elsewhere. A *Wall Street Journal* review of a memoir by Imre Kertész, the Hungarian writer who received the Nobel Prize for Literature in 2002, praised Kertész for surviving in 'a derivative, post-historical Western Europe'. What could this actually mean? Did history stop half a century ago? The prefix *post* too often signals simplistic thinking or clubby shorthand. When attached to *human*, the combo can have a portentous air, evoking Weltschmerz, malaise, ennui and anomie.

Literary precursors of posthuman studies suggest that the tensions people feel about their machines—an inevitable shadow of the Industrial Revolution—have created doubts about human nature itself. In *R.U.R.* (1923), which stands for 'Rossum's Universal Robots', the Czech playwright Karel Čapek dramatized the plight of two attractive robots, Helena and Primus, built from synthetic organic matter. During the play's finale, after a robot rebellion to supplant the human race, Helena bursts into real tears in a sudden display of emotion, and she and Primus flee the laboratory as the new 'Adam-Eve'. Is it only emotion that makes us human? And does human nature ever change? In post-apocalyptic novels such as *The Chrysalids* (1955), British writer John Wyndham struggled with these questions. 'The essential quality of life is living,' he observed, and 'the essential quality of living is change; change is evolution, and we are part of it.' Not always a reassuring thought. The dystopian nightmare of Philip K. Dick's novel *Do Androids Dream of Electric Sheep?* (1968) became a cult film after Ridley Scott adapted it for *Blade Runner* (1982). The threat comes from genetically engineered creatures, or 'replicants', who can't easily be distinguished from humans. Giving Čapek's concerns a thriller-like twist, the novel and film use a bounty-hunter hero to expose the replicants (empathy is the emotion they lack) before they conquer the weaker humans. Not simple entertainments, or esoteric speculations, such plots embody unconscious fears about the next stage of human evolution.

Despite the abundant writing associated with posthuman studies, it tends to neglect the supernatural and paranormal, including the world of vampires or zombies. Yet the supernatural often explores our deepest dreams and fears, which are crucial to what we mean by the word *human*. Most students I know get their sense of human nature from their popular culture. Since they haven't been required to study much history either in secondary school or at university, they are, in this sense at least, post-historical, and unfamiliar with the ways in which history can shed light on the difficult task of being human. Dependent on their iPads and iPhones, and worn down by the stress of juggling them, and multitasking, they are often devoted to futuristic video games and take comfort in genre fantasy—loving wizards, warlocks, all feats of magic. The non-human seems more exciting than the human, even more sympathetic.

It's a statistical commonplace that many young people today have been raised on psychotropic medications, and there's now a body of research concerning internet addiction. Are drugs and technology the best we can offer future generations? And is it only a coincidence that the American Academy of Arts & Sciences decided to release a grim study, *The Heart of the Matter* (2013), about the state of the humanities in North American universities? The recent emphasis on 'practical' disciplines has occurred at the expense of humanistic studies, disregarding rich speculations of centuries, while commercial pop culture thrives. Anyone who spends time in bookstores knows that the sections devoted to fantasy and sci-fi have exploded since the 1960s cult of Tolkien, which seems quaint by comparison. It's worth remembering that as literary genres fantasy and sci-fi only entered the academic curriculum in the 1970s; large numbers of readers now subsist on writing once dismissed as fringe. Do they sense that the arts and sciences have a great deal to say to each other?

In a mechanized world where human nature has been called into question, non-humans have come to dominate our popular culture. The late-twentieth-century craze for vampire fiction corresponded with the AIDS epidemic, and their connection seems obvious. Fear of contamination through sexual contact with a desirable 'other' plagued the readers of Anne Rice's vampire series (which included gay vampire protagonists). This fear suited such high-style films as *The Hunger* (1983), with glamorous Catherine Deneuve and David Bowie as star-crossed vampire lovers. The trend morphed into a television series, *Buffy the Vampire Slayer* (1997–2003), and television is now awash in undead characters like those of *Vampire Diaries* and *True Blood.* Following on Buffy, there's been Stephenie Meyer's ubiquitous *Twilight* series—also about teenage vampires—and its film adaptations. Fear of contamination was real enough for adolescents too. With the threat of terrorist plots and pandemics beyond the reach of our medical knowledge dominating the news, it's no surprise that the exotic vampire has had staying power. Iconoclastic film director Jim Jarmusch satirized this subject in his melancholy *Only Lovers Left Alive* (2013), where Adam and Eve, a cultured, world-weary vampire couple (Tilda Swinton and Tom Hiddleston), despair of the feckless human race—except for its nutritional value. Incidentally, they refer to humans as 'zombies'.

Humans, of course, are a restless lot, and historically we've enjoyed our own reflections. Although some novelists like Margaret Atwood prefer to call their work 'speculative fiction', which sounds tonier than 'sci-fi', the roots of their writing are as old as storytelling. The tale of Pygmalion, for instance, isn't just source material for George Bernard Shaw's play named after that myth (1912). Rather, it's a powerful enquiry into human aspiration. When the Roman poet Ovid recreated the Greek cosmology in *Metamorphoses* (circa 8 A.D.), where gods and humans intermingle with some strange transformations, his compendium challenged notions of empire and duty by emphasizing individual autonomy and pleasure. Yet Ovid wasn't promoting absolute freedom. His human characters are flawed beings that exist within the moral imperative to be fully human, and their behavior is not given only a psychological explanation. Pygmalion fails because of pride—he seeks a perfect partner, an idealized copy less than human. To be human, then, is seen as something wonderful, with an ethical dimension.

Postmodern variations on Pygmalion's quest replace the ethical model with a therapeutic or psychological one. In *Lars and the Real Girl* (2007), Ryan Gosling plays a troubled young man who takes an inflatable doll with him everywhere as a companion, and manages to get his world to go along with his delusion; the movie ends on a contrived fairy tale note. But good stories don't die so easily. Spike Jonze's film *Her* (2013) stars Joaquin Phoenix as another troubled guy who falls in love with a computer's operating system, names her Samantha (voiced by Scarlett Johansson) and loses all interest in real people. Rather than sculpting a marble statue—an act of creation—these fellows adore mass-produced objects. We've come a long way from Mary Shelley's *Frankenstein* (1818), titled after the doctor who creates the 'monster' from the body parts of corpses. That poor creature sought his own humanity through the act of reading, and no less a book than Milton's epic *Paradise Lost* (1667), where Satan's isolation mirrors the outsider's loneliness. We assume that our creations are like ourselves, with the same desires and fears. Are we now projecting these assumptions onto our machines?

Transhumanism may be part of the answer. The term is popular with futurists who contemplate something like the merging of humans with their machines. Who, or what, will we then be? Of course accounts of smart robots prefigure the posthuman interest in artificial intelligence. In Jacques Offenbach's *opéra comique*, *Les contes d'Hoffmann* (1881), the enchanting mechanical doll Olympia—her name echoing the classical home of the gods, a warning in itself—is, like Dr Frankenstein's monster, the creation of a mad scientist who ends up destroying his handiwork. Fooled by her human appearance, Hoffmann falls in love with the doll, and when the role is sung by a soprano with the right coloratura fireworks, Olympia does appear desirable, until her machinery breaks down. Closer to our time, the Spencer Tracy–Katharine Hepburn romantic comedy *Desk Set* (1957) dramatizes the anxieties about becoming redundant when a computer is installed in the library of a Manhattan media corporation. These anxieties fuel the sparing between Tracy's egghead inventor and Hepburn's defender of human intelligence. After the computer quickly retrieves obscure information, it's patted and praised as a 'good girl', but when it goes haywire, one of Hepburn's hairpins is used for a quick fix and all's well. That premise may now seem laughably naive—especially to moviegoers familiar with Samantha's seductive voice in *Her*—yet *Desk Set* portrayed a genuine mid-century fear of the future: will our computers be better than us?

How do we get from artificial intelligence to creatures with no intelligence at all—to the walking dead who have only the will to consume living flesh? Unlike Dr Frankenstein's creature, zombies long not for family and friends but for fuel; they're more nihilistic than the werewolf figure, who embodies the human fear that our animal nature might overpower us. Pop culture kitsch like old Hollywood B-films offers the best zombie stomping ground. One can see deeper meanings in movies such as *White Zombie* (1932), considered the first zombie film, or *Night of the Living Dead* (1968), than their phantasmagoria might suggest. Death, after all, frightens most people—even those who believe in an afterlife. This conundrum permeates zombie stories. As a send-up of the zombie cult, the bestselling novel *Pride and Prejudice and Zombies* (2009), 'by Jane Austen and Seth Grahame-Smith' (as proclaimed on the book's cover), turns the genre on its head. The book is in fact a clever parody, though the true fun of it isn't available to people unfamiliar with Austen. After the summer of 2013, when one of the largest American amusement parks included in its fall schedule a mass wedding ceremony where couples could register to be married by a 'zombie officiant', I asked my students about this fascination with zombies. They appeared puzzled, as if the appeal was self-evident, but then admitted that they feared there was no future for them, that the future had been used up. They weren't talking about employment opportunities or projected statistics for government spending, but expressing instead a vague sense of unease. Might this anxiety also be part of what is meant by the terms *posthuman* and *post-historical*?

Posthuman studies are a challenge to humanists. Those who accept the declining draw of the humanities as a done deal are discarding not only the wisdom of several millennia but perhaps the moral imagination as well. In *Machines of Loving Grace: The Quest for Common Ground Between Humans and Robots* (2015), John Markoff, who reports on technology for the *New York Times*, wrote that researchers and engineers 'grow uncomfortable when asked about the potential consequences of their inventions and frequently deflect questions with gallows humor'; and in December 2014, the eminent physicist Stephen Hawking warned that 'the development of full artificial intelligence could spell the end of the human race.' The taste for apocalypse—from born-again religionists to political ideologues to literary and pulp storytellers and, yes, to academic theorists—has a long history. No wonder the old figures of superstition, those vampires and zombies, remain alive amidst our technology revolution, attractive to some and still haunting us.

Postheroism

In the fall of 2016 a retrospective exhibition of Saskatchewan-born painter Agnes Martin (1912–2004) opened at Manhattan's Guggenheim Museum to glowing reviews. The headline for one of them, in the *New York Review of Books*, proclaimed: 'The Heroic Art of Agnes Martin'. Linked to the Abstract Expressionists, Martin had a difficult, solitary life, but her art—and her story—don't immediately evoke the word *heroic*. What does it mean here? Martin produced large-scale, delicate paintings, often of grid-like structures. Compressed for commercial printing, the images can appear like graph paper, but when actually seen Martin's lines vibrate almost mystically, a glimpse of an eternal design. Still, one might ask, how is this unmonumental art heroic? And who is the hero?

Since the publication of Jean François Lyotard's *The Postmodern Condition* in 1989, professors and professional pundits have told us that ours is a 'postmodern' era, with relativism the key to understanding it. In the last decade or so we've also been told that our time is a 'posthuman' one of advanced technologies, cyborgs and the like. Perhaps we're living in a postheroic age as well. Though Hollywood still loves a hero, and regularly turns out action-filled blockbusters based on the antics of comic-book characters, I'm puzzled by the appeal of these films. Once aimed at an audience of adolescent boys, afficionados of special effects and viewers nostalgic about teenage taste, such movies now dominate the international entertainment business and reach a vast market. While their grim, post-industrial settings and computer-generated heroics may draw on anxieties about the future, Superman, Batman, Spider-Man, Iron Man and Captain America haven't lost their currency.

Traditional heroes seek self-definition. The lives of figures like Oedipus, Moses, Buddha, Jesus, King Arthur, Beowulf and Parsifal (to name only a few) have similar patterns, whether the men are quasi-historical, mythic, military or religious heroes. The patterns shared by them have been studied in books such as *The Hero with a Thousand Faces* (1949), by

American mythologist Joseph Campbell, and *The Myth of the Birth of the Hero* (1909), by the Viennese psychoanalyst Otto Rank. Many heroes were born under mysterious circumstances, experienced conflict with father figures, withdrew from family life into solitude, overcame insurmountable obstacles, discovered a new identity and finally created fresh possibilities of perception. Not a strict checklist, the pattern can be updated to include almost any culture's favoured heroes—think of Abraham Lincoln or, closer to our time, Nelson Mandela.

In the last half century biographers and social historians have applied this pattern to the lives of prominent women (Joan of Arc, say; even Eleanor Roosevelt), while feminist writers have challenged its very nature as patriarchal and oppressive. But earlier literary writers such as Mary Ann Evans—better known as George Eliot (1819–80)—also examined the pattern in terms of women's lives. Eliot's most famous novel, *Middlemarch* (1871–72), opens with a prelude: 'Who that cares much to know the history of man, and how the mysterious mixture behaves under the varying experiments of Time, has not dwelt, at least briefly, on the life of Saint Theresa, has not smiled with some gentleness at the thought of this little girl walking forth one morning hand-in-hand with her still smaller brother, to go and seek martyrdom in the country of the Moors?' The question is a rhetorical device, but I think still sincere. As Eliot sketches the story of the Spanish saint, she posits that 'Many Theresas have been born who found for themselves no epic life wherein there was a constant unfolding of far-resonant action.' Eliot's dissatisfaction with the limited opportunities Victorian society offered an intellectual woman likely shaped her protagonist's fate, if not her own life. She understood that cultures don't always get the heroes they need.

The decline of the traditional male hero in the Western literary psyche coincided with the ascent of the secular, post-Enlightenment Romantic hero—often an anti-hero—who became a popular figure, thanks to the protean German writer Johann Wolfgang von Goethe (1749–1832). It may be difficult to believe that one book could change the pattern of a literary culture, but Goethe's *Sorrows of Young Werther* (1774) did just that. Considered to be the world's first bestselling novel, it recounts the misadventures of a super-sensitive young man who can find no direction for his idealism. Almost inevitably he falls into an impossible love triangle and, overwhelmed by emotion, kills himself, reputedly causing suicidal behaviour in troubled admirers of the novel. While many details of the plot were borrowed from Goethe's own youthful amours, he transformed them to create a story that spoke to the anxieties of his era. He intended the book to be a critique of the cult of sensibility, but it was often misread as a celebration of it.

As if Werther hadn't already damaged traditional heroism, the scandalous British poet Lord George Gordon Byron (1788–1824) embroidered details from his own love life with elements derived from the attractive but diabolical heroes of popular Gothic fiction. Thus he created the brooding Byronic hero, a handsome, moody, charismatic aristocrat who became fashionable in the nineteenth century as well as the prototype of literary heroes across the continent. Every national literature could give the figure a spin of its own. In Russia, for example, Alexander Pushkin (1799–1837) and Mikhail Lermontov (1814–1841) created the superfluous man. Almost bursting from the pages of Pushkin's verse novel *Eugene Onegin* (1828) and Lermontov's prose tale *A Hero of Our Time* (1839), this figure—a deeply bored man, too fine to hold any place in his world—engages in a pointless duel that echoes the close of *Werther.* (More than a century later, the restless young men played by James Dean in *Rebel Without a Cause* of 1955 and Dustin Hoffman in *The Graduate* of 1967, owe a debt to Goethe and Company.)

Meanwhile, artistic rebels like Vincent Van Gogh (1853–90) added another dimension to the figure of the Romantic hero, grounding him in the sufferings of misunderstood and unrecognized talent, or tragic genius. By the early years of the twentieth century, modernist writers had absorbed the classic pre-Romantic pattern as well as its more recent nineteenth-century variations. But after the First World War, heroic deeds seemed almost impossible, if not passé. The ideals that didn't die in the trenches of Europe were probably killed off by the then-shocking insights of Freudian psychoanalysis. Who could be a traditional hero now?

During the heady years of literary modernism, traditional heroism seemed irrelevant. The best challenge that André Gide could offer the hero of his novel *Lafcadio's Adventures* (1914) was a gratuitous act (*acte gratuit*), an unmotivated moment where, for no reason, Lafcadio pushes a man from a moving train to his death. Modernist protagonists could be artists (Stephen Dedalus, with his symbolic name, in Joyce's *A Portrait of the Artist as a Young Man*, 1916); sexual rebels (in Gide's *The Immoralist*, 1902); or war survivors (the impotent Jake Barnes in Hemingway's *The Sun Also Rises*, 1926). In contrast, women writers of that era—Colette and

Virginia Woolf, for example—found heroic possibilities, and even adventure, in the act of survival. At the end of *The Vagabond* (1910), Colette's protagonist chooses the life of a single vaudevillian rather than the confines of marriage, while in the closing lines of Woolf's *To the Lighthouse* (1927), the unmarried painter Lily Briscoe completes her work: 'Yes, she thought, laying down her brush in extreme fatigue, I have had my vision.' Perhaps the future of traditional heroism belongs to women.

Well, maybe. Yet the name of one man from the past continues to inspire me: Anton Chekhov (1860–1904). While the modern short story genre and much contemporary theatre would have been impossible without his work, it's the intertwining of Chekhov's courageous life with his wise, humane writing that claims my awe. His surname has given rise to an adjective—Chekhovian—which evokes a world of fading gentry lost in twilight lives, but Chekhov was the least 'Chekhovian' individual I can think of.

Born into a family that had been freed from serfdom by a paternal grandfather who managed to buy their way out of it, Chekhov grew up in grim poverty. One of six children, the smart, roguish boy assumed financial responsibilities far beyond his years. As a medical student he wrote humorous sketches for Moscow's popular magazines, and the more he wrote, the more innovative his work became. Torn between literature and medicine, Chekhov wore two hats, and his exceptional talent as a writer was recognized early on with the Pushkin Prize (1888). His short fiction portrayed a wide range of human types and experiences, all told with a directness that is forgiving: this is what people are and do and can dream.

By the age of twenty-four, Chekhov was coughing blood and had developed the first symptoms of tuberculosis (then called consumption), and as a doctor he could guess what lay ahead. Refusing the temptations of self-pity or despair, he continued to work as if a bright future beckoned. While his reputation grew, he decided to undertake an eleven-week journey from Moscow through Siberia to Sakhalin Island, a penal colony more than five thousand miles away. Travelling mostly by steamer, horse-drawn coach, barges and ferries and troikas, in conditions that would challenge any action hero, he recorded his encounters in *Sakhalin Island* (1895). With a sympathetic eye and a deep sense of irony, Chekhov told of the hardships he shared with the people he met along the way. In one early scene, near Tomsk, he had to ford a river through pounding snow and rain:

> But now the shoreline is closer and closer, and the oarsmen ply more cheerfully, little by little the weight falls from one's soul, and, when there are no more than three sazhens left to the bank, I become light-hearted and merry, and the thought occurs to me: 'It's good to be a coward! Not a great deal is necessary for him all of a sudden to become very happy!'

Coward indeed. Chekhov remained in the penal colony for three months, interviewing chain gangs and exiled settlers in an informal census, before making the arduous trip home.

When, at the age of thirty-two, Chekhov purchased Melikhovo, an estate of over five hundred acres, he moved his family there with him. Soon he was tending to the medical needs of the local peasantry, working to build schools and joining rural councils, all the while writing as if he could ignore his worsening disease. Finding his subjects in the lives around him, over the next twelve years he penned dozens of stories, novellas and the plays that have come to define *fin de siècle* Tsarist Russia. Chekhov's magnetic personality drew people wherever he went, and he struggled to make time for writing while helping an extended family, dependent friends and strangers in need. Since tuberculosis was then a death sentence, he hid his illness from the world. In the years before his death, at forty-four, he tried various cures, moved to Yalta for its gentler climate and even married, though he claimed that he could be a good husband only if he and his wife, the actress Olga Knipper, spent periods apart in different cities. ('As I shall lie in the grave alone,' he wrote in his notebook, 'so in fact I live alone.') In the last months of his life he was pressured to complete a new play for the Moscow Art Theatre, a company associated with his work, and miraculously finished *The Cherry Orchard* before dying in Badenweiler, Germany, at a health spa where he was making a final attempt at a cure.

While flashy heroics never caught Chekhov's imagination, many of his characters yearned for lives with greater possibilities than those in their surroundings. Olga, Masha and Irina, the Prozorov women in *Three Sisters*, long for Moscow and meaningful work, while in *Uncle Vanya* the world-weary Dr Astrov tends to the health of his rural district while mapping its lakes, woodlands, farmsteads and hamlets, since all he can do is record how 'everything's gone downhill because people have found the struggle for existence too much for them.' At the end of the play a young woman dreams of a better future:

We shall see all the evils of this life, all our own sufferings, vanish in the flood of mercy which will fill the whole world. And then our life will be calm and gentle, sweet as a caress. I believe that, I do believe it.

Did Chekhov? A clear-eyed realist, and early absurdist, he did give some of his characters hope, even hope against hope. In story after story they seek solutions to life's dilemmas and sorrows. When they fail, as invariably happens, they have at least tried to be more fully human. As readers we may shake our heads at their illusions, but how often do we truly understand our own? Sometimes I wonder what would have happened if Chekhov's consumption had been cured. Ahead, of course, was the Russian Revolution, and he would have been fifty-seven when it began. Would he have left Russia, like Ivan Bunin and Vladimir Nabokov? Or remained in Moscow, with the poet Anna Akhmatova (1889–1966)? She chose to stay with her people and her beloved language, and eventually wrote the elegiac 'Requiem' (circa 1935–40), arguably the greatest protest poem of the last century. It's pointless to speculate, yet irresistible.

What about Agnes Martin? Chekhov has shown how acts of personal heroism can make life bearable, and Martin's courage seems the stuff of fiction. Like the Prozorov sisters, she hated the life she'd been born to in rural Saskatchewan ('a land of no opportunity', she once said). After moving to Vancouver with her family, Martin uprooted herself to New York City—an amazing act for a young woman of her era—and, in 1941, studied to be an art teacher at Columbia University. But instead of the schoolroom, she turned to full-time painting. Solitary by nature, and less interested in romantic bonds than in creating time for her work, Martin travelled the United States alone, painting wherever she stopped, before settling in Taos, New Mexico. Was she searching for an 'epic life', as George Eliot called it, one of 'far-resonant action'? In 1957, with encouragement from the legendary art dealer Betty Parsons, Martin returned to Manhattan and discovered a group of like-minded experimental artists that helped her thrive; she also found acceptance in their company as a gay woman. Then, diagnosed with schizophrenia in her early fifties, she suffered periods of painful hospitalization. Against all odds, in 1967 she set out, alone, to restore her health. She lived in trailer parks before settling, again, in New Mexico, and finally returned to painting in 1974. More people would be artists, Martin observed, if they could tolerate solitude. She continued to look inward, hell-bent on serving her work, which has sometimes been called Minimalist, and its spiritual dimension. That it found an audience, and critical acclaim, came almost as a surprise. She painted until her death, at ninety-two. And now she's been called 'heroic'—perhaps for surviving.

The word *heroic* seems to have gone flat on us, and may even bring to mind the eighteenth-century saying, 'No man is a hero to his valet.' Yet the German philosopher Georg Wilhelm Friedrich Hegel (1770–1831) added to the quip: 'This is not because the hero is not a hero, but because the valet is a valet.' In any case, we can amuse ourselves with the exploits of cartoon supermen, but we know they're a fantasy. Newspapers overuse the term *hero* after the death of figures like the American astronaut John Glenn and English singer David Bowie, in 2016, but it's a formulaic tribute. Nor does it apply to the steady stream of victimhood memoirs—often by celebrities—about surviving various addictions and tribulations. I don't mean to discount the sufferings people inflict on each other, and themselves, but what do they show us? When Chekhov wrote, in his notebook, 'Man will only become better when you make him see what he is like', he didn't mean marketable confessions. And any new biography of a notable person from the past includes a debunking angle, something to 'humanize' the figure. Perhaps we've become too skeptical, even cynical, and have lost the desire to measure ourselves against people who refuse to be defeated by life's challenges and injustices. Heroism, by its nature, is a comparative quality, or virtue; it's seen in community. Heroes have always been singular, and they stand out—even above us—and can make us feel like lesser beings. Who wants that? But if we don't want it, we still need the idea of heroes and heroism, in order to ask more of ourselves than we think possible. Our world may be postmodern, and even posthuman, but a postheroic one? That would be an unthinkably bleak place.

The End of Beauty?
Some Notes, with a Nod to Susan Sontag

1. Half a century has passed since the publication of Susan Sontag's seminal essay 'Notes on Camp' (1964) with its focus on a sensibility that influenced the 1960s' love of playful artifice. The issue of beauty was central to her argument (in 58 notes) because Camp emphasizes surface rather than content, thumbing its nose at the latter. Sontag owed a considerable debt to Oscar Wilde, and his aesthete's inversion of the beauty/truth debate (with the former triumphant). To mark the essay's fiftieth anniversary, the Toronto-based filmmaker Bruce LaBruce wrote a short rebuttal, 'Notes on Camp—and Anti-Camp', arguing that Sontag's ideas are now irrelevant because Camp is no longer an esoteric style. Instead, it has become the style of our time—an interesting notion that suggests how, with the passing years, a radical style can be absorbed and even commercialized. (Recall how the startling innovations of early Surrealist photography were quickly taken over by advertising art.) In our popular mass culture, the knowing smirk of Camp is commonplace, and notions of beauty's radical potential seem beside the point.

2. During the decade when I directed my university's undergraduate program in creative writing, I often asked students in workshops and seminars for their definitions of beauty. This seemed a good icebreaker—a sensible way to begin a course—and an opportunity to bring values, assumptions and preferences into the open. Without exception, the students explained that beauty was personal and subjective: essentially the cliché, which many actually used, that it's in the eye of the beholder. Naturally a few of them made an association with sexual attraction, also deemed subjective. Since relativism has become the core of most secondary and post-secondary education, there was no reason to be surprised. Why would they think otherwise?

3. In the last few decades, courses in aesthetics, once common in universities, have largely vanished from the liberal-arts curriculum, while literary theory—focusing on matters of gender, race and class—predominates, bringing a quasi-sociological perspective, with aesthetics now deemed elitist and old-fashioned, if not downright oppressive in its apparent bias towards universality. Once postmodernism, and its relativism, became the preferred theoretical framework, beauty was passé because it assumes an absolute, or something very much like it, with a hierarchy of values. A rich and complex discourse has been marginalized, often by artists themselves. This matters because the sociological model has a utilitarian caste—even a puritanical edge—that seems uncomfortable with the association of beauty and pleasure, as if pleasure is inherently useless, or at best irrelevant to serious thought. I'm reminded of a scene in the Ernst Lubitsch/Billy Wilder classic film *Ninotchka* (1939). When night falls over Paris, Greta Garbo as Ninotchka, a Soviet commissar on official business, stands at the top of the Eiffel Tower overlooking the city's glittering lights. 'I do not deny its beauty,' she remarks, and, after a pause, adds, 'But it's a waste of electricity.' Without aesthetics, beauty can seem like a waste.

4. But fashions change, even in thinking. For a decade now I've noticed new books that attempt to return the idea of beauty to serious discourse: Denis Donoghue's *Speaking of Beauty* (2003), Umberto Eco's *History of Beauty* (2004), Howard Gardner's *Truth, Beauty, and Goodness Reframed: Educating for the Virtues in the Twenty-First Century* (2011), and David Konstan's *Beauty: The Fortunes of an Ancient Greek Idea* (2014). Meanwhile, critics frequently called 'conservative'—Hilton Kramer, for example, in *The New Criterion*—have continued to value aesthetics. But beauty isn't only a conservative or neo-conservative concern; far from it.

5. Beauty was an ancient preoccupation. We can't know exactly what was in the minds of our ancestors who painted the cave walls of Lascaux, but it's reasonable to assume that some kind of aesthetic decisions or choices were involved. Even if their paintings were part of religious rites and belonged to sacred spaces, we know that concepts of beauty have played an important role in religious art (think of Raphael's placid Renaissance Madonnas, of Bernini's ecstatic Baroque sculptures, or, closer to our time, of Mark Rothko's abstract modernist chapel in Houston, Texas).

Beauty has been among the earliest concerns of humans trying to understand their world—and not only in Plato, where the 'absoluteness' of beauty begins with the idea of beauty as universal and eternal, but also in the Bible (in the Song of Songs, for example). Since Plato, beauty has been seen as an absolute quality—a kind of divine measure—but today we're uncomfortable with such a concept and the hold on us that it implies.

6. Some notion of beauty has been the heart of any discussion of aesthetics, but as aesthetics gave way to historicized and sociological criticism, sophisticated writers often seemed embarrassed to speak of beauty. We're supposed to be influenced, even moved, by diversity—whatever that's taken to mean—with a kind of knowingness that disdains beauty. Since twentieth-century Modernist artists taught us to value a fractured perspective, like the multiple angles of Cubism, the notion that art has something to do with beauty has been upended. And can one speak, for example, of the beauty of an atonal or electronic composition? Perhaps a knowledgeable music critic might, but the word almost seems irrelevant here. Once Stravinsky, Picasso and Gertrude Stein embraced dissonance, and the partial or incomplete, traditional notions of beauty needed updating. While the natural beauty of an artist's subject or object might still touch us—the fragility of Picasso's models, the dancers who give movement to the ballet scores by Stravinsky, the rich meals that Stein dissects in her Cubist poems *Tender Buttons*—we know their subjects only indirectly, through works of art. This indirection also has the appearance of a spontaneity that we've come to value, preferring art that conceals skill and industry. And beauty, as well?

7. Often connected to freedom, ideas of beauty are taught—and learned. They naturally relate to worth, to value, and take on great power when some things (paintings, poems, pieces of pottery, even garments and faces and body shapes) are more valued than others. Here beauty can be confused with fashion, a realm that touches on it tangentially and temporally.

8. The older Platonic triad of truth, beauty and goodness has shaped the Western discourse about beauty. While the eighteenth-century German philosopher Immanuel Kant distinguished between choices that are

moral or aesthetic in *On Moral Reasoning*—there is no moral component in liking green, or preferring the colour blue, for instance—the Romantic poet John Keats wrote, in the famous closing lines of his 'Ode on a Grecian Urn' (1819): 'Beauty is truth, truth beauty;—that is all // Ye know on earth, and all ye need to know.' Yet Keats's lines are a half-truth, and apply mainly to the lovers painted on the urn, lovers who chase each other in perpetuity, never aging, never facing death; their beauty—a denial of time—remains forever youthful and fresh. But we humans age, and often not beautifully. (It was the painter Georgia O'Keeffe who once said that she liked tulips because they died so beautifully.)

9. Four curious cases:
As an undergraduate I bought my first copy of Glenn Gould's iconic recording of Bach's *Goldberg Variations* (1955), and have lived with it happily for almost half a century. It's an idiosyncratic performance, spontaneous and robust, and one that always leaves me feeling invigorated. Not long ago I purchased a new version of the *Goldbergs* by the great Hungarian pianist András Schiff, who brings to the variations a subtle touch, refined phrasing, a rich sense of detail and plush tone. Often I sit back, amazed at what I hear. How does he do that, I ask again and again. Yet after listening, I'm drained, even worn out. Such beauty can be exhausting.

Now if beauty can be exhausting, what else can it be? In a *New York Times* review of a Metropolitan Opera performance of Puccini's *Madama Butterfly*, in the production by the late Anthony Minghella, one critic remarked, 'The staging of her suicide was spectacular and almost indecently beautiful, as her red sash unravelled into ribbons of blood.' Indecent too?

If that's not enough of a puzzle, think of this conversation in Marcel Carne's acclaimed 1945 film *Les enfants du paradis*. When the Count offers to take the heroine Garance as his mistress, she asks, 'What if someone loved me?' He replies, 'You're much too lovely to be truly loved. Beauty is an exception, an affront to an ugly world. Men rarely love beauty. They pursue it to blot it out, forget it.' Yet before leaving her he apologizes, and adds, 'Your beauty alone is the cause of my confusion.' He is not a cynic, just another of the film's romanticists.

Keeping to the world of movies, a 2012 documentary about the Los Angeles artist Wayne White, directed and written by Neil Berkeley, was titled *Beauty Is Embarrassing*.

Exhausting ... indecent ... affront ... embarrassing.... How to explain this bundle of negative attributions? Our new triad doesn't help, likely relegating my question to the realm of high-art quibbles. The nineteenth-century French novelist Gustave Flaubert once wrote, 'You know that beautiful things do not admit description', and I'm tempted to trust him. But the Peruvian writer Mario Vargas Llosa refuted Flaubert in his fine study *The Perpetual Orgy: Flaubert and Madame Bovary*, arguing that his novels surpassed Romantic-era fiction where 'people, things and events are either beautiful or horrible, attractive or repellent.' Transforming the 'limbo' between them—in Vargas Llosa's words—'into "beauty" in *Madame Bovary*', Flaubert made a new kind of beauty, one that 'corresponds to the full, flat, dreary existence of ordinary people.' Both men are right yet wrong, having come up with half-truths, much like Keats's famous couplet. 'Beauty eludes description' might be a better way of putting things, and the paradox here is that attempts to describe beauty can sometimes themselves be beautiful, while descriptions of 'the dreary existence of ordinary people' can also partake of it.

10. Yet 'Beauty is strange,' wrote Charles Baudelaire. Yes, *strange.* If he's right, then beauty stands out in the world because the world is not beautiful and usually defeats it. As Oscar Wilde claimed in *The Picture of Dorian Gray*, 'Beauty is a form of Genius', needing no explanation. 'It is one of the great facts of the world, like sunlight, or spring-time, or the reflection in dark waters of that silver shell we call the moon. It cannot be questioned. People sometimes say that Beauty is only superficial. That may be so. But at least it is not as superficial as thought.... It is only shallow people who do not judge by appearances. The true mystery of the world is the visible, not the invisible.' Wilde's character argues with the flourish of rhetorical inversion. As a result, beauty embodies a kind of paradise and lives in tension with ordinary reality. So beauty can distance us from our world and create discontent. Alas, such beauty is never democratic; in fact beauty can be a reminder of the injustice around us.

11. This curious tension is addressed by Virginia Woolf in her essay 'A Room of One's Own' (1929), where she explored the plight not only of creative women but of all women throughout history—or, at least, the Western European past. According to historians and poets, she wrote, women have been portrayed as 'the spirit of life and beauty in the kitchen

chopping up suet'. The juxtaposition of beauty with a common culinary act is precisely her point, that the ordinary *almost* destroys the beautiful. Still, Woolf saw a challenge here, and imagined looking out of a Cambridge college window, down onto the domes and towers of the city: 'It was very beautiful, very mysterious in the autumn moonlight.' *Beauty* and *mystery* link up naturally, even inevitably, as the second word qualifies, or helps define, the first.

12. Eventually one has to ask some basic questions: What is an aesthetic sense? Is it a feeling for beauty? In her biography of the British novelist Penelope Fitzgerald, whose prose can fairly be described as beautiful, Hermione Lee quotes Fitzgerald's remark that her grandfather, an Anglican bishop, 'had no aesthetic sense whatever'. How can this be? Fitzgerald grew up in a low-church family, but not poverty-stricken; some idea of beauty had to shape their values. As a girl she was shown Burne-Jones's Pre-Raphaelite window in Birmingham Cathedral, and years later wrote that it was 'the first time I'd seen something that I realized was stunningly beautiful', though she claimed that her grandfather hardly noticed the window. Her excitement perhaps contained a reaction to her family, and an aesthetic sense can be built on rejection; it may be an alternate way of seeing and valuing what one sees. Still, a notion of that thing called beauty is involved, as if one has an idea of beauty in mind without being aware of it, has even been looking for it, and then the idea appears manifest in the physical world and one recognizes it. A sense of revelation animates Fitzgerald's phrase 'stunningly beautiful'. It's a cliché—how often is anyone actually stunned?—but she's stopped in her tracks by something that transforms her sense of possibilities. (And I'm tempted to wonder if the window had become all too familiar to her grandfather.) Such powerful beauty may even seem to have moral or spiritual weight. Perhaps we've returned to Plato's absolutes and are circling around them.

13. When Doris Lessing wrote about the phenomenon she called 'group think' in *Prisons We Chose to Live Inside*, she spoke only of social and political ideas, but her theory is relevant here. 'When we're in a group,' she argued, 'we tend to think as the group does: we may even have joined the group to find 'like-minded' people. But we also find our thinking changing because we belong to a group. It is the hardest thing in the

world to maintain an individual dissident opinion, as a member of a group.' Lessing's idea also implies that the aesthetics of any historical moment are a kind of group think, which leads me to another curious case: Having included films in some of the undergraduate courses I teach, I've lectured about *Casablanca* (1942) many times, and in the past ten years there has been a shift in student responses to it. I'm now told that the film, usually among the top five on great-film lists, is dull, talky, too slow, boring and old-fashioned. Some students have claimed that they couldn't watch it because black-and-white movies hurt their eyes, and one film-studies major patiently explained that he couldn't decide if the problem with *Casablanca* was its weak screenplay or its poor director. In their early twenties, these students are devoted to the latest social technologies, as well as to video games. Their aesthetic demands rapid pacing, quick cuts, short scenes and special effects. By such values *Casablanca* is hopelessly dated, hence inferior. They see in a certain way and appreciate what they know: group think. Styles evolve along with taste, but which comes first? Something new, not seen before, apparently satisfies a generation; group think takes over, and the new thing gives pleasure. Yet beauty, as embodied in works of art, can take time getting used to despite its newness. Before his death Van Gogh sold only one painting (to his brother); the first performances of Chekhov's *The Seagull* and *Three Sisters* were considered disasters, leaving the playwright ready to abandon his art; and Picasso famously said of his initial Cubist paintings that he was the first to attempt the style, so naturally it was ugly.

14. Earlier I mentioned several books that encourage a re-evaluation of our current discourse about beauty. In *Speaking of Beauty* Denis Donoghue surveys ideas from the last few centuries and discusses beauty as a value (like the true or the good), reaffirming its centrality to our lives. In his *History of Beauty* Umberto Eco, to confront the nature of beauty itself, compiles examples of works deemed beautiful for more than two millennia. Howard Gardner, in *Truth, Beauty, and Goodness Reframed*, asks how we judge beauty when it is treated as 'an outdated virtue', and reasserts its centrality to both social and philosophical thought. Finally, David Konstan's *Beauty: The Fortunes of an Ancient Greek Idea* argues that eros and erotic attractiveness were central to the ancient notion of beauty, reminding us that pleasure, and ideas about it, can lead us to a deeper appreciation and understanding of the world and its fragility (surely a

virtue). Taken together, these books are an important challenge to present group think.

15. How, then, can we use the term 'beauty' today? We might begin by accepting it as an essential part of our lives rather than as mere ornament, hence insubstantial. And then we might reclaim the study of aesthetics. While the gender, race and class triad was a necessary corrective to the New Critical approach that dominated literary studies half a century ago, when texts existed in a vacuum detached from history and culture, another corrective is needed today. As well, students were once required to take a course in art or music appreciation as part of a well-rounded undergraduate program, exposing them not only to the history of a discipline but to the idea of appreciation itself. Inevitably appreciation implies aesthetic issues, including the way ideas of harmony, balance, juxtaposition and the like occur in the creative works of different cultures and at different historical times. Without resorting to elaborate treatises about beauty, students saw and heard for themselves some of the recurring elements of the creative process, and of making beauty. The liberal arts are, in the end, all teachers; they have something to say about the world, and do this through their forms, genres and styles.

Teaching the classic tenets of aesthetics is one way of helping people understand what can be meant by the word *beauty*, at the same time keeping former ideas and representations of beauty alive. Like a museum curator or art restorer, an archivist or librarian, even a symphony conductor or dramaturge, a teacher has to have one foot in the past and one in the future, an awkward way to straddle the present. It may not seem like a beautiful stance, it's never steady or quite secure, but it serves to puncture group think and has, I trust, its own kind of beauty.

Bibliography

BOOKS

Apollinaire, Guillaume. *Alcools: Poems 1898–1913*. Translated by William Meredith. Garden City, N.Y.: Doubleday, 1964.

——. *Alcools*. Translated by David Revell. Hanover, N.H.: Wesleyan UP, 1995.

Augustine. *The Confessions of St. Augustine*. Translated by John K. Ryan. New York: Doubleday, 1960.

Avison, Margaret. *Concrete and Wild Carrot*. Toronto: Brick Books, 2002.

——. *The Dumbfounding*. New York: Norton, 1966.

——. *Selected Poems*. Toronto: Oxford UP, 1991.

Bailey, Paul. *Uncle Rudolf*. London: Fourth Estate, 2002.

Baker, Nicholson. *Double Fold: Libraries and the Assault on Paper*. New York: Vintage, 2002.

Baumbach, Jonathan, ed. *Writers as Teachers/Teachers as Writers*. New York: Holt, Rinehart & Winston, 1970.

Beauman, Nicola. *E.M. Forster: A Biography*. New York: Knopf, 1994.

Bellows, Barbara L. *The Talent for Living: Josephine Pinckney and the Charleston Literary Tradition*. Baton Rouge, La.: Louisiana State UP, 2006.

Benjamin, Walter. *Illuminations*. Translated by Harry Zohn. New York: Schocken, 1968.

Berberova, Nina. *The Italics Are Mine*. 1969. Translated by Philippe Radley. London: Vintage, 1993.

Bernanos, Georges. *The Diary of a Country Priest*. 1937. Translated by Pamela Morris. New York: Carroll & Graf, 1983.

Blais, Marie-Claire. *Deaf to the City*. 1981.Translated by Carol Dunlop. Toronto: Exile Editions, 2006.

——. *A Season in the Life of Emmanuel*. Translated by Derek Coltman. Introduction by Edmund Wilson. New York: Farrar, Straus & Giroux, 1966.

——. *Une Saison dans la vie d'Emmanuel*. Montréal: Editions du jour, 1965.

Boyd, Brian. *Vladimir Nabokov: The American Years*. Princeton, N.J.: Princeton UP, 1991.

Brown, Frederick. *Flaubert: A Biography.* New York: Little, Brown, 2006.

Byatt, A.S. *Ragnarok: The End of the Gods.* New York: Canongate, 2011.

Čapek, Karel. *R.U.R.* Translated by Paul Selver and Nigel Playfair. 1923. Anthologized in *Sixteen Famous European Plays,* compiled by Bennett A. Cerf and Van H. Cartmell. New York: Modern Library, 1943.

Capote, Truman. *Answered Prayers: The Unfinished Novel.* London: Hamish Hamilton, 1986.

Carhart, Thad. *The Piano Shop on the Left Bank.* New York: Random House, 2001.

Cather, Willa. *My Ántonia.* 1918. London: Virago Modern Classics, 1991.

Cervantes, Miguel de. *Don Quixote.* Translated by Edith Grossman. New York: Ecco, 2003.

Chase, Mildred Portney. *Just Being at the Piano.* Berkeley, Calif.: Creative Arts, 1985.

Chekhov, Anton. *Five Plays.* Translated by Ronald Hingley. Oxford: Oxford UP, 1980.

——. *Notebook of Anton Chekhov.* Translated by S.S. Koteliansky and Leonard Woolf. 1921. New York: Ecco, 1987.

——. *Sakhalin Island.* Translated by Brian Reeve. 1993. Richmond, Surrey, U.K. : Alma Classics, 2011.

Ciuraru, Carmela, ed. *Solitude: Poems.* New York: Everyman's Library/Knopf, 2005.

Clarke, Gerald. *Capote: A Biography.* New York: Ballantine, 1988.

Cozzens, James Gould. *By Love Possessed.* New York: Harvest/Harcourt, Brace & World, 1957.

Cutler, Laurence S., and Judy Goffman Cutler. *J.C. Leyendecker: American Imagist.* New York: Abrams, 2008.

Davis, Lydia. *The Collected Stories of Lydia Davis.* New York: Farrar, Straus & Giroux, 2009.

de Beauvoir, Simone. *The Second Sex.* 1953. Translated by Howard Madison Parshley. New York: Bantam, 1968.

——. *The Second Sex.* Translated by Constance Borde and Sheila Malovany-Chevallier. New York: Vintage, 2011.

DeMallac, Guy. *Boris Pasternak: His Life and Art.* Norman, Okla.: University of Oklahoma Press, 1981.

de Waal, Edmund. *The Hare with Amber Eyes: A Family's Century of Art and Loss.* New York: Farrar, Straus & Giroux, 2010.

Dick, Philip K. *Do Androids Dream of Electric Sheep?* 1968. New York: Ballantine, 1996.

Dizikes, John. *Opera in America: A Cultural History.* New Haven, Conn.: Yale UP, 1993.

Donoghue, Dennis. *Speaking of Beauty.* New Haven, Conn.: Yale UP, 2003.

Doody, Margaret Anne. *The True Story of the Novel.* New Brunswick, N.J.: Rutgers UP, 1996.

Dubal, David. *Reflections from the Keyboard: The World of the Concert Pianist.* New York: Summit Books, 1984.

Duczyńska, Ilona, and Karl Polanyi, eds. *The Plough and the Pen: Writings from Hungary, 1930–1956.* Toronto: McClelland & Stewart, 1963.

Echenoz, Jean. *Ravel: A Novel.* Translated by Linda Coverdale. New York: New Press, 2007.

Eco, Umberto, ed. *History of Beauty.* Translated by Alastair McEwen. New York: Rizzoli, 2004.

Eliot, George. *Middlemarch.* 1874. New York: Washington Square, 1963.

Figes, Orlando. *Natasha's Dance: A Cultural History of Russia.* New York: Metropolitan Books/Henry Holt, 2002.

Finn, Peter, and Petra Couvée. *The Zhivago Affair: The Kremlin, the CIA, and the Battle Over a Forbidden Book.* New York: Pantheon, 2014.

Fischer-Dieskau, Dietrich. *Reverberations: The Memoirs.* Translated by Ruth Hein. New York: Fromm International, 1989.

Flaubert, Gustave. *Madame Bovary.* Translated by Lydia Davis. New York: Viking, 2010.

——. *Madame Bovary.* Translated by Francis Steegmuller. 1957. New York: Vintage, 1992.

France, Peter, ed. *The Oxford Guide to Literature in English Translation.* Oxford: Oxford UP, 2000.

Fraser, Kennedy. *Ornament and Silence: Essays on Women's Lives.* New York: Knopf, 1996.

Freud, Sigmund. *Civilization and Its Discontents.* Translated by David McLintock. London: Penguin, 2002.

Frey, Stefan. *Emmerich Kalman: Laughter Under Tears, An Operetta Biography.* Translated by Alexander Butziger. Culver City, Calif.: Operetta Foundation, 2014.

Friedrich, Otto. *Glenn Gould: A Life and Variations.* Toronto: Lester & Orpen Dennys, 1989.

Fukuyama, Francis. *Our Postmodern Future: Consequences of the Biotechnology Revolution.* New York: Farrar, Straus & Giroux, 2002.

Furbank, P.N. *E.M. Forster: A Life.* Oxford: Oxford UP, 1979.

Gardner, Howard. *Truth, Beauty, and Goodness Reframed: Educating for the Virtues in the Twenty-First Century*. New York: Basic Books, 2011.

Gobard, Henri. *L'Aliénation linguistique*. Paris: Flammarion, 1976.

Goodman, Celia. *Living with Koestler: Mamaine Koestler's Letters 1945–51*. London: Weidenfeld and Nicolson, 1985.

Gordon, Mary. *Good Boys and Dead Girls and Other Essays*. New York: Penguin, 1992.

Gould, Glenn. *Selected Letters*. Edited and compiled by John P.L. Roberts and Ghyslaine Guertin. Toronto: Oxford UP, 1992.

Graffman, Gary. *I Really Should Be Practicing: Reflections on the Pleasures and Perils of Playing the Piano in Public*. New York: Doubleday, 1981.

Grahame-Smith, Seth. *Pride and Prejudice and Zombies*. Philadelphia, Pa.: Quirk Books, 2009.

Grosholz, Emily R., ed. *The Legacy of Simone de Beauvoir*. New York: Oxford UP, 2004.

Haffenden, John. *Novelists in Interview*. London: Methuen, 1985.

Halberstam, David. *The Fifties*. New York: Random House, 1993.

Hammer, Langdon. *James Merrill: Life and Art*. New York: Knopf, 2015.

Haraway, Donna. *Simians, Cyborgs and Women: The Reinvention of Nature*. New York: Routledge, 1991.

Harvey, James. *Movie Love in the Fifties*. New York: Knopf, 2001.

Hayles, N. Katherine. *How We Became Posthuman: Virtual Bodies in Cybernetics, Literature, and Informatics*. Chicago: University of Chicago Press, 1999.

Hazlitt, William. *Hazlitt: Selected Essays*. Edited by George Sampson. Cambridge, U.K.: Cambridge UP, 1917.

——. *Anne Hébert: Collected Later Novels*. Introduction by Mavis Gallant. Translated by Sheila Fischman. Toronto: House of Anansi, 2003.

Hébert, Anne. *Kamouraska*. Translated by Norman Shapiro. Toronto: Musson, 1973.

Herrera, Hayden. *Arshile Gorky: His Life and Work*. New York: Farrar, Straus & Giroux, 2003.

Hingley, Ronald. *Pasternak: A Biography*. New York: Knopf, 1983.

Hirsch, Foster. *Otto Preminger: The Man Who Would Be King*. New York: Knopf, 2007.

Hirshler, Erica E. *Sargent's Daughters: The Biography of a Painting*. Boston: MFA Publications, 2009.

Hollinger, Veronica, and Joan Gordon, eds. *Edging into the Future: Science Fiction and Contemporary Cultural Transformation*. Philadelphia, Pa.: University of Pennsylvania Press, 2002.

Hong Kingston, Maxine. *The Woman Warrior: Memoirs of a Girlhood Among Ghosts.* 1976. New York: Vintage, 1989.
Hutner, Gordon. *What America Read: Taste, Class, and the Novel 1920–1960.* Chapel Hill, N.C.: University of North Carolina Press, 2009.
Ingersoll, Earl G., ed. *Conversations with May Sarton.* Jackson, Miss., and London: University Press of Mississippi, 1991.
Isacoff, Stuart. *A Natural History of the Piano: The Instrument, the Music, the Musicians—from Mozart to Modern Jazz, and Everything in Between.* New York: Knopf, 2011.
Ivinskaya, Olga. *A Captive of Time: My Years with Pasternak.* Translated by Max Hayward. New York: Doubleday, 1978.
Ivry, Benjamin. *Maurice Ravel: A Life.* New York: Welcome Rain, 2000.
Jacobs, Jane. *The Girl on the Hat.* Toronto: Oxford UP, 1989.
Joyce, James. *A Portrait of the Artist as a Young Man.* 1916. New York: Viking, 1965.
——, Stephen Hero: Part of the first draft of *A Portrait of the Artist as a Young Man.* London: Jonathan Cape, 1944.
Kawabata, Yasunari. *House of the Sleeping Beauties and Other Stories.* Translated by Edward Seidensticker. New York: Kodansha International, 1980.
Klinenberg, Eric. *Going Solo: The Extraordinary Rise and Surprising Appeal of Living Alone.* New York: Penguin, 2012.
Koestler, Mamaine. *Living with Koestler: Mamaine Koestler's Letters 1945–51.* Edited by Celia Goodman. London: Weidenfeld and Nicolson, 1985.
Kogawa, Joy. *Obasan.* Boston, Mass.: Godine, 1984.
Konstan, David. *Beauty: The Fortunes of an Ancient Greek Idea.* New York: Oxford UP, 2014.
Korolenko, Vladimir. *Selected Stories.* Translated by Suzanne Rosenberg. Moscow: Progress Publishers, 1978.
Kroetsch, Robert. *The Lovely Treachery of Words: Essays Selected and New.* New York: Oxford UP, 1989.
Leavitt, David. *While England Sleeps.* New York: Viking-Penguin, 1993.
Lee, Hermione. *Penelope Fitzgerald: A Life.* New York: Knopf, 2014.
Lessing, Doris. *The Fifth Child.* London: Jonathan Cape, 1988.
——. *Prisons We Choose to Live Inside.* New York: Harper & Row, 1987.
Levertov, Denise. *The Poet in the World.* New York: New Directions, 1973.
Loesser, Arthur. *Men, Women & Pianos: A Social History.* New York: Simon and Schuster, 1954.
Lowell, Robert. *Imitations.* 1985. New York: Farrar, Straus & Giroux, 1990.
Lyotard, Jean-François. *The Postmodern Condition: A Report on Knowledge.*

Translated by Geoff Bennington and Brian Massumi. Theory and History of Literature, Vol. 10. Minneapolis, Minn.: University of Minnesota Press, 1989.

Macdonald, Dwight. *Masscult and Midcult: Essays Against the American Grain.* 1962. New York: New York Review Books Classic, 2011.

Mach, Elyse. *Great Pianists Speak for Themselves.* New York: Dodd, Mead, 1980.

Madsen, Axel. *Stanwyck.* New York: HarperCollins, 1994.

Mann, Thomas. *Essays of Three Decades.* Translated by H.T. Lowe-Porter. New York: Knopf, 1957.

Markoff, John. *Machines of Loving Grace: The Quest for Common Ground Between Humans and Robots.* New York: HarperCollins, 2015.

Marlyn, John. *Under the Ribs of Death.* 1957. Toronto: McClelland & Stewart, 1990.

Marquand, John P. *B.F.'s Daughter.* Boston: Little, Brown, 1946.

Marquez, Gabriel Garcia. *Memories of My Melancholy Whores.* Translated by Edith Grossman. New York: Knopf, 2005.

Marvell, Andrew. *The Poems of Andrew Marvell.* Edited with an introduction by Hugh MacDonald. London: Routledge and Kegan Paul, 1972.

McCarthy, Mary. *Occasional Prose.* New York: Harcourt Brace Jovanovich, 1985.

McClatchy, J.D., ed. *Recitative: Prose of James Merrill.* San Francisco: North Point, 1986.

McGrath, Charles, ed., et.al., *Books of the Century: A Hundred Years of Authors, Ideas and Literature.* New York: Random House, 1998.

Merrill, James. *The Changing Light at Sandover.* Edited by J.D. McClatchy and Stephen Yenser. New York: Knopf, 2013.

——. *Collected Poems.* Edited by J.D. McClatchy and Stephen Yenser. New York: Knopf, 2013.

——. *A Different Person: A Memoir.* New York: Knopf, 1993.

Merton, Thomas. *Entering the Silence: Becoming a Monk & Writer. The Journals of Thomas Merton. Volume Two: 1941–1952.* Edited by Jonathan Montaldo. San Francisco: HarperCollins, 1996.

Metalious, Grace. *Peyton Place.* 1956. Boston: Northeastern UP, 1999.

Meyers, Jeffrey. *Edmund Wilson: A Biography.* 1995. New York: Cooper Square, 2003.

Moffat, Wendy. *A Great Unrecorded History: A New Life of E.M. Forster.* New York: Farrar, Straus & Giroux, 2010.

Monroe, Marilyn. *Fragments: Poems, Intimate Notes, Letters by Marilyn Monroe.* Edited by Stanley Buchtal and Bernard Comment. New York: HarperCollins, 2010.

Montaigne, Michel de. *The Complete Essays of Montaigne.* Translated by Donald M. Frame, Stanford, Calif.: Stanford UP, 1958.

Moretti, Franco. *The Bourgeois: Between History and Literature.* London: Verso, 2013.

Mott, Michael. *The Seven Mountains of Thomas Merton.* Boston: Houghton Mifflin, 1984.

Nichols, Roger. *Ravel.* New Haven, Conn.: Yale UP, 2011.

Nicolson, Harold. *Some People.* 1927. London: Constable & Co., 1958.

Olsen, Tillie. *Silences.* New York: Delacorte, 1978.

Ovid. *Metamorphoses.* Translated by Rolfe Humphries. 1955. Bloomington, Ind.: Indiana UP, 2008.

Page, P.K. *Evening Dance of the Grey Flies.* Toronto: Oxford UP, 1981.

——. *A Flask of Sea Water.* Toronto: Oxford UP, 1989.

——. *The Glass Air: Selected Poems.* Toronto: Oxford UP, 1985.

——. *The Glass Air: Poems Selected and New.* Toronto: Oxford UP, 1991.

Pasternak, Boris. *Doctor Zhivago.* Translated by Max Hayward and Manya Harari. New York: Pantheon, 1958.

——. *Doctor Zhivago.* Translated by Richard Pevear and Larissa Volokhonsky. New York: Pantheon, 2010.

——. *Safe Conduct: An Autobiography and Other Writings.* New York: New Directions, 1958.

Pasternak, Josephine. *Tightrope Walking: A Memoir.* Bloomington, Ind.: Slavica, 2005.

Perényi, Eleanor. *The Bright Sword.* New York: Rinehart & Company, 1955.

——. *Green Thoughts: A Writer in the Garden.* New York: Random House, 1981.

——. *Liszt: The Artist as Romantic Hero.* Boston: Little, Brown, 1974.

——. *More Was Lost.* 1946. New York: Helen Marx, 2001.

Peters, Margot. *May Sarton: A Biography.* New York: Knopf, 1998.

Philip, Marlene NourbeSe. *She Tries Her Tongue, Her Silence Softly Breaks.* Charlottetown, PEI: Ragweed, 1989.

Pirozhkova, A.N. *At His Side: The Last Years of Isaac Babel.* Translated by Anne Frydman and Robert L. Lusch. South Royalton, Vt.: Steerforth, 1996.

Plante, David. *ABC: A Novel.* New York: Anchor, 2008.

——, *The Accident.* New York: Ticknor & Fields, 1991.

——. *American Ghosts.* Boston: Beacon, 2005.

——. *Annunciation.* New York: Ticknor & Fields, 1994.

——. *Becoming a Londoner.* New York: Bloomsbury, 2013.

——. *The Catholic.* 1985. New York: Atheneum, 1986.

———. *The Country*. 1981. Boston: Beacon, 2004.
———. *The Darkness of the Body*. London: Jonathan Cape, 1974.
———. *Difficult Women: A Memoir of Three (Sonia Orwell, Jean Rhys, Germaine Greer)*. New York: Atheneum, 1983.
———. *The Family*. New York: Farrar, Straus & Giroux, 1978.
———. *The Foreigner*. New York: Atheneum, 1984.
———. *The Ghost of Henry James*. Boston: Gambit, 1970.
———. *The Native*. New York: Atheneum, 1988.
———. *The Pure Lover: A Memoir of Grief*. Boston: Beacon, 2009.
———. *The Woods*. New York: Atheneum, 1982.
———. *Worlds Apart: A Memoir*. New York: Bloomsbury, 2015.
Purdy, James. *In a Shallow Grave*. 1975. New York: Arbor House, 1977.
Puschmann-Nalenz, Barbara. *Science Fiction and Postmodern Fiction: A Genre Study*. New York: Peter Lang, 1992.
Rabassa, Gregory. *If This Be Treason: Translation and Its Discontent: A Memoir*. New York: New Directions, 2005.
Raine, Kathleen. *Defending Ancient Springs*. London: Oxford UP, 1967.
Rich, Adrienne. *On Lies, Secrets, and Silence: Selected Prose 1966–1978*. New York: Norton, 1979.
Roberts, John P.L., and Ghyslaine Guertin, eds. *Glenn Gould Selected Letters*. Toronto: Oxford UP, 1992.
Rodriguez, Richard. *Days of Obligation: An Argument with My Mexican Father*. New York: Viking, 1992.
Rollyson, Carl, and Lisa Paddock. *Susan Sontag: The Making of an Icon*. New York: Norton, 2000.
Rose, Norman. *Harold Nicolson*. London: Pimlico, 2006.
Rose, Phyllis. *A Year of Reading Proust: A Memoir in Real Time*. Washington, D.C.: Counterpoint, 2000.
Rosen, Charles. *Piano Notes: The World of the Pianist*. New York: Free Press, 2002.
Rosenberg, Suzanne. *A Soviet Odyssey*. Toronto: Oxford UP, 1988.
Ross, Alex. *The Rest Is Noise: Listening to the Twentieth Century*. New York: Farrar, Straus and Giroux, 2007.
Roth, Henry. *Call It Sleep*. 1934. London: Penguin, 1977.
Rubinstein, Arthur. *My Young Years*. New York: Knopf, 1973.
Rubin, Joan Shelley. *The Making of Middlebrow Culture*. Chapel Hill, N.C.: University of North Carolina Press, 1992.
Rukeyser, Muriel. *The Speed of Darkness*. New York: Random House, 1960.

Sacks, Oliver. *Musicophilia: Tales of Music and the Brain.* Toronto: Vintage, 2008.

Said, Edward W. *On Late Style: Music and Literature Against the Grain.* New York: Pantheon, 2006.

Sarton, May. *After the Stroke.* New York: Norton, 1988.

——. *As We Are Now.* 1973. New York: Norton, 1982.

——. *At Seventy.* New York: Norton, 1984.

——. *Eighty-Two: A Journal.* New York: Norton, 1996.

——. *Encore: A Journal of the Eightieth Year.* New York: Norton, 1993.

——. *Endgame: A Journal of the Seventy-Ninth Year.* New York: Norton, 1992.

——. *The House by the Sea: A Journal.* New York: Norton, 1977.

——. *Mrs Stevens Hears the Mermaids Singing.* 1965. New York: Norton, 1975.

——. *Plant Dreaming Deep.* New York: Norton, 1968.

——. *Journal of a Solitude.* New York: Norton, 1973.

Schiff, Stacy. *Véra (Mrs Vladimir Nabokov).* New York: Random House, 1999.

Schiffrin, André. *The Business of Books.* New York: Verso, 2001.

Schonberg, Harold C. *The Great Pianists: From Mozart to the Present.* New York: Simon and Schuster, 1963.

Shelley, Mary. *Frankenstein.* 1818/1831. Edited by M.K. Joseph. Oxford: Oxford UP, 1992.

Sherman, Russell. *Piano Pieces.* New York: North Point, 1997.

Sherman, Susan, ed. *Dear Juliette: Letters of May Sarton to Juliette Huxley.* New York: Norton, 1999.

——. *Selected Letters: 1916–1954.* New York: Norton, 1997.

——. *Selected Letters: 1955–1995.* New York: Norton, 2002.

Silvera, Makeda. *Silenced: Talks with Working Class Caribbean Women.* Toronto: Sister Vision, 1989.

Simmonds, Posy. *Gemma Bovery.* London: Jonathan Cape, 2001.

Sontag, Susan. *Against Interpretation and Other Essays.* 1966. New York: Picador, 2001.

Spacks, Patricia Meyer. *On Rereading.* Cambridge, Mass.: Harvard UP, 2011.

Steegmuller, Francis. *Flaubert and Madame Bovary.* Revised edition. Chicago: University of Chicago Press, 1968.

Steiner, George. *After Babel: Aspects of Language and Translation.* Oxford: Oxford UP, 1975.

Stone, Grace Zaring. *The Bitter Tea of General Yen.* 1930. New York: Vintage, 2014.

——. *The Cold Journey.* 1934. New York: Bantam, 1946.

——. *Escape.* Boston: Little, Brown, 1939.

——. *The Grotto.* New York: Harper & Brothers, 1951.

——. *Reprisal.* Boston: Little, Brown, 1943.

——. *The Secret Thread.* New York: Harper & Brothers, 1948.

——. *Winter Meeting.* Boston: Little, Brown, 1946.

Storr, Anthony. *Solitude: A Return to the Self.* New York: Free Press, 1988.

Tallman, Richard. *The Turning Year.* Marmora, Ont.: Northern Light, 2012.

Tolstoy, Leo. *Anna Karenina.* Translated by Richard Pevear and Larissa Volokhonsky. New York: Viking, 2001.

Thorne, Diana. *Drawing Dogs.* New York: Studio Publications, 1940.

Tranströmer, Tomas. *The Half-Finished Heaven.* Translated and selected by Robert Bly. Minneapolis, Minn.: Graywolf, 2001.

Traubner, Richard. *Operetta: A Theatrical History.* New York: Oxford UP, 1983.

Traver, Robert. *Anatomy of a Murder.* New York: St. Martin's, 1958.

——. *Anatomy of a Murder.* Introduction by Robert Traver. New York: St. Martin's, 1983.

Truong, Monique. *The Book of Salt.* Boston: Houghton Mifflin, 2003.

Vargas Llosa, Mario. *The Perpetual Orgy: Flaubert & Madame Bovary.* Translated by Helen Lane. New York: Farrar, Straus, & Giroux, 1986.

Waddington, Miriam. *Apartment Seven: Essays Selected and New.* Toronto: Oxford UP, 1989.

——, ed. *Canadian Jewish Short Stories.* Toronto: Oxford UP, 1990.

——. *The Last Landscape.* Toronto: Oxford UP, 1992.

White, Edmund. *Caracole.* New York: Dutton, 1985.

White, Edward. *The Tastemaker: Carl Van Vechten and the Birth of Modern America.* New York: Farrar, Straus & Giroux, 2014.

Wilde, Oscar. *The Uncensored Picture of Dorian Gray.* Edited by Nicholas Frankel. Cambridge, Mass: Harvard UP, 2011.

Wilson, Edmund. *O Canada: An American's Notes on Canadian Culture.* New York: Farrar, Straus & Giroux, 1965.

Wilson, Victoria. *A Life of Barbara Stanwyck, Steel-True 1907–1940.* New York: Simon & Schuster, 2013.

Woolf, Virginia. *The Death of the Moth.* 1942. London: Hogarth, 1981.

——. *The Diary of Virginia Woolf.* Volume Two: 1920–1924. Edited by Anne Olivier Bell. New York: Harcourt Brace Jovanovich, 1978.

——. *A Room of One's Own/Three Guineas.* 1929 and 1938. London: Penguin, 1993.

——. *To the Lighthouse.* 1927. Oxford: Oxford UP, 2008.

Wyndham, John. *The Chrysalids.* 1955. New York: New York Review Books Classics, 2008.

Yardley, Jonathan. *Second Reading: Notable and Neglected Books Revisited.* New York: Europa, 2011.

Yezierska, Anzia. *Bread Givers.* 1925. New York: Persea, 1975.

ARTICLES, ESSAYS, INTERVIEWS, REPORTS AND MUSICAL SCORES

Albert, Dora. 'Dogs Made Her Famous'. *Saturday Night,* December 28, 1929, 13–14.

Als, Hilton. 'The Heroic Art of Agnes Martin'. *New York Review of Books,* July 14, 2016.

American Academy of Arts & Sciences. 'The Heart of the Matter'. Cambridge, Mass., 2013.

Angell, Roger. 'Two Emmas'. *New Yorker,* June 8 & 15, 2009, 65.

Bakerman, Jane S. 'Work Is My Rest: A Conversation with May Sarton' in *Conversations with May Sarton,* ed. Earl G. Ingersoll. Jackson, Miss., and London: Mississippi UP, 1991.

Bast, Andres. 'A Translator's Long Journey, Page by Page'. *New York Times,* May 25, 2004, B1, B5.

Bowman, David. 'Read It Again, Sam', Sunday Book Review. *New York Times,* December 2, 2011.

Bulliet, C. J. 'Respectability in Chicago'. *New York Times,* Feb. 22, 1931, 105.

da Fonseca-Wollheim, Corinna. 'A Met Debut as That Besotted Geisha, Adamant That He Will Be True'. *New York Times,* Jan. 18, 2014, C5.

Dalley, Jan. 'Life after "Nemesis"'. *Financial Times,* June 24, 2011.

Duchen, Jessica. '"To Thine Own Self Be True": Interview with András Schiff'. *International Piano,* Jan./Feb. 2012, 58–61.

Ellenzweig, Allen. 'In with the Worldly Set'. *Gay and Lesbian Review,* January-February 2016, 29–31.

Fountain, Henry. 'An Artist's Best Friend? Giraffe, Monkey, Etc.', *New York Times,* July 18, 2006, Arts, 28.

Fox, Margalit. 'Alexis Weissenberg: Pianist of Fire and Ice, Dies at 82'. *New York Times,* January 10, 2012, A19.

Gates, David. 'Now, Read It Again'. *Newsweek,* July 13, 2009.

Glazer, Sarah. 'Lost in Translation'. *New York Times Book Review,* August 22, 2004, 13.

Glueck, Grace. 'Out of the Kennel and into the Gallery: The Artist's Best Friend'. *New York Times,* July 7, 2006, B29.

Itzkhoff, Dave. 'Arts, Briefly ("Philip Roth Gives Up Reading Fiction")'. *New York Times*, June 28, 2011, C3.

Jack, Ian, ed. 'Best of Young American Novelists'. *Granta 54*, Summer 1996.

Jewett, Eleanor. 'These Are the Dog Days at Show by This Artist', *Chicago Daily Tribune*, May 23, 1930, 37.

Kehr, Dave. 'Mystery Endures After Verdict Is In'. *New York Times*, March 11, 2012, Arts 7, 22.

Klinkenborg, Verlyn. 'Marvel and Persistence'. *New York Times*, March 13, 2011, 9.

——. 'Some Thoughts on the Pleasures of Being a Re-Reader'. *New York Times*, May 29, 2009.

LaBruce, Bruce. 'Notes on Camp—and Anti Camp'. *The Gay and Lesbian Review*, March–April 2014, 10–13.

Lewis, Zachary. 'Living a Mozart Dream with Orchestra'. *Plain Dealer*, April 4, 2012, E4.

Liptak, Adam. 'Treasury Department Is Warning Publishers of the Perils of Criminal Editing of the Enemy'. *New York Times*, February 28, 2004, A8.

Lodge, David. '"O Ye Laurels" The Best of Young American Novelists'. *Granta 54*, Summer 1996. *The New York Review of Books*, August 8, 1996, 16–20.

Michaels, Anne. 'What the Hand Sees' in *The Etty Drawings* by Claire Weissman Wilks. Toronto: Excelsis Group, 2015.

Munson, Sam. 'His Own Holocaust'. *Wall Street Journal*, August 3–4, 2013, C8.

Nichols, Steve. 'The Post-Human Manifesto'. *Games Monthly*, 1998.

Paci, Frank. 'Interview with Joseph Pivato' in *Other Solitudes: Canadian Multicultural Fictions*, eds. Linda Hutcheon and Marion Richmond. Toronto: Oxford UP, 1990.

Palmer, Willard A., ed. *J.S. Bach Interventions and Sinfonias*. Van Nuys, Calif.: Alfred Publishing Co., 1991.

Parker, Peter. 'Ripple effect'. *Times Literary Supplement*, January 10, 2014, 22.

Patchett, Ann. 'And the Winner Isn't ...'. *New York Times*, April 18, 2012, A25.

Paz, Octavio. 'Octavio Paz—Nobel Lecture: In Search of the Present'. Translated by Anthony Stanton. Nobelprize.org.

Perényi, Eleanor. 'A Thoroughly Highbrow Cruise'. *Harper's*, December 1962, 37–43.

——. 'After Hours'. *Harper's*, September 1962, 21, 23–4, 26.

——. 'Art's Sake'. *Town & Country*, March 1947, 126, 198, 200.

——. 'The Bloom Is Off'. *New York Review of Books*, March 29, 1984.

——. 'Carl Van Vechten'. *Yale Review*, Summer 1988, 537–43.

——. 'Dear Louisa'. *Harper's*, October 1955, 69–71.

——. 'Wilson'. *Esquire*, July 1963, 80–5, 118.

Plante, David. 'The Accident'. *New Yorker*, August 2, 1982.

——. 'Tales of Chatwin'. *Esquire*, October 1990, 183–90.

Rich, Motoko. 'Translation of Foreign to U.S. Publishers'. *New York Times*, October 18, 2008, C1, C8.

Rosen, Charles. 'The Super Power of Franz Liszt'. *New York Review of Books*, February 23, 2012, 19–21.

Schweitzer, Vivien. 'Pride at the Piano'. *New York Times*, September 16, 2011, AR 67.

Smith, Patrick J., Under 'Book Reviews'. *High Fidelity*, July 1975, MA 36–37.

Staff. 'By the Book: John Irving'. *New York Times Book Review*, June 10, 2012, 8.

Staff. 'Dog Quits Modeling to Lead Her Own Life'. *New York Times*, March 6, 1928, 29.

Staff. 'Keeping Posted: Among Other Things'. *Saturday Evening Post*, May 23, 1942, Vol. 214, Issue 47, 4.

Steiner, George. 'Glenn Gould's Notes'. *New Yorker*, November 23, 1992, 137–41.

Talese, Gay. 'Where Are the Italian-American Novelists?'. *New York Times Book Review*, March 14, 1993: 1, 23–29.

Thorne, Diana. 'Look Doggish, If You Please'. *Christian Science Monitor Magazine*, July 15, 1936, 8–9.

Turner, Jenny. 'In the Potato Patch'. *London Review of Books*, December 19, 2013, 6.

Van Gelder, Robert. 'An Interview with Grace Zaring Stone'. *New York Times Book Review*, May 3, 1942, 2, 14.

Vidal, Gore. 'Everything Is Yesterday'. *New York Review of Books*, February 28, 2002.

Wilson, Edmund. 'Doctor Life and His Guardian Angel'. *New Yorker*, November 15, 1958, 213–37.

——. 'A Fairy-Tale Castle in Hungary'. *New Yorker*, March 9, 1942, 98, 101.

Wyall, Edward. 'Ending Editorial Oversight at Treasury'. *New York Times*, September 29, 2004, A26.

——. 'Tolstoy's Translators Experience Oprah's Effect', *New York Times*, June 7, 2004, B1, B5.

CDS, DVDS AND VHS TAPES

Bach. *Goldberg Variations.* Glenn Gould, pianist. 1955. Sony Classical.

——. *Goldberg Variations.* András Schiff, pianist. ECM New Series.

Chabrol, Claude (director). *Madame Bovary*, 1991. Republic Pictures Home Video.

Chopin, Frédéric. *The Complete Preludes.* Rafal Blechacz, pianist. Deutsche Grammophon.

——. *The Nocturnes.* Maria João Pires, pianist. Deutsche Grammophon.

——. *Polonaises.* Arthur Rubinstein, pianist. Naxos.

Curzon, Clifford. *Mozart/Schubert.* Great Pianists of the 20th Century, No. 22. Philips/Decca.

Geuden, Hilde. *Hilde Gueden Sings Operetta Evergreens.* Classic Recitals. Vienna State Opera Orchestra, Robert Stolz, conductor. Decca.

Gillespie, Craig (director). *Lars and the Real Girl.* 2007. Twentieth Century Fox.

Hadley, Jerry. *The World Is Beautiful: Viennese Operetta Arias.* Munich Radio Orchestra, Richard Bonynge, conductor. RCA Victor.

Hampson, Thomas. *Operetta Arias.* London Philharmonic Orchestra, Franz Welser-Möst, conductor. EMI Classics.

Haskil, Clara. *Beethoven/Mozart/Schubert/Schumann.* Great Pianists of the 20th Century, No. 44. Philips/Deutsche Grammophon.

Jarmusch, Jim (director). *Only Lovers Left Alive.* 2013. Sony Pictures Classics.

Jarre, Maurice. *Doctor Zhivago.* Rhino Records Inc.

Jonze, Spike (director). *Her.* 2013. Warner Bros.

Kálmán, Emmerich. *Csárdás Furstin.* Anneliese Rothenberger, Nicolai Gedda, Willy Mattes, conductor, Symphonie-Orchester Graunke. EMI Classics.

——. *Gräfin Mariza.* Anneliese Rothenberger, Nicolai Gedda, Willy Mattes, conductor. Symphonie-Orchester Graunke. EMI Classics.

——, Kálmán Conducts Kálmán. Complete Radio Broadcast of May 5, 1940. The Music of Emmerich Kalman, Vol. 2. Operetta Archives.

Keenlyside, Simon, and Angelika Kirchschlanger. *Dein Ist Mein Ganzes Herz.* Tonkünstler Orchester Niederösterreich, Alfred Eschwé, conductor. Sony.

Lang, Walter (director). *Desk Set.* 1957. Fox Video.

Lehár, Franz. *Der Zarewitsch* (The Tsarevich). Teresa Stratas, soprano. Unitel Classic Video.

Lipatti, Dinu. *Dinu Lipatti*, Vol. 2. EMI.

Lubitsch, Ernst (director). *Ninotchka.* 1939. Warner Bros.

Minelli, Vincente (director). *Madame Bovary.* 1949. Turner Entertainment Co.

Mozart, Wolfgang Amadeus. *Piano Concertos No. 20, K 466* & *No. 27, K 595*. The Cleveland Orchestra with Mitsuko Uchida, pianist and conductor. Decca.

Offenbach, Jacques. *Les contes d'Hoffmann*. André Cluytens, conductor. EMI.

Preminger, Otto (director). *Anatomy of a Murder*. 1959. The Criterion Collection.

Ravel, Maurice. *Oeuvres pour piano*. Jean-Philippe Collard, pianist. EMI Classics.

Schumann, Robert. *Symphonische Etüden*. András Schiff, pianist. Teldec.

Schwarzkopf, Elisabeth. *Operetta Arias*. Philharmonia Orchestra, Otto Ackermann, conductor. EMI Classics.

——. *A Viennese Evening*. Orchestre de Radio Canada, conducted by Willi Boskovsky. Video Artists International, 2006.

Scott, Ridley (director). *Blade Runner*. 1982. Nelson Entertainment.

Scott, Tony (director). *The Hunger*. 1983. Warner Bros.

Thompson, Danièle (director). *Avenue Montaigne*. 2006. THINKFilm.

Wheelock, Martha, and Marita Simpson (directors). *A World of Light: Portrait of May Sarton*. Ishtar Films, 1980.

About the Author

Richard Teleky is an author, editor and educator who has published a dozen books of poetry and prose (both fiction and non-fiction), including, most recently, *The Blue Hour* (Exile Editions, 2017) and *The Hermit in Arcadia* (Exile Editions, 2012). His novel *The Paris Years of Rosie Kamin* (Steerforth, 1998) won the Harold Ribalow Prize. He is a professor in the Humanities Department of York University and lives in Toronto.